PENGUIN BOOKS AND BLUE SALT
DIAL D FOR DON

Neeraj Kumar is one of the most distinguished police officers of the country. He completed his post-graduation from St. Stephen's College, Delhi University, and joined the Indian Police Service in 1976. In 2013, he retired as the commissioner of police, Delhi. Earlier, he served in the Central Bureau of Investigation (CBI) first as DIG and then as joint director. During his nine-year tenure in the CBI, he investigated several sensational cases and conducted a number of important transnational operations, involving terrorism, organized crime, economic offences and corruption. He was later joint commissioner of police, Special Cell of the Delhi Police—mainly responsible for tackling Pakistan-sponsored terrorism—and the director general of prisons, Delhi.

In an illustrious career spanning thirty-seven years, Kumar dealt with a range of high-profile assignments and ushered in novel initiatives, like a literacy and placement programme for prisoners; a programme called YUVA, for youth susceptible to crime; Aapka Update, a scheme for providing regular updates on police action to complainants; and Jan Sampark, a platform for members of the public to meet senior police officers.

Kumar represented India at the UN Convention on Transnational Organized Crime and later to draft the UN manual on countering kidnapping and extortion. The Government of India recognized his work by awarding him the Police Medal for Meritorious Service in 1993 and the President's Police Medal for Distinguished Service in 1999. Kumar is presently the chief adviser to the Anti-Corruption and Security Unit of the Board of Control for Cricket in India (BCCI).

ADVANCE PRAISE FOR THE BOOK

'Neeraj Kumar's *Dial D for Don* is a riveting account of the evolution of India's underworld, particularly in Mumbai. From organized crime to match-fixing and finally, terrorism. Narrated in graphic detail by the man who investigated some of its most sensational episodes'—Aroon Purie

'Neeraj Kumar prises open a world of crime and policing through his debut book, *Dial D for Don*, in a manner that is both John Le Carré and James Hadley Chase, except, his eleven stories are for real. The accounts have been part of India's crime history, bordering on folklore. His easy style, an incredible memory and deftness of purpose make this book a compelling read. The reader is transported into a world she knew existed but had no insights into. He reveals a closet full of solved cases which he helped bring to closure. It is in this book that we come to terms with a reality that has been part of our lives, and yet one we've remained so distant from'—Suhel Seth

'Neeraj Kumar's *Dial D for Don* makes for fascinating reading. It's fast, furious and some of the stuff is pretty hair-raising. It's a great insight, first-hand, into the world of match-fixing, terrorism and the underworld. It's a must-read that goes at T20 pace'—Ravi Shastri

Dial D for DON

Inside Stories of CBI Missions

NEERAJ KUMAR

BLUE SALT

PENGUIN BOOKS

PENGUIN BOOKS
Published by the Penguin Group
Penguin Books India Pvt. Ltd, 7th Floor, Infinity Tower C, DLF Cyber City,
Gurgaon 122 002, Haryana, India
Penguin Group (USA) Inc., 375 Hudson Street, New York,
New York 10014, USA
Penguin Group (Canada), 90 Eglinton Avenue East, Suite 700, Toronto,
Ontario, M4P 2Y3, Canada
Penguin Books Ltd, 80 Strand, London WC2R 0RL, England
Penguin Ireland, 25 St Stephen's Green, Dublin 2, Ireland
(a division of Penguin Books Ltd)
Penguin Group (Australia), 707 Collins Street, Melbourne,
Victoria 3008, Australia
Penguin Group (NZ), 67 Apollo Drive, Rosedale, Auckland 0632,
New Zealand
Penguin Books (South Africa) (Pty) Ltd, Block D, Rosebank Office Park,
181 Jan Smuts Avenue, Parktown North, Johannesburg 2193, South Africa

Penguin Books Ltd, Registered Offices: 80 Strand, London WC2R 0RL,
England

First published by Penguin Books India and Blue Salt 2015

ISBN 9780143424420

Typeset in Bembo Std by Manipal Digital Systems, Manipal
Printed at Replika Press Pvt. Ltd, India

A PENGUIN RANDOM HOUSE COMPANY

*To Amma and Papa, who would have been proud of me this
day, as they always were;
To countless police martyrs who lay down their lives in the line
of duty—unknown and unsung;
And, to darling Aishwarya, my two-year-old granddaughter,
who, when she grows up, should know what her grandpa was up
to in his younger days!*

'The time has come,' the Walrus said,
'To talk of many things:
Of shoes—and ships—and sealing-wax—
Of cabbages—and kings—
And why the sea is boiling hot—
And whether pigs have wings.'

Through the Looking-Glass,
Lewis Carroll

Contents

Foreword

When I joined the police, we were taught that there is no crime that cannot be solved and that if you are focused and determined, you can scale any peak. Even in the Intelligence Bureau, where I worked for over fifteen years, the implicit understanding always was that there is nothing you cannot accomplish if you set your mind to it. The CBI is no less, as I discovered when I served in the organization. This book also conveys it in so many words. You can literally feel the passion and savour the author's success as he takes on one intractable case after another, facing all kinds of obstacles. No wonder Neeraj writes in 'Operation Desert Safari' that it was one of the most thrilling and satisfying cases of his life. Also, the lavish acknowledgement and gratitude that he and the CBI received from the Gujarat government and the Gujarat Police when they apprehended the mafia don Abdul Latif, whose notoriety seemed to be coming close to Dawood Ibrahim's. Not to forget the elation he and his team felt when they finally brought back Yakub Memon's family from Dubai, and a little later his wife and their month-old daughter, fighting all odds created by the ISI. I have known Neeraj as a soft-spoken person, not given to any drama or temper tantrums. But the hard slap he gave to Romesh Sharma, an underworld thug whom he later arrested, should be resoundingly applauded even by a diehard civil rights activist.

All stories (and true stories, mind you) in this book are grippingly narrated as though like a whodunit novel. You can't help but breathtakingly participate in the progress of the cases and join the author in jumping with joy on their dramatic conclusion. You repeatedly discover that Neeraj was not just a passive leader but often led from the front, at times even risking his life. His restlessness is amply reflected when he recounts a case getting stalled, which he says left him with no choice but to play a direct, hands-on role. Investigations, whether by the CBI or the police, call for not just skill, which one needs in enormous measure, but also immense patience, perseverance, passion and luck.

Although different in the level of action compared to other cases, the narrative on Dawood Ibrahim, the legendary gangster of gangsters, is no less interesting, especially the personal exchanges between him and Neeraj. The son of a police constable, Dawood did not get the head start other children of middle-class or affluent families get. Yet he not only emerged as the top gangster of India and acquired a notorious and even mysterious halo, he also had to seek safe haven in Pakistan when things became too hot for him here. Even while in India, he established a highly successful and well-oiled global network of dedicated compatriots, inspiring fear, awe and their inevitable loyalty. Dawood's major mistakes could be his falling out with Chhota Rajan, joining hands with Pakistan and playing a major role in the Mumbai blasts of 1993. Otherwise, he could have continued to lord over his criminal empire in India and would not have had to bolt to Pakistan. His gang could have by now been among the world's deadliest and most powerful, posing a serious challenge to all other global criminal networks. All said and done, he is now but a fugitive, as though trapped in Pakistan.

Coming to the CBI, I am sure readers will appreciate after reading this wonderfully written book that it is not entirely a caged parrot or a mere handmaiden of the Central government. When netas or bureaucrats have no stakes or are under no pressure themselves, they can be quite non-interfering and let the CBI be. They generally don't even care what the bureau is up to. But when the situation is different, they can be quite a handful to manage for the agency's top brass.

There is no doubt that despite all its shortfalls, the CBI commands enormous nationwide credibility. Hence, the not infrequent demand for a CBI inquiry into almost anything under the sun. Very few people know that the CBI is a small, understaffed organization with too much on its plate. When saddled with sensational cases or cases of national importance, it has no choice but to stall its normal work and shift focus almost entirely to an individual case. In the Rajiv Gandhi assassination case, for instance, the CBI had to close all normal operations in Chennai, Hyderabad, Bengaluru and Thiruvananthapuram and draft almost the entire staff of these units to the team investigating the case.

Another matter that Neeraj has repeatedly highlighted and deserves mention is the enormous synergy that can occur when cases call for joint action by the CBI, the state police, the foreign service and/or civil administration. All unnecessary impediments are easily overcome when various wings of the government join hands to achieve a common objective. And the resultant success can be phenomenal.

However, Neeraj's narration also brings out, though somewhat mutedly, the anxiety that he had to undergo due to personal jealousy of fellow officers in the CBI and the police. It is a shame that we human beings are such imperfect entities, capable of spite, deceit and needless one-upmanship. Neeraj weathered them stoically and with dignity. He refrains from taking names of his tormentors in his recollections. On the other hand, he has shown unmistakable grace in giving fulsome credit to a great number of his colleagues and junior officers who were involved in his investigations.

One thing that has often bothered me over time, and it seems appropriate to articulate it here, is that India's prisons are not correctional institutions, which they ought to be, where a criminal can be reformed. On the contrary, prisons are places where criminals, whether in judicial custody or serving a term, come in contact with other criminals and develop bonds. They exchange notes and ideas, and learn new modus operandi. They develop nexus with other hardened criminals, and even first-time offenders hone their skills in criminality under the tutelage of more seasoned felons lodged in the same jail. So prisons become breeding grounds for more crime and unwittingly breed fraternity among criminals, which they put to use when they are released. Even the courts unwittingly become venues of opportunity for such unholy nexus. Take the case of Aftab Ansari (see chapter 'Gifts from the Gulf'), who was jailed for his involvement in abduction and extortion but became a jihadi and a terrorist after he came in contact with other jihadi criminals while in custody. The government needs to ponder over this inherent flaw in our system and devise measures to permanently plug such opportunities that foster crime. Maybe only those criminals who serve life term or long sentences of seven years or more should be allowed to stay together, and thereby be prevented from influencing first-timers and petty criminals to gang up with them once out of jail. Also, technology should be increasingly used inside our prisons to maintain surveillance over hardened criminals to ensure their segregation from those new to the world of crime. Commission of crime from within the four walls of a prison, which we often hear about, should be curbed at all costs.

As Neeraj's accounts also demonstrate, riots, especially of the communal kind, invariably leave a trail of anger, bitterness and a thirst for revenge. India has paid and still pays a heavy price for the communal riots that occur frequently in the country. And almost always, the minorities and the lower strata of society have to bear the brunt. Since the majority community and the upper class are larger in number or more powerful, they are able to hit harder. It is the bitterness among the weak minority that not infrequently turns them into terrorists. Pakistan is always there to exploit this fault line in our country, both to give us a bad name and to inveigle the minority community into terrorism against India. Most political parties, some more than others, indulge in divisive politics to win votes and come to power. Our political leadership needs to deeply introspect and change their attitude alongside their electoral posturing, if at all they care for the masses they represent. Sanity lies in assimilation. If only their hearts can be won over.

One last word: I find that the author has based this book almost entirely on his phenomenal memory, with no notes, no documents and no background papers. For this, too, he deserves our congratulations.

Raja Vijay Karan
Former commissioner of police, Delhi, and
former director of the CBI

Preface

Sometime in early 2014, I received a call from the publishers of S. Hussain Zaidi's *Byculla to Bangkok*, requesting me to come for its book release. I was also informed that following the book launch, I would be in conversation with the author. Rather intrigued about why the publishing house had thought of me, I inquired of the caller why I was being asked to do the honours. The gracious lady said: 'Sir, it is the author's desire.'

I had not met Hussain Zaidi before but knew of him because of his book *Black Friday* on which the eponymous film was made. The publishers sent me a copy of *Byculla to Bangkok* a day before the event. Having dealt with the underworld of Mumbai (earlier known as Bombay) during my nine-year stint at the Central Bureau of Investigation (CBI), and familiar with the dramatis personae, the book made for fascinating reading. I finished it in a couple of sittings and was ready to be 'in conversation' with the author.

The book release passed off delightfully. My conversation with the author was interesting and enjoyable, even though most of the time I was finding faults with the book. From typos to facts, I didn't hold back any punches. In the process, I might have annoyed both the organizers of the event and the author.

The following day, Zaidi Sahib called to inform me that he had met Chiki Sarkar, the editor-in-chief of Penguin Random House, who was keen to publish my memoirs. I thought it was a bit of a joke—I, writing my memoirs, and that too for such a reputed publishing house. But, lo and behold, in a matter of a few days, a contract from Penguin arrived in my mail. Caught totally by surprise, I wondered how this had come about when neither Chiki nor Hussain Zaidi had read a word written by me. But, the fact staring me in the face was that I had been served a fait accompli and I had to get down to putting pen to paper. The struggle that followed has been both trying and exhilarating.

The idea of writing my memoirs did not appeal to me in the least, nor did it excite me. I feel it requires extraordinary courage to lay bare the truth about oneself, to disclose the many dark secrets of one's personal and professional lives, which are best left alone. Though it's done frequently, for writing honest memoirs one has to be a Gandhi or a Bertrand Russell to say it all. Further, many a memoir written by police officers has gone completely unnoticed and ended up adorning the bookshelf of the author himself or gathering dust in sundry police libraries. Most of them are full of 'I did this in this district and I did that in that range'. After all, who is interested in reading such inanities about a cop's life? Details of interesting investigations might still engage readers. I discussed with the publishers and proposed writing accounts of police operations I participated in during my tenure in the CBI instead. They were game and I set out on a journey of reminiscing and nostalgia. Since I had not retained any documents connected with the concerned cases, most of what I have recounted is based on memory with a little bit of help from colleagues who were my partners in these adventures.

In the pages that follow, I have attempted to document eleven operations carried out by CBI teams under my leadership and supervision. Of the several such operations, I have chosen eleven on account of my direct and hands-on involvement with them. Also, hopefully, they make good crime stories with interesting characters operating across transnational jurisdictions. Seven of them relate to the Mumbai underworld, one to a Sikh terrorist, one to a murder committed in Dubai, one to a notorious gang targeting young foreign tourists visiting India, and the last to a cricket bookie turned fixer.

Till my superannuation at the end of July 2013, my career in the police spanning thirty-seven years has been an exciting mix of both rough and fulfilling. The cadre allotted to me in the IPS was AGMUT (Arunachal, Goa, Mizoram and other Union Territories). I have served in the three states which give the acronym AGMUT its first three letters and have fond memories of my tenures there. Most of my working years have been in Delhi, including my last assignment of thirteen eventful months as the commissioner of police. However, the nine years spent on deputation with the CBI, first as DIG and later as a joint director, have been the most satisfying of my career.

The CBI never ceases to attract media and public attention. Always mired in one controversy or the other, the common perception of the CBI is difficult to fathom. What baffles an outsider is why there is demand for a CBI inquiry or investigation in a case despite the enduring criticism of the bureau being a 'caged parrot' or a handmaiden of the Centre. Be that as it may, I found it to be an organization where I could pursue investigative work without the distractions of day-to-day firefighting work typical of the local police. My tenure in the CBI offered me the opportunity to work in diverse areas of policing like counterterrorism, organized crime, economic crime and anti-corruption. Towards the later part of my stint, I also had the occasion to supervise cases of wildlife crimes, antique thefts, fake currency and others—all fascinating areas of police work. Fortunately for me, except on two or three occasions, I faced no persistent political interference, otherwise considered an occupational hazard of working in the CBI. But, I must confess, when on a couple of odd occasions such interferences did come up, it was quite testing and intense. One case I handled in the CBI follows me till today and will perhaps chase me to my grave. However, that story doesn't figure in this book as it is still being fought in the courts.

But, the best part of my tenure was to conceive police operations, largely transnational in character, and execute them with the support of numerous agencies. Synergizing the efforts of law enforcement from different areas, eliciting their support, travelling overseas, interacting with our diplomatic corps, seeking the cooperation of Interpol and doing things hands-on had thrills that arguably no other job in the police could have provided. I was lucky to have supportive bosses and extraordinary team members. I hope I have done justice to their role in the operations recounted in this book.

A word or two more about my impressions of the CBI: its strength is its singular objective of investigating crimes and pursuing investigation. At every step of its work, legal help is at hand which keeps it on course. Final decisions are taken either by the director or the special director, depending on the enormity of the case. Officers have enough latitude to express their opinion on file and most decisions are taken collectively. But what is special and unique about the organization is its in-built system of following up on the prosecution in court. Besides government counsels, it can engage the best lawyers in the country, and sometimes even abroad, if a case so demands. Like any other organization, a lot depends on who the leader is; in the CBI's case, it's the director. He sets the tone of investigations and also determines their quality. If he is weak, unprofessional or dishonest, it amply reflects in the standard of investigation and the reputation the organization acquires. I was fortunate to have able and professional directors to serve under and supportive immediate superiors. From them I learnt lifelong lessons in courage, righteousness and integrity.

That said, the CBI has its fair share of weaknesses. Its processes make its working painfully slow. The sense of urgency, an inherent quality of crime investigation, is generally conspicuous by its absence. Investigations drag on for ever and the trials go on for decades. For instance, the L.N. Mishra (then the railway minister) assassination case took forty years to come to a conclusion. The serial blasts case of Mumbai in 1993, which figures frequently in the stories that follow, was tried by a special designated court not dealing with any other matter. Yet the trial went on for twelve years and appeals in the apex court for a year. Eleven accused died as the trial lingered. We are yet to hear the last on it as seven accused arrested later are still under trial.

Most accused die during the course of the trial; others, if convicted, are often in their seventies and eighties by then. I have seen some of them arrive in Tihar Jail during my stint as director general (prisons). Most had to be taken to the Jail Hospital straightaway on arrival, so emaciated and aged were they. The delay in disposal of cases is on account of our judicial system, the dilatory tactics adopted by defence lawyers and huge pendency that courts are saddled with.

The other weakness in the CBI, linked with its slow pace of work, is on account of too many cases and too few officers to investigate them. The agency has its own cadre officers as well as officers who come on deputation from state police forces and other police and enforcement agencies. Most officers who come on deputation at the inspector and DSP level are not equipped to undertake investigations as they are from paramilitary forces or agencies where no investigation is done. Some of them pick up the work quickly but most remain out of sorts throughout their tenures.

The CBI's own cadre of investigating officers is remarkable. They can investigate a case in any part of the country from start to finish. The only drawback they have is that sometimes, while investigating what in CBI parlance are called 'special crimes', they lack the confidence that a regular local field police officer has. But when faced with challenges, my experience was that they rose to meet expectations even in the face of trying circumstances. My stories reveal both sides of this predicament.

The nature of the CBI's work is such that often the rich and the powerful need to be probed. This class of society has access to patronage from the highest and the mightiest in the land coupled with the best legal support. The accused in this category can block investigations at every stage by securing political interference and judicial intervention. If the case does reach the trial stage, proceedings can be stalled by adopting dilatory tactics like seeking endless adjournments on flimsy grounds. For instance, two cases investigated and charge-sheeted by my team have not had a single hearing for the last thirteen years. The intervention of superior courts, even before the trial commenced, has thwarted progress in trial for over a decade now. All an accused needs is tons of money to engage top lawyers, and connections at the right places to keep the law at bay. As mentioned earlier, I had the unique opportunity of dealing with terrorists and underworld elements on one hand, and on the other I dealt with cases involving serious economic offenders and corruption in high places. Oftentimes I sensed that the underworld elements and 'regular' criminals have an unwritten code not to target the law enforcement officers who investigate them. They somewhere have an innate fear of the police and recognize that they (the police) are only performing their bona fide duties. However, during the course of official work, if the police take on the rich and the powerful, as they sometimes have to, it is taken as an affront and made personal. You are a 'marked' man thereafter for all time to come. Baseless and vexatious litigations are launched against you and you may end up appearing in courts every fifteen days or so to answer ridiculous charges. While you anxiously defend yourself, the accused, on the other hand, makes merry after securing bail. But what hurts the most is when the organization you serve in disowns you and you are left to fend for yourself and face such litigations alone. I have faced this betrayal and continue to confront it even today.

Nonetheless, on the whole, I have pleasant memories of my run in the CBI as the stories that follow will testify. Those times were good while they lasted—exciting and adventurous—each day bringing its share of surprises and challenges. After all, what more can a police officer ask for?

I have penned down the accounts of the CBI operations I was blessed to be part of with considerable trepidation. Aware that they may ruffle some feathers, and matters, long dead and buried, may raise their controversial heads all over again, I plodded on. Equally troubling was the self-doubt lurking at the back of my mind about my writing abilities, which are admittedly limited. What kept me going was the desire to give readers a taste of the thrill of chasing down hardened criminals and a glimpse of the life-threatening situations in which the police in general and the CBI in particular work. At no stage has the desire for self-glorification motivated me to write any part of the book. I am content with all that my profession has given me and need no further recognition. On the contrary, my attempt has been to highlight the stellar work done by my colleagues who were go-getters and brought me plaudits without ever letting me down.

I sincerely hope that the unexpected nudge that Hussain Zaidi gave me and the confidence my publishers have reposed in me do not go in vain.

Acronyms

ACP	assistant commissioner of police
ASI	assistant sub-inspector
ATS	Anti-Terrorism Squad
BSF	Border Security Force
CBI	Central Bureau of Investigation
CID	Crime Investigation Department
CMD	chairman and managing director
COFEPOSA	Conservation of Foreign Exchange and Prevention of Smuggling Activities Act
DCP	deputy commissioner of police
DGM	deputy general manager
DGP	director general of police
DIG	deputy inspector general
DSP	deputy superintendent of police
GM	general manager
IAS	Indian Administrative Service
IMEI	International Mobile Equipment Identity
IO	investigating officer
IPC	Indian Penal Code
IPL	Indian Premier League

IPS	Indian Police Service
ISI	Inter-Services Intelligence
IST	Indian Standard Time
JCP	joint commissioner of police
MP	member of Parliament
MTNL	Mahanagar Telephone Nigam Limited
PCO	public call office
SSP	special superintendent of police
SP	superintendent of police
STF	Special Task Force
TADA	Terrorist and Disruptive Activities (Prevention) Act
UAE	United Arab Emirates
USP	unique selling point or proposition

1

Gifts from the Gulf
The rise and fall of Aftab Ansari

William Ewart Gladstone (1809–1898), a British Liberal politician, served as prime minister four times, more than any other person in Great Britain's history. His supporters affectionately gave him the monikers 'People's William' and the 'Grand Old Man'.

Known for his robust health and indefatigable energy, he was once asked the secret of his long and healthy life. 'I chew every morsel of food twenty times so my stomach doesn't do what my teeth need to,' he disclosed.

Alas! DSP M.C. Sahni of the CBI and six members of his team found it hard to stomach, literally, Gladstone's words of wisdom on mastication and healthy living, while camping at Santalpur in Patan district of Gujarat. The sleepy, one-horse town of Santalpur is less than, as the crow flies, forty-five kilometres from the Indo-Pak border.

The team was on a mission to trail the movement of a huge cache of arms, ammunition and explosives smuggled into India from across the border. The food served to them in sundry wayside eateries always had irksome sprinklings of sand, thanks to the dust-laden winds blowing over the arid landscape. The trick, therefore, was to somehow swallow what they ate rather than masticate.

But even as our hard-nosed investigators found it difficult to chew on every morsel of their sandy servings, they decided to sink their collective teeth deep into a top-secret operation in late October of 2001. The mission the DSP and his team were pursuing was a joint operation of the BSF and the Economic Offences Unit-V (EOU-5) of the CBI. The BSF and the CBI, both federal organizations of the Government of India, had worked together on several such joint operations in the years 2000 and 2001, thanks to the trust and mutual coordination developed painstakingly between the then Director General, BSF, Ram Mohan, his Inspector General (Ops) V.N. Rai and yours truly of the CBI. All such missions involved 'controlled deliveries' across the Indo-Pak border.

'Controlled deliveries' are operational tactics often adopted by law enforcement agencies wherein contraband consignments of drugs or arms or fake currency, etc., are allowed to 'flow' under controlled conditions. They are not intercepted even though there is definite information on their illicit movement. The objective behind such tactics is to get to the eventual recipient, usually the big fish of a smuggling ring. Couriers and other intermediaries are, usually, mere foot soldiers who earn paltry sums of money.

Sometimes they may not even know who the ultimate beneficiaries are or what the consignment contains. If one or more of such foot soldiers can be won over or compromised, either at the source or at any other stage of the supply chain, the consignment can be trailed, the entire racket busted and the kingpins brought to book. Of course, the deal between law enforcement officers and the informer often is to let the latter go scot-free once his task is completed, besides rewarding him suitably.

The EOU-5 of the CBI was one of the many branches of the Economic Offences Wing under my charge, of which I was then the joint director. This branch, in collaboration with the BSF, spearheaded four operations involving 'controlled deliveries'. On 24 February 2000 twenty-three kilos of high-grade heroin were seized from one Haji Gul Khan, a Pakistani, and Abdullah, an Afghan national. The contraband was hidden in secret cavities of giant-sized aluminium *degchee*s, or cooking utensils. The capture took place opposite Filmistan Cinema in Old Delhi and was one of the biggest drug seizures of those times.

The same team of officers apprehended four Mumbai-based criminals on 24 July 2000 at Ahmedabad and recovered twenty-five pistols, fifty magazines, 200 cartridges and 6.325 kilos of high-grade heroin concealed in a truck's spare wheel. Interrogation of the arrested criminals disclosed that the Dawood Ibrahim gang was behind the consignment that was sent with the blessings of the notorious Pakistani agency, the ISI. The weapons were meant for underworld operations in Mumbai and the drugs to fund the operations.

In yet another collaborative effort between the BSF and CBI, a truck headed for Punjab was intercepted on 14 July 2000 at Libaspur, north-west Delhi. A steel trunk and a Rexene bag were recovered with two AK-56 rifles, twenty pistols, large quantities of ammunition, detonators, timers, cordex fuse and match fuse, all meant for Babbar Khalsa, a deadly terrorist outfit in Punjab. Two couriers, Gurbachan Singh of Ajnala and Baldev Singh of Gurdaspur, were arrested from the truck.

However, we did not in the least expect that a similar operation involving a controlled delivery at Santalpur would eventually link us to a ruthless, transnational underworld network that had systematically spread fear among India's business community through a series of kidnappings for heavy ransom. Indeed, some of the members of this gang were the newly appointed *bhai*s, or dons, of Dubai, originally from India but working closely with the ISI and militant outfits in India's western neighbourhood. We could not have anticipated that in the months to come, as a fallout of our operation, a rising star on the firmament of terror and organized crime in India would be stopped in his tracks.

~

At about 1.30 a.m. on the night of 26–27 October 2001, the CBI team headed by M.C. Sahni spotted a truck bearing registration number RJ-02-XXXX parked opposite Hotel Nagraj in Santalpur on National Highway 15 (NH 15). It was the vehicle the CBI boys had been looking for since they arrived in the area a fortnight before, based on the tip-off of a BSF informer. The eight-member team fanned out in the cover of darkness and approached the vehicle stealthily. However, they could not escape the alert eyes of the truck's occupants who had spotted suspicious-looking men surround them. The miscreants opened fire on the CBI team. Inspector V.K. Shukla returned fire. The smugglers immediately drove the truck away on NH 15 towards Radhanpur, the next township on the highway. The CBI team hopped on to two jeeps, requisitioned locally from government departments, and followed the truck. Since the truck had a head start on our men, it took some time before it could be reached.

After five kilometres, when the miscreants saw their pursuers closing in on them, the truck jerked to an abrupt halt. Its occupants, four in number, jumped off and fled into the thorny shrubbery of the sparse landscape, just like in our Bollywood potboilers. The CBI boys followed them undaunted, despite the alien and hostile terrain, until they reached atop a *bandh*, or a small embankment. The miscreants were nowhere to be seen despite the advantage of the elevation of the embankment. The local police was informed, their help taken and the entire area combed, but to no avail. Our men had lost the smugglers and had no option but to return, a dejected lot, to the truck abandoned on the highway.

A search of the truck led to the discovery of two military kitbags hidden between the driver's and the cleaner's seats. Two AK-56 assault rifles with 524 rounds of ammunition, two pistols, 296 pistol cartridges, six pistol magazines, detonators, fuses, remotes for improvised explosive devices (IEDs), wireless sets and four kilos of explosives were found in the kitbags. The cache of arms, ammunition and explosives was enough to carry out scores of terror attacks and other serious crimes.

Besides the deadly consignment, the couriers, to our good fortune, left behind enough clues for us to chase them down. Registration papers of the truck showed its ownership in the name of one Yunus Khan, a resident of Alwar in Rajasthan. A few mobile numbers were found randomly scrawled on dirty soiled papers lying in the glove compartment. Analysis of the call details of these cell phones led us to a property dealer with his office in Jaitpur, south Delhi. He confirmed having received calls from mobile number 98102-xxxxx found in the truck. The number, he said, belonged to one Ashabuddin, who had purchased a plot of land through him. Further, Ashabuddin was likely to meet him in a day or two to close the deal.

Our boys lay in wait at the business premises of the property dealer. On 3 November, a week after the mess-up in Santalpur, Ashabuddin walked into our trap. He was accompanied by another person identified as Abdul Subhan, who turned out to be the driver of the truck we had trailed the other night. Both Ashabuddin and Abdul Subhan are from the Mewat area of Haryana bordering Delhi. They had come to the property dealer's office in a Maruti car. (Interestingly, this car was later connected with Kolkata-based shoe baron Partha Pratim Roy Burman's kidnapping, which figures later in the story.)

During interrogation, they disclosed that their other two accomplices were Yunus Khan, the truck's owner, and one Akhtar, also a resident of Mewat region. Subhan further confessed to having hidden some arms and ammunition from an earlier consignment at his home in village Ghummat Bihari of Gurgaon district. Based on his disclosure, two AK-56 rifles with ammunition were recovered, buried under the *chulha*, the earthen cooking fire burner, in his village home.

A CBI team was dispatched to locate and arrest Yunus Khan, the owner of the truck, who was also one of its four occupants on the fateful night of 26–27 October 2001 when the operation had commenced. The team traced Khan to his village in Alwar district of Rajasthan. Upon questioning he confessed to his involvement in the case. However, the fourth accused, Akhtar, was nowhere to be found despite several raids at his village and elsewhere. He continued to evade arrest till as late as 2012 when he surrendered in court.

Ashabuddin, Abdul Subhan and Yunus, during their interrogation, disclosed that they all worked on the directions of one Aquib Ali Khan from Alwar. According to them, Aquib had left Delhi for Bhopal by car, a Santro, with registration number DL-4C-XXXX. Aquib's girlfriend, Humeira Firdaus, lived in the Ghoda Nikas area of Madhya Pradesh's capital and, presumably, he had gone to Bhopal to spend time with her. A CBI team headed by Inspector Jagdish Prasad was dispatched to look for Aquib.

~

Our boys reached Bhopal on the night of 5 November
2001 and fanned out in the Ghoda Nikas area. It is a thickly
populated, congested area in old Bhopal city, teeming with
people from a minority community, packed in houses like
sardines. The CBI team spotted the Santro parked in a
narrow lane and mounted a night-long vigil over it. They
guessed Aquib was somewhere close by, probably with his
paramour, and would emerge soon. Sure enough, a young
man came to the car the following morning. He began to
drive through the congested lanes, negotiating his way past
countless rickshaws, handcarts and pedestrians. Inspector
Jagdish Prasad, even though sleep-deprived, followed the
car on foot, often having to break into a sprint. Experienced
cop that he was, he wanted to be absolutely sure that it was
Aquib at the wheel, not someone else. He saw the young
man stop his car and walk into a photo studio. Prasad and
his team intercepted and detained him when he came
out. The inspector went into the studio and checked its
register. The last entry, made minutes earlier, was of the
name Aquib Ali Khan. We had got the next important link
in the chain we were trying to bust.

~

Aquib Ali Khan aka Firasat was brought to Delhi. He was
a young man in his early thirties, and I was present when
he was interrogated. He disclosed that he worked for Asif
Raza Khan, a gangster from Kolkata, and it was at Asif's
behest that he was overseeing the smuggling of arms from
across the Indo-Pak border. He further said Asif had been

arrested by the Delhi Police only a few days earlier and gave the name of a Hindi newspaper and the rough date when he had seen a report on his arrest.

The news item on Asif's arrest was retrieved. It mentioned his having been arrested at Lodhi Garden by a team headed by ACP Ravi Shankar of Delhi Police's Crime Branch on 29 October 2001. I reported the developments to my director, P.C. Sharma, and requested him to speak with his batchmate Ajai Raj Sharma, the then commissioner of police, Delhi. We needed to interrogate Asif Raza Khan, who was still in the custody of Delhi Police. Very soon, I got a call from the then JCP (crime) that we were welcome to interview Asif at the Crime Branch office complex in Chanakyapuri.

During interrogation, Asif disclosed to us that he was a member of a gang headed by Aftab Ansari, originally from Varanasi. He confessed to working with Aftab in several sensational kidnappings for ransom like those of jeweller Bhaskar Parekh of Rajkot and Partha Roy Burman of Kolkata. Aftab, he said, operated under various aliases— including Abdal, Farhan Malik, Guptaji, Azhar, Hero, Amaan, and so on—and was based in Dubai. The name Farhan Malik somehow stuck at the back of my mind. Asif further disclosed that the weapons were meant for terrorist activities in India and had been sourced from Pakistan. Asif confessed that he himself was a jihadi and had received training in terror camps in Bahawalpur, Pakistan.

On my return to the CBI headquarters, I briefed my director on Asif Raza Khan's interrogation. The big picture that had emerged, I felt, was that of a gangster named Aftab

Ansari who was steeped in jihadi ideology and had the potential to cause terror strikes using his vast, organized criminal network. 'Sir, a new star is rising on the horizon of the Indian crime scene, with all the makings of another Dawood Ibrahim. His gang in India is a well-organized hierarchy of desperate criminals with bases in Dubai and Pakistan,' I reported. My boss thought I was indulging in hyperbole and was rather dismissive of my inferences.

A few days after our interrogation of Asif Raza Khan, the Rajkot Police took Asif's custody from the Crime Branch of Delhi Police to probe his role in the Bhaskar Parekh kidnapping case of November 2000. Asif confessed to having committed a number of sensational crimes in the company of Aftab Ansari, Amir Raza Khan (Asif's younger brother) and other gang members, including Harpreet Singh aka Happy of Delhi. He further admitted to having jihadi leanings and undergoing training at various terror camps in Pakistan. In one such camp, he had overheard that a module was being readied to attack the Indian parliament. Rajkot Police shared the information with the concerned agency immediately but the input seems to have got lost somewhere in the maze of intelligence bureaucracy.

Asif made another startling revelation. His boss Aftab Ansari had shared the ransom money collected in the Burman kidnapping case with Omar Sheikh—one of the three terrorists who had been flown out of jail on 31 December 1999 when India had to trade them for securing the safe release and return of Indian Airlines flight 814 passengers held hostage in Kandahar. Earlier, on 24 December 1999, the flight destined for Delhi from Kathmandu had been hijacked by

Harkat-ul-Mujahideen terrorists who took the flight to Afghanistan via Amritsar, Lahore and Dubai. Sheikh was subsequently involved in the killing of journalist Daniel Pearl, then with the *Wall Street Journal*. Part of the ransom money received in the Burman kidnapping—about USD 100,000 (at the time Rs 48 lakh)—had later found its way from Omar Sheikh to Mohammad Atta, the chief of the 9/11 attackers. Asif Raza Khan further disclosed to us that both Aftab Ansari and Asif himself had jihadi proclivities. They had visited Lashkar headquarters in Bahawalpur, Pakistan. Aftab had even met Azam Cheema, the launching commander of Lashkar-e-Taiba for India, in February 2000.

On 7 December 2001 Asif Raza Khan was killed in an encounter with the Rajkot Police when he tried to escape from custody. Perceived as a fake encounter by Aftab Ansari and Amir Raza Khan, the incident would set off a chain reaction in the nether world of organized crime and terror. The Indian parliament was attacked less than a week later. Though the attack was executed by operatives of the Jaish-e-Mohammad, not directly connected with Aftab and Asif, it was the beginning of a decade of terror strikes by new jihadi groups who in fact owed their origin to the killing of Asif Raza Khan and the quest for vendetta for this 'murder'. One such incident would take place a little over a month later in Kolkata.

~

On 22 January 2002 Director, CBI, P.C. Sharma hosted a breakfast at Hotel Ashok for Robert S. Mueller, Director,

Federal Bureau of Investigation (FBI), who was visiting Delhi. I too was invited and was seated next to Union Home Secretary Kamal Pande. As the meeting proceeded, I overheard an aide whisper into Pande's ears that the American Center in Kolkata had been attacked by terrorists. The name Farhan Malik figured in the muted conversation between the Home Secretary and his aide. I thought I must get going right away as, willy-nilly, I was privy to many disparate bits of information that all seemed to add up. Taking leave of the director after apprising him of the developments, I rushed to my office in the CGO Complex on Lodhi Road.

I was soon on the line with Rajeev Kumar, SSP (CID) of West Bengal, based in Kolkata. Rajeev had been in touch with me for some time prior to this incident in connection with the sensational kidnapping of Partha Pratim Roy Burman, chairman–cum–managing director of Khadim Shoes in July 2001. Rajeev had done extensive legwork in the kidnapping case and interrogated Asif Raza Khan in Rajkot. He had heard hours of recorded conversation between Aftab Ansari, negotiating the ransom amount from Dubai, and the Burman family based in Kolkata. He had obtained a scanned copy of Aftab's Pakistani passport and had all its details, which he had shared with Interpol, Delhi, and me. He had told me Aftab had a passport issued from the Regional Passport Office in Patna. I had deputed an officer to proceed to Patna and seize Aftab's original passport file in the CBI's Santalpur arms case.

Rajeev's team had arrested most of the perpetrators of the Burman kidnapping case except the ringleaders

Aftab Ansari and Asif Raza Khan. During our protracted interactions, we had hit it off well and developed a good rapport with each other. I had carefully catalogued the stray bits of information on Aftab that Rajeev had given. Many other details about Aftab had emerged during Asif Raza Khan's interrogation in the Santalpur arms case. My batchmate Sudhir Sinha, then the commissioner of police, Rajkot, was investigating the Bhaskar Parekh kidnapping case. He too had shared several inputs on Aftab and his gang with me. I put them all together and prepared a dossier on Aftab, appending to it a copy of his passport file obtained from Patna Passport Office.

When I spoke with Rajeev on the morning of 22 January 2002, he gave me the details of the attack in Kolkata, in which four policemen had been killed and several others injured. The terrorists had come riding two motorcycles at 6.30 a.m. and opened fire indiscriminately on the policemen deployed at the American Center while the change of guard was in progress. The policemen were caught totally by surprise and couldn't react. Rajeev had received a call at his residence on his landline from one Farhan Malik claiming responsibility for the attack. Having heard Aftab's recorded voice during the Burman kidnapping case investigations, Rajeev addressed him by his real name. That caught the caller by surprise and he hung up. Aftab then called *Anand Bazar Patrika*, a Kolkata newspaper, posing as Farhan Malik and claimed responsibility for the terror attack. It was this news that was flashed all over and had reached the Home Secretary's ears at the breakfast table in Hotel Ashok that morning.

Rajeev quickly ascertained the calling number from the Kolkata telephone exchange. It was the same number from which the Burman family had received calls for ransom. At that time the caller had identified himself as Aftab Ansari. It was more than certain that he and Farhan Malik were the same person. The mobile number from which calls had been placed to Kolkata was passed on to me and I, in turn, shared it with K.C. Singh, the Indian ambassador in Abu Dhabi (UAE).

During the course of the day, I suggested to my director that the matter be brought to the notice of the highest office in the government. The man behind the Santalpur arms trafficking case was also the mastermind of the attack on the American Center in Kolkata. It was time we involved the Americans in nabbing Aftab Ansari in Dubai. There was a probability they would respond positively as one of their own overseas facilities had come under attack. I suggested to the director that he should meet the prime minister and request him to use his good offices to convey a message to the US authorities. The director took my suggestion and sought an appointment with the PM on an urgent basis.

The same evening Director Sharma called me on my mobile at around eight, soon after I returned home from work. He said he had met the PM and briefed him. PM Vajpayee had immediately summoned his principal Secretary, Brajesh Mishra, and asked him to get the Americans in the loop. When Brajesh Mishra said he would call the US ambassador to his office the following day, the PM retorted that it needed to be done immediately.

Presumably, before the director telephoned me, the US ambassador had been spoken to and had agreed to help. He was waiting at the US Embassy for a dossier on Aftab Ansari before proceeding further. The director asked me if I could get the dossier from my office and hand it over to the US ambassador. I said the dossier was with me in my briefcase and I could deliver it in five minutes. I lived in Chanakyapuri then, in a government accommodation, close to the American embassy.

When I reached the embassy on Shanti Path, I was taken to its Banquet Hall. A dinner was being hosted in honour of the visiting FBI chief by the US ambassador to India, Robert Blackwill. The dossier, with a photograph of Aftab Ansari, his Dubai mobile number, passport details, etc., was received by a senior embassy staffer on behalf of the ambassador. I returned home a contented man. We had pulled out all the stops and done everything possible to nab the fugitive.

~

On 5 February 2002 I was in a meeting with the Joint Intelligence Committee in their office on Parliament Street when Ambassador Singh called me on my mobile from Abu Dhabi. I excused myself from the meeting to take his call. '*Aap ka banda pakad liya hai, aap jaldi Dubai aa jao* (Your guy has been arrested. Come to Dubai soon),' said the ambassador in a matter-of-fact and officious manner. I returned to the conference room, took leave of the chair and rushed to the CBI headquarters.

The director was in a meeting with senior officers in the CBI's conference hall but I decided to walk in anyway. I conveyed the news of Aftab's arrest in Dubai by whispering it into his ears. He asked me to wait until he wound up the meeting. After hearing the details of my conversation with K.C. Singh he spoke to the ambassador himself. Thereafter, I was directed to leave for Dubai post-haste.

The Indian Airlines flight to Dubai leaving Delhi in the evening was full. Nonetheless, I went to the airport to take my chances. At the airlines counter I was informed again that finding a seat on the flight was out of the question as there were no cancellations. I had to throw my weight around as a senior CBI officer on a special mission and told the airlines authorities that I must reach Dubai, even if it meant travelling in the cockpit! Somehow, they accommodated me in the plane and I was on my way.

~

The following morning I met senior Dubai officials at Ambassador Singh's office. They wanted evidence from me to determine the identity of the man in their custody and confirm that he was indeed Aftab Ansari. I handed over a dossier prepared by the Delhi Police with Aftab's fingerprints. Aftab's passport file obtained from Patna with his thumb impression was also given. The Dubai officers asked Ambassador Singh and me to wait until the process of confirming Ansari's identity was completed and further orders from their higher-ups had been received.

It was then that the ambassador informed me that Aftab Ansari aka Farhan Malik had been arrested at the Dubai International Airport on 23 January 2002, the day after the Kolkata attack. He was attempting to leave for Islamabad by an Emirates flight and was travelling on a Pakistani passport, J-872142, issued at Lahore in the name of Safeer Mahmood Rana. The details of the passport were the same as those I had shared with Ambassador Singh and Ambassador Blackwill. We shall never know how much the Americans contributed in getting Dubai to locate and arrest Aftab, but my own sense is that involving the Americans did, in all probability, help in getting Dubai to react fast. The Dubai authorities had kept the news of Aftab's arrest close to their chest from 23 January till 5 February.

My anxious wait continued for the remainder of 6 and 7 February, during which I was deluged with phone calls from Delhi. My bosses wanted to know the progress almost every half an hour as the Government of India was getting impatient. Finally, on 8 February, I was given the good news by our ambassador that I could take Aftab Ansari back to India as his deportation had been cleared by the Dubai government. I conveyed the information to my director with the request that a government aircraft be sent to bring the captive back to Delhi.

Our consulate in Dubai had put me up at Hotel Sheraton Jumeirah Beach with spectacular views of the waterfront, except that I had no time to stand and stare. It so happened that a horde of press reporters from Delhi were staying in the same hotel to cover an international conference. I ran into one of them in the hotel lobby. The word of my presence spread among the others. They all wanted to know what was going on and what had brought me to Dubai. I somehow warded them off, saying I was there for an Interpol meeting.

On the morning of 9 February, I was taking a walk on the corniche near the hotel when I was informed by my director that a special aircraft of the Government of India was on its way to Dubai. I was ecstatic. When the flight arrived later the same day, a team of five CBI officers, headed by DIG A.K. Gupta of Delhi Interpol, deputed to assist me, was brought by the consulate staff to the hotel where I was staying. I briefed the officers that they had to lie low and, as far as possible, stay indoors. We did not want any fly on the wall, or a mole in the hotel, scuppering our master plan!

The following morning, that is 10 February, we were driven to a relatively less used terminal of the Dubai International Airport in consulate vehicles. Reserved for chartered planes and flights leaving for Pakistan, it wore a deserted and eerie look. In fact, it was this terminal where Aftab had been arrested before he could board a flight to Islamabad. We were seated in the VIP lounge of the terminal, not sure of what was going to happen next and when.

After about half an hour of waiting, our consulate staff, accompanied by local plainclothes police officers attired in their traditional robes, asked us to follow them. We were taken to a Gulfstream plane, which had flown in from Delhi. My team members were asked to board the aircraft while I was asked to wait on the tarmac. Not unlike a scene from a racy thriller, a long luxury bus approached us leisurely from the far end of the tarmac. It shimmered in the hot April sun of the Gulf, much like a mirage in a desert. When it came to a halt near our aircraft, two blindfolded men in handcuffs were escorted out. When their blindfolds were removed, Aftab Ansari and his Gujarati compatriot Raju Anadkat stood unveiled before me. Staggered by the sudden sharp sunlight, both men raised their handcuffed arms to shade their eyes. On regaining focus they saw a surreal scene before them—plainclothes policemen all around and a waiting aircraft. It took them some time to make sense of it all. They eventually realized they were on their way to face the law of the country to which they

The last and final call: Raju Anadkat (left), Aftab Ansari (centre) and I after the handover in Dubai.

belonged. Their jaws dropped and a look of despair and despondency spread across their faces. They didn't have the faintest idea that the morning of 10 February 2002 would spell their doom.

Aftab, a bearded, barely five-and-a-half-feet tall, frail, sophisticated-looking, pleasant thirty-four-year-old, was the complete antithesis of the persona anyone would conjure of a mafia don behind sensational kidnaps and terror strikes. Raju, on the other hand, with his robust build and scruffy face, looked every bit the crook we had known him to be. He was in a loose and crumpled white shirt and a pair of grey pants and was clearly sleep-deprived.

A shiny black Mercedes drove in just then with Ambassador Singh and a senior Dubai official. It was this official who had helped us get all the clearances required to take Aftab and Raju back. Getting Raju along with Aftab was a huge surprise for us and a most welcome bonus. He was wanted in a fake currency case from 2001, registered in the Jaipur branch of the CBI, besides several other cases of kidnappings in Gujarat, Kolkata and other parts of India. He was an important member of Aftab's gang and a key participant in most cases of kidnapping committed by it.

The Dubai Police handed them over to us without any fuss and they were taken aboard the waiting plane. I thanked Ambassador Singh for the stellar role he had played in the operation and the Dubai authorities for their magnanimity. Much embracing and hand-shaking between our embassy officials and me preceded our take-off with two of the most wanted rogues of India who, sitting in Dubai, had wreaked havoc in our country for far too long.

The air of celebration that normally follows a well-deserved triumph prevailed on board the aircraft. Wide smiles were written over the faces of my colleagues. The joint efforts of a large number of officers from Kolkata Police, Delhi Police, Gujarat Police, senior functionaries of the government, our diplomatic corps based in the UAE, particularly Ambassador K.C. Singh and the CBI, had paid off. Having been at the centre of these efforts, the feeling of euphoria and elation for me was very special.

Inside the aircraft I sat opposite Aftab, got his handcuffs removed and began to talk to him while Raju Anadkat sat on the other side of the aisle with DSP M.C. Sahni. The Dubai authorities had given us a packet of Aftab's medicines, which included insulin. On learning that he was a fellow diabetic, my attitude towards him softened. I have often found that, contrary to popular belief prevalent within the police and elsewhere, most criminals open up faster when spoken to decently than when interrogated in a rough-and-ready manner. Aftab was no exception. Despite the cataclysmic

Homebound: Aftab Ansari seated in the aircraft

turn his life had taken that morning, he soon felt at ease
and was forthcoming as I continued to draw him out. We
talked all through the three-hour-long flight. He narrated
to me the story of his life, which, buttressed with a few
facts here and there collected during further investigation
and interrogation, was something like what follows.

~

Born in 1968 in the Lallapura area of Varanasi, Aftab had
a widowed mother, an elder brother and four sisters. The
word Aftab in Urdu means the sun. His parents perhaps
expected him to shine bright in life and bring glory to the
family. Shine he did, but in a bad light.

He graduated from Banaras Hindu University and joined
a course in journalism. But he soon realized journalism
was not his calling in life as it was crime that fascinated
and beckoned him. His elder brother Anwar Ahmed, a
part-time advocate and journalist, who had already cut
his teeth in crime, introduced Aftab to Dinesh Thakur,
a notorious criminal of Varanasi. Thakur saw something
special in Aftab and decided to take him under his wing.
Together they committed several kidnappings for ransom
and Aftab, under Thakur's tutelage, learnt the tricks of the
trade, including spotting wealthy targets, studying their
daily routine and habits, acquiring 'safe houses' for keeping
prospective abductees, the art of negotiating ransom, and
safe methods of collecting and moving ransom money.

In July 1995, they came to Ashok Vihar in Delhi to
collect Rs 2 lakh as extortion money from Girish Arora, a

businessman. The Delhi Police, alerted by Arora, laid a trap for the extortionists and Dinesh Thakur was gunned down in a shoot-out with the police. For once, the mentor and his pupil had slipped up in their modus operandi and paid the price for it.

Aftab was arrested and lodged in Tihar Jail where he stayed from July 1995 to November 1998. During this period Aftab came to know several fellow inmates involved in cases of terror. Talking to them for hours, he was exposed to jihadi ideology and came under its overpowering and indelible influence. Interactions with jihadi inmates in jail gradually converted this extortionist into an Islamist.

Among the people he met in jail were Kashmiri militants, each with his own woeful tale of the militant struggle in the Valley. He also became intimate with one Asif Raza Khan, a young criminal turned hard-core militant from Kolkata, who was linked to Hizb-ul-Mujahideen, a dreaded terrorist outfit. Asif was doing time in a case of 1994 of Adarsh Nagar Police Station of Delhi under TADA and the Explosive Substances Act. Aftab and Asif became close friends in prison and remained so for several years after their release from jail.

Asif introduced Aftab to the infamous Omar Sheikh while on a visit to the jail hospital. Sheikh, a London School of Economics graduate, was doing time for the kidnapping of four Western tourists—three British and one American—in October 1994, in cahoots with Kashmiri militants. He was linked to various Islamist militant groups like Jaish-e-Mohammad, al-Qaeda, Harkat-ul-Mujahideen, Harkat-ul-Ansar and the Taliban. As mentioned before, he was released from jail and flown to Kandahar in December 1999 along with Maulana Masood Azhar (founder of Jaish-e-Mohammad) and Mushtaq Ahmed Zargar, both dreaded terrorists. Sheikh was convicted for the murder of journalist Daniel Pearl and received a death sentence. Currently, he is in a Pakistan jail, awaiting execution.

Conversations with Omar Sheikh in Tihar Jail had a profound effect on Aftab Ansari. Adding to Aftab's radicalization was the company of his cellmate Akhtar Hussain aka Hashim Bhai, a hard-core militant sympathizer. Akhtar hailed from a village in Gurgaon district, not far from Delhi, and kept himself engrossed in religious books and prayers for hours every day. Aftab was deeply influenced by Akhtar's religiosity and became quite close to him. Aftab, Akhtar and Asif Raza Khan joined forces on their release from jail and worked together to commit several crimes. Aftab and Akhtar happened to meet again in a terrorist training camp some years later. This is the same Akhtar who was present in the truck in Santalpur on the night of 26–27 October 2001—the starting point of this story—when the CBI intercepted it. Akhtar evaded arrest by the CBI until 2012 before surrendering in court.

Aftab was released on bail in 1998 in the Ashok Vihar extortion case. He, however, had to keep attending court and was in dire need of money to meet his legal expenses. It was during one such visit to the court that he met Harpreet 'Happy' Singh, a specialist kidnapper, who had already carved a niche for himself in the world of crime. He, like Aftab, was also in need of money and when Aftab proposed to Happy that they should plan to kidnap a wealthy person together to make quick money, he jumped at the offer.

Happy knew Sanjay Khanna aka Chunky of the Babloo Srivastava gang, notorious for kidnappings for ransom in urban settings (see the story 'Operation Desert Safari'). He got in touch with Chunky and asked him to send seed money to fund kidnappings that Happy was planning with his fellows. Sanjay sent Rs 7 lakh, in two instalments, with which two second-hand cars—a Maruti 800 and a Maruti van—were bought. Happy roped in his trusted associates to augment the gang and was ready for action.

Anand Aggarwal, a coal merchant from Varanasi, was targeted for the first kidnapping as Aftab had prior knowledge of Aggarwal's overflowing coffers. Two houses were taken on rent: one in Ashok Vihar in Varanasi and another in Hyderabad Colony in Lucknow—both to be used as safe houses. On 5 August 1999, Aftab Ansari, Happy and others impersonated CBI officers and abducted Anand Aggarwal from his house. The ransom collected was Rs 3 crore, negotiated by Aftab and Happy's compatriots—Raju Anadkat and Chunky—both then in Dubai. With this kidnapping Aftab Ansari resumed his career in crime as a gang leader of crooks specializing in extortion.

The next big target was Niranjan Shah, a Mumbai-based wheeler-dealer, who in partnership with Raju Anadkat had sent a consignment of drugs to Canada. When it came to dividing the booty, Shah claimed that the consignment was seized by the Canadian police en route and refused to pay Raju his share. Raju decided to recover his share by kidnapping Shah. He instructed Aftab Ansari and Asif Raza Khan to kidnap Shah in Kathmandu during one of Shah's business visits there. He was kept in confinement for fifty-five days in Maharajganj, Kathmandu. Several leading lights of the underworld like Fazl-ur-Rehman, O.P. Singh, Chhota Rajan intervened on Shah's behalf with Raju Anadkat to peacefully settle the dispute and release Shah. Eventually, Raju Anadkat and Aftab Ansari agreed to settle for Rs 20 lakh and released Shah on Darbar Marg in Nepal's capital.

But the mother of all kidnappings was yet to come. In July 2001, they targeted Partha Pratim Roy Burman, chairman–cum–managing director of Khadim Shoes in Kolkata. Aquib Ali Khan aka Firasat was tasked to procure weapons and a car from Delhi, which he did. Five armed men blocked Burman's Tata Safari multi-utility vehicle with a Maruti van on C.N. Roy Road, Tiljala, near his factory in the southern outskirts of the city. Burman was forcibly dragged out of his vehicle and bundled into the kidnappers' Maruti van. When he tried to resist and escape, one of the abductors shot at Burman, wounding him in the arm.

Burman was taken to a safe house in Haroa in North 24 Parganas district, near the Indo-Bangladesh border, where the abductors had his injuries treated. He was kept in confinement while the Burman family negotiated with Aftab Ansari, the mastermind behind the kidnapping, who was then in Dubai. Eventually, a ransom of Rs 4 crore was paid to Ansari through 'hawala' from Hyderabad.

(Hawala operators receive and send money across the world through non-banking channels for a commission using a system of coded words and numeric clues such as the last three digits of a particular currency note that must be verified at the other end. Typically, the receiver of the money shares the numerals of a currency note he possesses with the sender who lets his hawala dealer know of the number. The dealer then informs his counterpart at the receiving end before whom the recipient of the money must produce the currency note bearing the same number. These operators have a worldwide network and money travels both ways.)

Burman was released after eight days of captivity and left on the roadside in Dum Dum area, several kilometres away from his Salt Lake residence. As mentioned earlier, part of the ransom money collected in this case was used in funding the 9/11 attack on the World Trade Center in New York. The fact that Aftab gave Rs 49 lakh to Omar Sheikh who passed it on to Mohammad Atta, the mastermind behind the terror attack, was mentioned in the testimony of John S. Pistole, deputy assistant director, Counterterrorism Division, FBI, before the Senate Committee on Terrorist Financing in July 2003 at Washington DC.

Aftab also narrated how the attack on the American Center in Kolkata was planned and executed, primarily to avenge the killing of Asif Raza Khan by the Gujarat Police. It was also meant to send a message to the USA and was timed to coincide with the FBI chief's visit. Both he and Asif's younger brother Amir Raza Khan had collaborated with their gang members in India to carry out the terror attack in the name of Asif Raza Khan Commando Force. This outfit would later become the Indian Mujahideen which continues to trouble Indian law enforcement agencies till date. Amir Raza Khan runs its affairs from Pakistan.

Aftab confessed to have called Rajeev Kumar, the SSP (CID), West Bengal, and *Amrit Bazar Patrika*, a local newspaper of Kolkata, soon after the attack on the American Center.

~

The flying time between Dubai and Delhi whizzed by, thanks to the engaging conversation with Aftab. Raju Anadkat, meanwhile, was being interrogated by my other colleagues on board. We were soon flying over Delhi, awaiting clearance to land. When our Gulfstream touched down at Delhi, with the aircraft still taxiing, I switched my mobile on. Almost instantaneously, it began to ring. Rajdeep Sardesai, then working with NDTV, was on the line. He wanted to know whether I had arrived with Aftab Ansari. I tried to be evasive and asked him why he wanted the information. He said Prime Minister Atal Behari Vajpayee had announced at a public meeting in Meerut that the man behind the attack on the American Center in Kolkata had been apprehended in Dubai and was being brought to Delhi. So the news of this successful operation had already been conveyed to the people of India by the prime minister himself! After all, the PM had played a small but critical role in the operation leading up to the fugitive's arrest. I had no option but to confirm the news to Rajdeep.

I got off the aircraft jumping with joy, almost as if I had scored the winning run for India in a Cricket World Cup final! Some of my colleagues from the Delhi Police and the Intelligence Bureau were waiting on the tarmac. They were not only my colleagues but also my well-wishers, who were genuinely proud of and happy with my success. While the two captives were taken by other members of my team to the CBI headquarters, I drove to my residence with the colleagues who had come to receive me. My wife had arranged a huge cake to celebrate my return and the successful accomplishment of the mission. We all helped ourselves generously to the cake and there was much rejoicing at home that evening.

The mood in the CBI headquarters was similarly upbeat. After all, not often are such arrests made. Officers from other intelligence agencies were keen to speak to Aftab Ansari first. We allowed it without any ado. Meanwhile, I debriefed my director on all that had transpired in Dubai. He asked me to proceed to the Press Information Bureau at Shastri Bhavan where a joint press conference was to be addressed by officials from the ministries of home and external affairs to announce the arrest and deportation of Aftab Ansari. Needless to say, TV channels and newspapers the following day were full of stories on the prize catch.

Aftab's interrogation threw up a huge database on Lashkar-e-Taiba, the location of their training camps, the number of recruits under training, and so on. He also gave information on his associates and their current locations. Interrogation reports for both Aftab and Raju were painstakingly prepared, and continue to be storehouses of information on both the underworld and Pak-based Islamic terrorism.

~

There is an interesting aside that I can't help but mention. The Kolkata Police took Anadkat in custody soon after we brought him back to Delhi. They had to interrogate him in the Partha Roy Burman kidnapping case. The CBI brought Raju back once they were done. After his custodial interrogation in the Jaipur fake currency case of the CBI, he was remanded to judicial custody and kept in the Jaipur Jail. Several production warrants were pending against him from different courts of India. For some strange reason, maybe in an inadvertent slip-up, those pending warrants went missing when his judicial remand in the Jaipur fake currency case was over and he was released on bail. Raju Anadkat realized that the jail officials were committing a grave error as he was still wanted by several police forces of the country and warrants were pending against him. He asked the jail staff to not release him. They thought he had dubious reasons for staying on or was trying to act smart with them. They pushed him out of the jail premises forcibly without verifying what he told them.

Once thrown out of jail, Raju called Inspector V.K. Shukla of the CBI, the investigating officer of the Jaipur fake currency case, from the nearest telephone booth and apprised him of the piquant situation he was in. Taken totally by surprise, the CBI officer asked him to come to Delhi and report to him. Since the following day was a Sunday, Raju asked the inspector if he could visit the Pushkar Ji Temple of Lord Vishnu, located a couple of hours away from Jaipur, and then come to him on Monday. The inspector, though in a quandary, sensed honesty and earnestness in what Raju said. He acquiesced and approved of his plan.

Lo and behold, come Monday morning and Raju was seen waiting outside the CBI headquarters in Delhi! When asked to explain his rather unbelievable and least expected behaviour, Raju told Inspector Shukla he wanted to face trial in all the cases against him and be done with them once and for all. He was tired of running from the law and wanted to lead a normal life. He was prepared to go back to jail, if the courts so ordered. It was high time, he said, that he did penance for his misdeeds and then spent his life peacefully with his children.

This was a rarest of rare situation in the history of Indian crime when an underworld don had decided to atone for his past errors. Usually hardened criminals like Raju Anadkat elude the CBI or law enforcement in general. Yet here was a man who was willing to tell it all, instead of hiding and running or fighting in courtrooms for long years.

Today, Raju Anadkat leads a normal life in Rajkot. He is still facing trial in a few cases in which he is on bail. His daughter studies at one of the Indian Institutes of Management, arguably the most coveted business schools in India. His son has a flourishing shipping business. The

Court of the Almighty seems to have accepted his penance and granted him divine pardon!

Aftab Ansari, in the interim, has been sentenced to death in the American Center attack case and awaits execution lodged in Alipore Central Jail, Kolkata. His accomplice in the Partha Roy Burman kidnapping case, Harpreet Singh aka Happy, was killed on 5 May 2014 by a fellow inmate in Presidency Jail, Kolkata. Happy was serving the life sentence he had received in the kidnapping case when Nizamuddin, another prisoner, battered him to death with a brick while he was doing yoga.

~

I consider the operation leading up to the arrests of Aftab Ansari and Raju Anadkat as one of the most satisfying of my career. Never had I imagined that the seizure of arms, ammunition and explosives in a remote area of Gujarat would lead us to the perpetrators of a serious terror attack in Kolkata, over a thousand miles away. Our hunt for the mastermind led us to the Gulf, from where we brought him back in a rather dramatic fashion. And the discovery that one of the captives was linked with the funding of the 9/11 terror attack of 2001 added a global dimension to the operation.

We had traced the backward and forward linkages meticulously and, most importantly, in close coordination with the police officers of several states, our diplomatic corps and the PM himself. By sheer providence, I was the fulcrum of these efforts. It further reinforces my undying belief that in synergy, mutual trust and cooperation lie the key to success in law enforcement. The contours of the operation also underscore the necessity for a federal agency, which can act as the pivot around which all action can revolve. Whether there is such an agency in our country today is a moot question.

2

Operation Desert Safari
The story of an anti-kidnap operation

When Thekkat Siddhique arrived at the Indira Gandhi International Airport in Delhi in the wee hours of 11 March 2001, he could hardly contain his excitement. An Abu Dhabi–based entrepreneur, always ready to venture into uncharted territories, he was in the capital on the invitation of one Vijay Rathore, whom he had never met. Claiming to be a prosperous Delhi-based businessman, Vijay had contacted him repeatedly on his mobile phone and through emails, inviting him to Delhi for business negotiations in the export–import of ceramics. The mere thought that he had been sought out by Rathore was enough to make Thekkat undertake this journey.

As he stepped out of the arrival lounge he could sense spring in the Delhi air, which was still cool and crisp. The spring in his own step was no less apparent. Vijay Rathore

had informed him that he would be received by his secretary
Amar, who would be carrying a mobile phone with the
number 98101xxxxx. He rang up Amar and they decided
to meet at the main exit of the airport. Amar informed him
that Vijay was waiting for him at his office-cum-residence.
They were soon on their way in a silver Hyundai Accent
with Amar at the wheel. Thekkat called his wife in Abu
Dhabi and informed her of his safe arrival in Delhi, assuring
her he would be home soon.

Thekkat Siddhique originally hailed from Calicut in
Kerala and had shifted to Abu Dhabi about twenty-two
years ago in search of greener pastures. In his mid-forties,
wheatish complexioned, and of medium height, he had an
amiable and respectable personality, ideal for the liaison work
he did for several companies. He had done reasonably well
for himself but was given to braggadocio about his wealth,
unmindful of the unwanted attention that could attract.

As it turned out, a Dubai-based gangster had received
news of Thekkat's 'boundless riches' and plotted to have
him abducted during his visit to India, aware that such
adventurism in the Gulf was foolhardy to attempt. The
gangster had enough 'connections' in India to implement
his plans.

As the Hyundai Accent sped through Delhi's chaotic
traffic, Thekkat was lost in his thoughts. So deep were
his reveries that neither the city's notorious smog nor the
boorish driving of Delhi's motorists made any impression
on him. As Delhi's landscape whizzed by, snapshots of
his own life flashed in his mind. He pinched himself to
remember the gifts he had planned to buy for his dear wife.

Half an hour later the Accent came to a halt outside a
well-appointed bungalow in a posh south Delhi colony.
Thekkat was smiling to himself when he walked on to
the premises, hoping that the soil of Delhi would catapult
his financial fortunes, and his life would change forever.
As he neared the entrance, he expected he would soon
be shaking hands with tony businessmen in well-cut dark
suits and designer ties, and, of course, wearing very broad
smiles. But hopes often slip away like quicksilver. Once
inside the bungalow, he came face-to-face with a bunch of
shabbily dressed and unkempt men. It not only seemed that
they had never smiled in their lives, but from their hostile
stares it also appeared to Thekkat that talking business was
the last thing on their minds. There was no customary
exchange of greetings either. As hope vanished, and fear
grew, things happened in a blur. Very soon they did make
him sit, but in an odd way, pushing him roughly towards a
chair. Almost immediately after, there was much slapping
and shoving, and then a torrent of blistering underworld
invective came his way, most of which sounded very alien
to his rapidly reddening ears. Instead of feeling welcome
and relaxing with a set of friendly business counterparts,
Thekkat was now trembling before a bunch of dangerous
abductors, one of whom was pointing a handgun straight at
him. Would he see his family again? Would the abductors
make him disappear? Would they torture him endlessly?
As his mind was caught in a whirl of unwanted thoughts,
his body began to stiffen with fear and his muscles started
paining from the generous thrashing he had received.
Thekkat wondered why he had not done any background

checks before taking the flight to Delhi. But it was too late now.

The captive was informed that a ransom of $2 million (over Rs 12 crore) would have to be paid if he wanted to be set free. Thekkat was quick to realize that the exaggerated bluster about his affluence was coming home to roost. When he said he didn't have that kind of money, he was beaten even more mercilessly. He was made to speak to his wife in Abu Dhabi and notify her of his abduction and the ransom demand for his release. Within minutes Thekkat's life and the lives of his family members had gone topsy-turvy; the castles he had built in the air came crashing down.

On 12 March, the day following the kidnapping, Thekkat's distraught family members met K.C. Singh, India's ambassador in Abu Dhabi, seeking his help. The ambassador promptly took a written complaint from the victim's wife and faxed it to R.K. Raghavan, the then director, CBI.

Twelfth March 2001 was a Monday and a hectic week lay ahead for me. The thrill of an enjoyable round of golf the previous day was still fresh in my mind. But the days ahead had thrills of a different order in store for me that not even golf could match. Soon after I reached office, I received a call from Abu Dhabi. Ambassador Singh was on the line. He gave me the details of the incident as reported to him and informed me that he had directed two close relatives of Siddhique, one of whom was a retired police officer from Kerala, to reach New Delhi and meet me.

Ambassador K.C. Singh and I had known each other for nearly a decade. In the mid-1990s, he was Joint Secretary, Consular, Passport and Visa (CPV) Section in the ministry of external affairs when I was handling the Mumbai bomb blasts case. We met frequently then in connection with official work. I always found him very responsive and positive to our requirements and, I guess, he liked me as well.

Thekkat Siddhique's relatives met me on 15 March and narrated the kidnap story. The enormity of the crime dawned on me with all its transnational dimensions. It was a live kidnap situation with a non-resident Indian's life hanging tenuously by a thread. The ransom calls were being received overseas while the hostage was somewhere in India, though not necessarily in Delhi. Since a satellite phone was being used to call Thekkat's family members we could not rule out the possibility of Thekkat having been taken out of Delhi.

I was not too sure how to respond. The CBI, its sterling reputation notwithstanding, was not equipped to handle such cases. Adept at dealing with cases of corruption and economic crimes, its capabilities in tackling a live kidnap situation had never been tested. It was a job cut out for the local police or one of their specialized units like the Crime Branch or the Special Cell/Anti-Terrorism Squad. Following the ambassador's call, the options before me were to either direct Thekkat's relatives to the Delhi Police, refer them to the Special Crimes Division of the CBI or take up the case in one of my own branches in the Economic Offences Wing of the CBI, of which I was then the joint director. The last option was the most tempting but was fraught with inherent risks. At the same time, I was conscious of the faith reposed in me by our ambassador in Abu Dhabi, whom I was loath to disappoint. Also, the case involved rescuing an NRI and had the potential for providing a fair amount of adrenaline rush, thrills and adventure, which every police officer craves, or should crave, if he is worth his salt.

At this stage, it is important to mention that the CBI has three divisions: the Anti-Corruption Division, the Economic Offences Wing and the Special Crimes Division. Cases of murder, robbery and kidnappings are usually investigated by the last, which has branches located in different parts of the country, just as the other two divisions do. As already mentioned, the CBI undertaking a case that involved a live hostage situation requiring search-and-rescue operations was unheard of. Volunteering to investigate such a case and, that too, a branch of the Economic Offences Wing, was sticking one's neck out a bit too far.

My career's track record thus far had earned me, by God's grace, ample laurels and medallions. I had had the privilege of leading investigations into sensational crimes, often involving the underworld. Then why was I racked by worries and imaginary fears instead of just going ahead with this case? At the same time, why take it up and risk my own reputation along with that of the CBI? If things did not fall into place, the consequences could be enormous. The media would run me down for years, as would my own colleagues. I was coveting the excitement of action, but couldn't throw prudence and discretion out of the window.

I was still mulling over the details given by Siddhique's relatives and the strange dilemma I was in, when, by a happy coincidence, Rajbir Singh, an assistant commissioner of the Delhi Police, Special Cell, walked into my office. Rajbir had worked with me in the Delhi Police when I was DCP of south Delhi district and was well known for his detective and operational skills. Earlier, too, I had coordinated with him and his team in several operations undertaken by me in the CBI and we had always come up trumps. I asked for his opinion on what I should do after sharing with him all the available details of the case. His opinion was unequivocal; such challenging cases should not be allowed to go elsewhere. He also expressed his keenness to be associated with the investigation if I decided to take it up. From providing technical support to armed back-up, he would be an invaluable partner in a case such as this. He had a crack team under him, comprising tried and trusted go-getters, which he offered to place at my disposal, along with his own services and expertise. His immediate superiors in the Delhi Police, DCP Ashok Chand and Special Commissioner S. Ramakrishnan, had given him carte blanche where collaborating with me was concerned.

Whatever little doubt lurked in my mind vanished. I rushed to P.C. Sharma, then special director and my immediate superior, and brought the matter to his notice. He too was absolutely clear that we should indeed take up this case in one of our branches in the Economic Offences

Wing and investigate it. He was very sure that, like several other operations undertaken in the EOW during my tenure, we would succeed again. His confidence in me was inspiring and I became determined to rise to his expectations one more time.

The first and foremost job was to get the director to assign this case, which in the normal course of events would have gone to a Special Crimes unit, to me. P.C. Sharma immediately got that done and the fax sent by our ambassador in the UAE to the director reached my desk within minutes. But, to my horror, the two relatives who had come to liaise with us did not want the case to be registered formally. Perhaps they didn't wish to go through the full run of the Indian legal system. Their desire was to secure Thekkat's release without getting into legal formalities. This, coming from a man who was a former police officer, was particularly distressing. However, our position was very clear; a complaint had been received from our ambassador and we had no option but to register a case. A case of abduction for ransom with threat to cause death (Section 364-A of the IPC) and criminal conspiracy (Sec 120-B, IPC) was registered on 16 March and investigation formally taken up. The joint operation of the CBI and the Special Cell of the Delhi Police to rescue Thekkat Siddhique was codenamed Operation Desert Safari.

Five days after Thekkat had been abducted, my mobile phone rang late in the evening. It was Siddhique's elder brother, Ahmed Koya. Thekkat had been made to speak to him by the kidnappers to disclose the ransom amount. During the conversation, Thekkat had managed to speak a few words in his mother tongue, Malayalam. He had cleverly managed to slip in a few stray and incoherent bits of information while talking to his brother: he was being held hostage on the second floor of a building in the vicinity of a shop with the phone number 6683899; also, he could hear aircraft flying right over his head all the time; and a public telephone booth was located close by.

I immediately rang up 197, the public phone inquiry number, to ascertain the address where a phone with the number 6683899 was installed. I was informed that it was F-73, Begumpur, Malviya Nagar. I shared the information with ACP Rajbir Singh and asked him where the two of us could meet to follow up on the lead. He asked me to stay at home while he took up the preliminary fieldwork.

Shortly after midnight, Rajbir called. He sounded terribly excited; he had located not only the shop but also a house close by which matched the description given to Koya by Thekkat. We decided to meet at Essex Farms, a commercial banquet hall, near the Indian Institute of Technology, Delhi. I informed Ramnish, the investigating officer, and Hitesh Awasthy, my DIG in the CBI, and asked them to reach the rendezvous point immediately.

My wife saw me taking my .22 Walther PPK pistol out of my cupboard and knew something big and dangerous was on. It was perhaps the first time during my tenure in the CBI that she had seen me leaving home armed, that too past midnight. Ordinarily, if I were serving in the Delhi Police in the same rank, I would have over a thousand men to fall back on. But in my current assignment things were different. The CBI is a perpetually understaffed and lean organization. Most things are best done yourself, hands-on. In the bargain you learn a lot but at times it can land you in situations you are not used to. So here I was, leaving home past midnight with only my pistol for company. Like any concerned spouse, my wife too was worried and asked me to be careful. There was no time to wait for my official vehicle to arrive so I left in my private car, driving myself.

When I reached Essex Farms, the rendezvous point, Rajbir was already there with about twenty of his best team members, including Inspector Mohan Chand Sharma, his right-hand man in the Special Cell. The enthusiasm and motivation of Rajbir's men had to be seen to be believed. Wearing bulletproof jackets, and armed to the teeth with AKs and semi-automatics, they presented a picture of determination and supreme confidence. They also carried powerful torches and a long ladder. The body language of the boys was electric and inspiring.

Begumpur is one of the many urbanized villages of Delhi. It is on the erstwhile agricultural land of such villages that posh residential colonies in India's capital city have come up. Most high-end colonies in the city, therefore, are invariably juxtaposed with such villages, which themselves have grown in a most unplanned and haphazard manner. Houses are both pucca and semi-pucca, with poor municipal amenities of sewerage and roads. The village residents have retained their old lifestyle. It is fascinating to see old men sitting on cots outside their homes, wearing traditional clothes with *saafaa*s (head wraps) and smoking hookahs, while the womenfolk, veiled in their dupattas, pass by. Cows and buffaloes vie for space with automobiles and two-wheelers in the narrow lanes. Every village has a head, usually called a *pradhan*, whose writ runs large in the village. The residents retain their earthy ways, struggling to keep urban modernity at arm's length. Such rural settings are usually less than fifty metres away from tony colonies that the BMWs and Mercedes of the super-rich gentry flit in and out of.

Begumpur, one such village, sits between Sarvodaya Enclave and Sarvapriya Vihar, both posh residential colonies. A few beautiful historical monuments, largely lying uncared for and decaying by the day, dot the area, seemingly amused with the changing times.

~

Rajbir had thought it wise to wake up Inspector Rajendra Bakshi of the Delhi Police, who happened to be a resident of Begumpur. Inspector Bakshi, an ace investigator in his own right, had in turn contacted the local pradhan and sought his help. While carrying out any police operation in Delhi's urbanized villages it is always advisable to take a local authority along as a facilitator. It makes things easier and safer. Inspector Bakshi and the pradhan were waiting for us when we reached Begumpur, approaching it from the Aurobindo Marg end, across Sarvodaya Enclave, a colony located to the west, overlapping the village.

The pradhan informed us that he knew of the premises Rajbir had located, which belonged to an exporter of garments and handicraft. He also knew that the exporter had regular business dealings with Dubai and had several people from the Gulf visiting him from time to time. Some of them, according to him, looked suspicious. This only strengthened our conviction that we were on the right track.

The Begumpur house had a huge courtyard at the back. There was no way to reach its second floor from there, even if we used the ladder we were carrying. This left us with no option but to raid it from the front. The front door was solid teak and breaking it open would only alarm the inmates and neighbours alike. On our request, the pradhan rang the doorbell while we hid ourselves. First the lights on the first floor came on. A Nepali servant peeped out and spoke to the pradhan. Despite requests from the pradhan, he refused to open the door and switched off the lights. Then the lights on the second floor came on and we heard a flurry of activity. We knew that the time to move in had arrived and broke open the front teak door. What had looked impregnable was gone in seconds. Homes are meant to be your castles—unless the cops are at the gates and decide to barge in! We rushed in and scrambled up the stairs. But, to our utter disappointment, all we found on the first and second floors were frightened labourers hailing from Nepal. It came to light that the caretaker, who had earlier spoken with the pradhan, was scared to open the door because he had allowed a handful of fellow Nepalese to stay on the premises. This was not in the knowledge of his employer, who also owned the building. Thus, our first raid had proved futile, even though the

Begumpur house entirely matched the description given by the victim.

We continued to scour the area, checking house after house, while planes kept flying overhead, reminding us that we were close yet not quite there. In most houses that we checked, young students preparing for the entrance examination to the coveted IITs were staying as paying guests. They were rudely woken up by our past-midnight knocks. We decided to call off the search at the break of first light—sleepless and disappointed, unable to comprehend why we could not reach our target despite seemingly specific and reasonably pin-pointed leads.

Once home, I tried to snatch a wink or two but to no avail. I worried endlessly for the man who was being held hostage by desperate transnational criminals. At the same time, I must admit, I fretted for my own reputation, which, I felt, was in grave jeopardy. I asked myself: *Have I, on this occasion, bitten more than I could chew?* In case anything went wrong and the abducted man was found killed somewhere, would it not bring a bad name to the CBI and to me? Imaginary fears had begun to get the better of me.

Ahmed Koya called me at about eleven the same morning. Thekkat had been made to speak to his family again by the kidnappers and, in the course of the conversation, had slipped in more clues—white plastic flowerpots and green net on the terrace of the premises where he was being held. Some clothes had been kept out in the open to dry. A couple of mosques with their round domes were visible in the vicinity.

Ahmed Koya made it very clear to me that his brother was under tremendous duress. Whatever his kidnapped brother was conveying to him was quite garbled and whatever Koya was telling us was based on what he could make out of their conversation. In the meanwhile, Koya played for time with the kidnappers.

Considering that it would not be proper to bother the Delhi Police boys, who had been up all night, I decided to set off on my own. I mainly concentrated on the Sarvodaya Enclave area where I found that every other flat seemed to match most of the description given by the hostage. If it had flowerpots, the green net was not in sight. If both were present, there was no dome-like structure nearby. Exasperated, I reached the residence of Inspector Rajendra Bakshi, the Begumpur resident who had helped us the previous night, and sought his help. He immediately came with me and we searched many flats in Sarvodaya Enclave and Begumpur with the help of local property dealers, but to no avail.

~

Meanwhile, we had commenced work on the technical aspects of the case. We had managed to get Thekkat's international roaming mobile number 97150641xxx from his family who, on our request, had got a printout of the calls made and received by this number from the UAE mobile service provider. The analysis of the call log showed that it had been in touch with a satellite phone number 0087376275xxxx. Thekkat's telephone book in

Abu Dhabi showed this number in the name of a Vijay Rathore of Delhi.

Inquiries made with the mobile service providers in Delhi showed that Thekkat, on reaching Delhi, had called a Delhi mobile number 98101xxxxx. Location parameters of both the numbers on the morning of 11 March, at the time Thekkat's flight arrived in Delhi, indicated their location to be around IGI Airport. We analysed the call details of the Delhi mobile phone and took it under interception. We found that the user was in touch with a girl in Vasant Kunj and attempting to fix a date with her soon.

Further analysis of these mobile numbers and other connected numbers that figured in their call details revealed that the user of 98101xxxxx was also using two other mobile numbers 981020xxx8 and 981002xxx9. Thus, the concerned gangster had three mobile handsets with IMEI numbers 33212935923xxxx, 44519946137xxxx and 44736687469xxxx. One more IMEI, 44912387152xxxx, appeared in the call details of mobile 98101xxxxx. The most significant finding was that the location parameters of 98101xxxxx showed that it was constantly in and around Begumpur, the area in which we were desperately hunting for the kidnappers and their victim. To some extent, it reassured us that we were on the right track.

The Special Cell boys, who had earlier investigated a kidnapping case in which one M.C. Mahajan of Desh Bandhu Gupta Road had been abducted on 23 November 2000, were able to connect that the same IMEI number, 44912387152xxxx, had been used in that kidnapping as well. Mahajan had subsequently been rescued and eight kidnappers arrested. They were all from Uttar Pradesh. The gangster using that mobile had been identified as Virender Pant aka Chhotu, a dreaded underworld criminal who was a close associate of Babloo Srivastava's, a mafia don from UP. The interception of Pant's telephones in the Mahajan case had revealed that he had been calling Abu Salem under the code name 'Rathore'. The name Vijay had also been used in that case.

We were now more or less certain that Thekkat Siddhique was in the hands of Virender Pant, who usually operated in tandem with his close associate Sanjay Khanna aka Chunky. Virender Pant belonged to a respectable family from Himachal Pradesh. He had studied at Rai University in Haryana. Although a keen sportsman, bad company had brought him into crime. He was young, handsome and sophisticated-looking, fluent in both Hindi and English.

His inseparable partner in crime was Chunky, who belonged to a decent south Delhi family that owned a sprawling bungalow in Safdarjang Development Area. Chunky was equally presentable and glib. The duo made a formidable pair of kidnappers who usually carried out hatchet jobs for more 'senior' criminals. They and their gang had the expertise and the gumption to abduct wealthy persons in urban settings and extort huge sums of money. Given their suave and presentable personas, they could operate in cities with considerable ease and facility. Killing hostages, if the ransom was not paid, was part of their modus operandi. They had committed several kidnappings in the past for Babloo Srivastava, Abu Salem, Fazl-ur-Rehman (or Fazlu), Ali Budesh, Aftab Ansari, etc., in different big cities in India like Delhi, Kolkata, Mumbai, Lucknow and so on.

These revelations were cause for further worry. Was it now necessary and prudent for me to request the commissioner of police, Delhi, to put the entire might of the Delhi Police behind this case so that the kidnapped person could be rescued and his precious life saved? I was also beginning to ask myself why I had followed the advice of a maverick ACP and taken up the investigation of a kidnapping case involving a rescue operation. After all, I was in the CBI, a joint director handling economic offences. What business did I have getting involved in a case of kidnapping with hardly any resources of my own to handle such an operation? If anything went wrong, no fingers would be pointed at the ACP or the Delhi Police. The entire blame would lie at my door and the CBI's.

Meanwhile, quite understandably, the tone and tenor of Koya's calls from Abu Dhabi kept changing for the worse. He was gradually sounding aggressive and reproachful. He said he had committed a grave error by reporting the matter to the Indian police, the CBI included, who in any case are not known to be professionally competent and efficient. If any harm came to his brother, the entire responsibility would be mine. On 17 March, six days after his brother was kidnapped, he disclosed that his family had negotiated the ransom amount and decided to pay US$700,000 (over Rs 4 crore) the following day, get his brother released and be done with it.

When all our efforts to trace Thekkat drew a blank till late that night, I decided to talk it over with Rajbir and tell him about my assessment of the situation. He was quick to sense my serious apprehensions and did his bit to assuage them. He reminded me that one of the gang members was already on our radar and was going to meet his Vasant Kunj girlfriend soon. If nothing else worked, Rajbir said, we could easily pick him up at a time of our choosing and extract the details of the place where the hostage was being kept. His sense of confidence and calm did its bit to make me think positively. I returned home, a trifle reassured, yet restless and apprehensive.

~

An early-morning call the following day from Koya, reiterating his family's decision to pay $700,000, jolted me out of bed. As per the deal with the kidnappers, Koya was to travel to Dubai in the afternoon to deliver the ransom amount to the money changer deputed by the abductors to be the recipient of the booty. There was no way I could dissuade him from doing so. I told him he was free to proceed to Dubai from Abu Dhabi, but suggested that he check with me once before delivering the money, in case there had been some development at our end by then. He mockingly told me he had lost all hope and that enough was enough. How could I convince him that not only was I totally empathetic with every member of the Siddhique family but almost equally concerned about Thekkat's well-being. More importantly, I was anxious to rescue him from the clutches of the kidnappers at the earliest.

It was 18 March 2001, a Sunday, but certainly not a day to laze around at home or play golf. Bundle of nerves that I was, I once again set out on my own, looking for the elusive flat. I thought of checking out Adhchini village in south Delhi where I had seen mosques with domes while conducting an operation in 1995, which had led to the arrest of Jagtar Singh Tara, the first accused to be apprehended in the sensational assassination case of Sardar Beant Singh, the then chief minister of Punjab (read more about it in the story *'Baitha hai, sir, baitha hai!'*). I drove through the village slowly, looking around, but in vain. I proceeded towards Shivalik, another south Delhi colony. Both Adhchini and Shivalik are in close proximity of Begumpur and many flats there matched quite a few clues the hostage had given. Both localities lie in the air funnel, with planes flying overhead frequently. Ruins of mosque-like structures, as mentioned by the hostage, were aplenty in their vicinity. In almost sheer desperation, I parked my car and scoured the entire neighbourhood on foot, including Sadhana Enclave, again located in that general area. Several two-storeyed flats overlooked dome-shaped structures and quite a few of them had flowerpots on their terraces, but some other vital details like the presence of a green net or a telephone booth nearby were missing. My anxiety was rising by the minute.

I decided to drive to the Lodhi Colony office of the Special Cell to meet up with Rajbir and take fresh stock of the situation. I found two other officers of the Delhi Police present there: Inspector Rajendra Bakshi of the Crime Branch and Inspector Harcharan Verma, then posted as a station house officer in a south Delhi police station. Both of them were assisting us without keeping their superiors informed. They were doing so purely out of their goodwill for Rajbir and respect for me. Had they sought the permission of their superiors, it would never have come. For a local police force to get involved with the CBI, several formalities have to be fulfilled. The CBI must share all the details of the case and make a formal request which has to be approved by the police chief. Where was the time for all this? Involving more people meant greater risk of information leaking to the media and so on. I once again impressed upon them that it was time to involve the Delhi Police and get the local police and police control room vans to conduct house-to-house searches in the area. This had become imperative, I felt, as we were getting nowhere. If anything were to go wrong, we would be blamed for keeping all the information to ourselves and not involving the Delhi Police sooner to widen the scope of the searches.

Rajbir and the other two officers present were opposed to the idea. Verma said that the police station staff and the police control room vans would not handle the searches with the finesse that was required. Their ham-handedness would only expose the hostage to risks that could prove fatal. They reassured me once again that we were on the right track and the best thing to do was to press ahead patiently.

I returned home for lunch, still edgy and knotted up with the gravity of the situation. I got another call from Koya that his brother had been made to speak to him once again, maybe for the last time. The kidnappers had decided that enough was enough and were taking him out of the safe house where he was being held captive thus far. They would drive him in the general direction of the airport. In case the ransom was paid in Dubai as had been mutually agreed, Thekkat would be dropped at the airport and his passport returned. Adequate money would be given to him for his ticket and incidental expenses. And if the ransom was not paid, he would be shot and his body thrown on the roadside in a remote area.

Koya added that Thekkat was sobbing during the conversation but, once again, had managed to convey a few clues about his location: a wedding ceremony was under way in close proximity of the kidnappers' hideout; loud music could be heard from the venue; a car with a canvas cover was parked across the street. A red-coloured multi-storeyed building was also in view from where he was confined.

I quickly passed on the information to Rajbir who, in turn, informed the search teams already combing the area. One of these teams spotted a marriage function in progress in a park in Sarvapriya Vihar. Loud music, too, was playing at the location. One thing was clear: while we had focused our searches on the Begumpur and Sarvodaya Enclave areas, the captive was being held hostage, in all probability, in adjacent Sarvapriya Vihar. The clue given by the hostage about the landline number had kept us

going around Begumpur and Sarvodaya Enclave, ignoring
Sarvapriya Vihar altogether.

Rajbir informed me of the development and we
decided to meet at the Hauz Khas Police Colony located
on Outer Ring Road, close to the IIT crossing. Sarvapriya
Vihar was only a stone's throw away.

We gathered at the meeting point in no time. It was
about four-thirty in the afternoon. We left in unmarked
cars for Sarvapriya Vihar and regrouped again in a park.
Our presence aroused the suspicion of a few watchmen
of the colony. It was broad daylight and it was most
unusual for them to find strangers in such numbers talking
animatedly to each other. One thing was clear—the
hiding place, taking into account the latest clues, was in
Sarvapriya Vihar and not in Begumpur. But the million-
dollar question was *where* in Sarvapriya Vihar? It's a fairly
large colony with hundreds of houses located cheek by
jowl. There was no option but to check each house in
every lane to see which one fully matched the description
given by the hostage. We were closer to our destination
but not yet there.

I took Rajbir aside and discussed with him the plan
I had in mind. Every member of the team needed to be
reminded once again what we were looking for. All clues
received from the hostage had to be reiterated to everyone.
Given that we were out in broad daylight, we had to do
our best to remain as inconspicuous as possible. The only
way to do so was to walk in ones and twos. Since flats
in every lane had to be checked out for the clues, it was
decided that one person would approach a lane from one

end and the second from the other side. In case anyone found something of interest he would call Rajbir on his mobile, who in turn would inform me. We would all meet at a spot closest to the premises identified and collectively decide our next move. I made it amply clear that in case we decided to raid a certain building or apartment, the final go-ahead would be given by me.

A brief pep talk to the boys pumped them up. Even though I was technically not their boss, they all knew that it was, at the end of the day, my operation and they were working to assist me. They all knew me as I had served in the Delhi Police for long and was not exactly an unpopular officer in the rank and file. Also, we had worked together on a couple of operations earlier and met with success.

Like men possessed, more than twenty of us scattered in predetermined directions. Since it was a Sunday, most menfolk in Sarvapriya Vihar were at home watching TV or catching forty winks. The lanes and by-lanes were practically deserted. Every now and then, people would step out of their apartments and eye us with suspicion. The time at our disposal was limited before somebody called up the police control room and siren-wailing vans converged on the spot, ruining everything.

We were drawing a complete blank. No flat seemed to fully match the description. Word was spreading in the colony that some strangers were on the prowl. We were beginning to lose heart when out of sheer despair I broke away from the main team and went about fifty yards or so eastwards. Suddenly, another row of houses, which we had failed to notice hitherto in our determination to keep close to the marriage venue, emerged before me as a mirage would in the distant horizons of a desert. As I took a few steps into the lane I noticed a green net on a rooftop and below it were rows of white flowerpots with beautiful red roses in full bloom. A car, covered with a canvas sheet, was parked opposite this house. The red-coloured multi-storeyed building, mentioned by Thekkat, also stood to the east from where I had entered that lane. And, of course, the marriage venue and the dome-shaped monuments were all there.

As I walked down this lane, I was seized by a sensation that is hard to describe. Whether it arose out of too much fatigue and stress or over-obsession, I don't know. I had felt a similar sensation on earlier occasions too, when nearing the successful culmination of difficult and complicated operations. Sometimes I have wondered whether it is something supernatural or some kind of 'message from above'. Countless thoughts reverberated in my mind. *Is this going to be another successful operation? Is this the turning point?*

I saw Sub-Inspector Mehtab Singh, a young officer of the Special Cell, walk down the lane from the other end and the two of us met almost halfway, close to the house with the green net on its terrace. We exchanged looks and I pointed out to him all that I had observed. Almost simultaneously, Rajbir emerged at the far end of the lane. On being shown the telltale signs, he began to shake me by my hand, congratulating me for completing the mission. I told him to remain focused on the job at hand till it was done with.

TOWARDS QUTUB MINAR

ROUTE OF RAIDING
TEAM ON DAY 1, 12 Oct

AUROBINDO MARG

SARVODAYA ENCLAVE

PARK

AUROBINDO
ASHRAM

TOWARDS BEGUMPUR

PARK

RUINS OF
QASR-E-HAZAAR-SUTOON

BEGUMPURI
MASJID

BEGUMPUR VILLAGE

PARK

BEGUMPUR VILLAGE

F-73, Begumpur

DHOBI /
WASHERMAN

PARK

R E D   B U I L D I N G

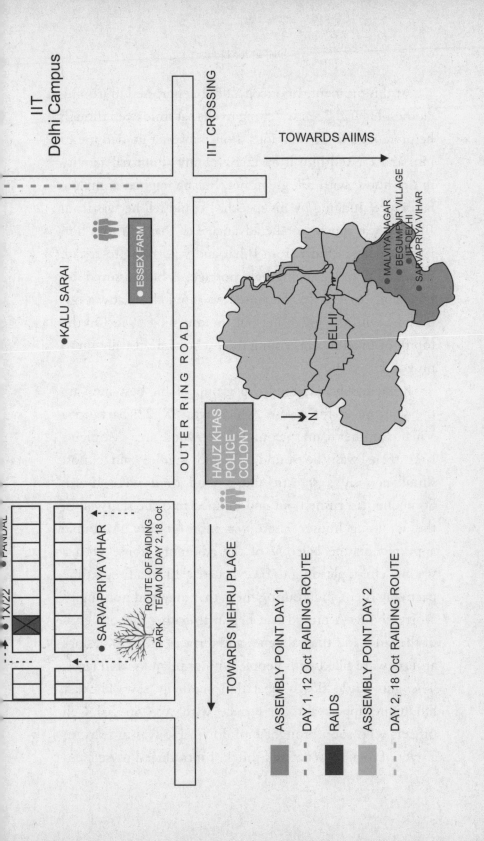

IIT
Delhi Campus

IIT CROSSING

TOWARDS AIIMS

KALU SARAI

ESSEX FARM

OUTER RING ROAD

HAUZ KHAS
POLICE
COLONY

MALVIYA NAGAR
BEGUMPUR VILLAGE
IIT DELHI
SARVAPRIYA VIHAR

DELHI

N

PANDAL

1X/22

SARVAPRIYA VIHAR

ROUTE OF RAIDING
PARK   TEAM ON DAY 2, 18 Oct

TOWARDS NEHRU PLACE

ASSEMBLY POINT DAY 1

DAY 1, 12 Oct RAIDING ROUTE

RAIDS

ASSEMBLY POINT DAY 2

DAY 2, 18 Oct RAIDING ROUTE

At this moment, I noticed a dhobi engrossed in ironing clothes. He had been watching us all that time even though he pretended to be oblivious. Police instinct guided me to him and I asked him if he knew of any abnormal activity in the house with the green net, but he feigned complete ignorance. Judging by his speech, I could tell he was from Bihar. I was quick to take advantage of that and told him I was a police officer from Bihar and was trying to rescue someone who was being held hostage. A bit reassured, he reluctantly told us that the house we should look at was not the one with the green net but the one next to it. On the top floor lived several young men who were usually up to no good.

Immediately, Rajbir led a group of his best men up the staircase of the house, which was 1X/22, Sarvapriya Vihar. Another team surrounded the whole area. Moments later there was the sound of rapid gunfire and almost simultaneously a scream and a loud thud were heard. Someone had rushed out and jumped into the stairwell of the adjoining house. There was more gunfire. A couple appeared on the balcony of the adjoining house with a wailing child, pleading to be evacuated. I had a tough time pacifying them and assuring them that they had nothing to worry about. A crowd had begun to gather at both ends of the lane, and the balconies and terraces of the buildings around were filled with people with grim and scared faces. The gun battle slowly abated. I suddenly saw Thekkat Siddhique appear on the terrace with two Special Cell officers who soon brought him down. He was in tears, in a state of total disbelief and shock. I introduced myself and dialled his brother's number from my mobile. Expectedly, there was untold relief and jubilation at the other end. Everyone in Thekkat's family spoke to me, expressing gratitude. Koya apologized for having been rude and impatient with me. He was full of praise for the CBI and the Delhi Police for what we had done.

When Thekkat recovered control of his senses, he informed us that two of his tormentors had left in a car shortly before we arrived. Amar, the person who had received him at the airport, had gone to see off an accomplice at the railway station. Quite incredibly, just then, a car drove into the lane where we stood, unmindful of the crowd that had gathered. Thekkat shouted that it was the same car. Some of us ran and caught the man at the wheel. He identified himself as Rakesh Saraha and the person whom he had seen off was Santosh Acharya, a notorious gangster of Mumbai belonging to the Fazlu–Ali Budesh gang.

Rajbir took me upstairs where two gangsters lay dead with their weapons beside them. They were none other than Virendra Pant aka Chhotu and Sanjay Khanna aka Chunky. The man whose body was found in the stairwell was later identified as Sunil Nathani who had no criminal record. It was unfortunate that he and two of his friends, Kartik and Vipin Chaudhary, had unwittingly got mixed up with this gang of kidnappers. They all belonged to respectable families. This had perhaps happened because they had befriended Rakesh Saraha, ignorant of his criminal antecedents. It was Rakesh who, on Virendra Pant's behest, had approached Kartik and Vipin seeking permission to use their flat for a few days to keep a kidnapped person.

They had gone along with him for reasons best known to them. All through Thekkat's captivity, they had known what was going on but had decided to look the other way, despite Thekkat's pleas for help. They were charged with and convicted for conspiracy to commit the crime and abetment.

I informed Special Director P.C. Sharma who immediately arrived at the spot and patted all of us on our backs. He was extremely delighted at our success but not unduly surprised—such was his faith in us. It was this supreme confidence in our abilities, and his unique non-interfering and encouraging leadership style, which had played a crucial role in the success of the operation.

Our work, however, was not over yet. We immediately obtained details of the train, the coach and seat numbers of Santosh Acharya from Rakesh Saraha and passed them on to D. Sivanandhan, my batchmate from the Mumbai branch of the CBI. Famous for his exploits against the Mumbai underworld in his earlier capacity as JCP (Crime), Siva was on the job straightaway. In a joint operation with the Mumbai Police, Acharya was caught when the August Kranti rolled into Mumbai Central the following morning. The joint team had boarded the train at one of the earlier stations, Vapi, spotted their man and kept him secured until the train reached Mumbai.

We quickly raided B-6X, South Extension, Part II, another hideout of the kidnappers, on Saraha's lead. This was where Thekkat had been driven on his arrival in Delhi and detained after being assaulted. Some important evidence was collected from there too.

By now the media was hounding us. A press conference was organized in the CBI headquarters during which Thekkat broke down. After composing himself, he gave a vivid account of the sequence of events. During captivity he had gradually won the confidence of his abductors who allowed him occasional strolls on the terrace of the flat in the company of one of the captors. It was during these 'outings' that he had noticed clues connected with the location of the flat, which he kept passing on in Malayalam to his family, whenever possible. The kidnappers were initially opposed to his speaking in his native language on the phone. But he had cleverly convinced them that if they wanted their ransom money they would have to allow him to speak in his mother tongue to his family members as that was the language they understood best. He had noticed the first clue about the shop with the telephone number 6683899 on a calendar hanging in the kitchen of the flat, a misleading clue which had given us a false start at the beginning of the operation.

While addressing the media, Thekkat praised the CBI and the Special Cell of the Delhi Police to the skies and said that he was alive because of us. Contrary to expectations, he returned to India to depose during the trial, which led to the conviction of all the surviving accused, who were awarded life sentences. It is not common for victims of crime, particularly those based overseas, to return to depose in courts of law in India, which often results in the culprits going scot-free. Thekkat, fortunately, proved to be an exception.

~

Operation Desert Safari is easily one of the most thrilling and satisfying experiences of my professional life. I headed a team that had volunteered to undertake a risky operation in which a private citizen had to be rescued from the clutches of desperate gangsters. We were racing against time and any delays would have proved fatal. Anything that went wrong would have attracted severe criticism officially, and caused disappointment and regret at a personal level. Constant inflow of clues about the location of the kidnappers' hideout, that too from the victim himself, added to the uniqueness of the operation. That we eventually succeeded in rescuing the hostage from the jaws of certain death and, in the process, eliminated two of the most wanted criminals of the country, added another dimension to our sense of professional and personal achievement. We had also succeeded in pre-empting an unnecessary fear psychosis in the minds of the NRI community that visiting India for business was unsafe. Incidentally, a list of twenty-five NRIs was found during the search of the Sarvapriya Vihar house, along with a satellite phone and four mobiles. Thekkat had been told that the gang intended to abduct more NRIs in future in a similar fashion.

The case was unique in several other ways too. The first information had been lodged overseas—with the Indian ambassador in Abu Dhabi. The victim, though of Indian origin, was settled abroad and had travelled home to India in search of greener pastures. While kidnapped and held hostage in his home country, his next of kin were to pay the ransom in Dubai. As subsequent investigations revealed, the entire conspiracy was the handiwork of criminals based abroad. All told, it was a classic case of transnational organized crime tackled with the urgency and the finesse it required.

The response to the challenge posed by this case was equally noteworthy. Our ambassador knew exactly how to respond to the first information report of the crime lodged with him. Rather than send the complaint through the customary bureaucratic maze, as is usually the practice in diplomatic circles, he cut to the chase by informing the CBI directly. We were equally quick to get our act together and involve the Special Cell of the Delhi Police, who have the requisite expertise and capability to handle such operations. That there was perfect synergy and understanding between the two teams is a sign of the espirit de corps that still exists in our country's police community. The use of technical data and swift fieldwork were some of the other highlights of the operation. No amount of praise is sufficient for ACP Rajbir Singh without whose involvement and commitment this operation would not have succeeded.

And, last but not least, it is my firm belief that everything went off well in the end not only on account of our efforts but also because of Divine Grace that guided us at every stage.

With deep regret, I have to inform readers that three members of the dramatis personae of this story, namely ACP Rajbir Singh, Inspector Mohan Chand Sharma and Sub-Inspector Mehtab Singh have since departed from this world; one falling to a bullet on account of personal enmity, and the other two in the line of duty. I remember them fondly while recording my recollections of this police operation and pay them homage. They were exceptional police officers, the likes of whom are difficult to find today. I continue to miss them. May they rest in peace. And yes, in the first week of July 2015, a few months before going to print, I learnt that Rajbir's son Rohit Singh has become an officer of the Indian Police Service, a service that gave me everything I have in life today. Rohit is now a policeman like his father and grandfather. There's one thing I'm sure he'll not fail to demonstrate in ample measure during his career—courage. His DNA has COURAGE coded in its double helix.

3

Dial D for Don
My conversations with
Dawood Ibrahim

In the afternoon of 23 July 1993 an unmarked car of the Delhi Police Crime Branch weaved its way through the chaotic traffic on New Delhi's Sardar Patel Marg. The eyes of Inspector Prithvi Singh—leader of the police team— were fixed on a sky-blue Maruti driving ahead. The officer waited patiently as the two cars crossed Dhaula Kuan roundabout and were now on National Highway 8. He asked his police driver to go in for the kill as he found the flanks on the left of the road wide enough. The man at the wheel knew the drill only too well. He overtook the car, swerved left suddenly and forced it to stop. The police team jumped out of their vehicle with their handguns aimed at the Maruti's occupants and ordered them to come out. Amit Tyagi, a notorious gangster of western

Uttar Pradesh wanted in several cases of murder, armed robbery and other crimes, realized his game was up and came out with his hands raised as if in prayer. His young associate Anil Tyagi and a third person, who disclosed his name as Shyam Kishore, also gave themselves up. A search of their persons and that of the car, however, led to no incriminating recoveries.

The Crime Branch informer had been spot on in his tip-off on Amit Tyagi. The two Tyagis were on their way to the airport to drop Shyam Kishore leaving for Mumbai. But who was Shyam Kishore? The name did not ring a bell in the veteran inspector's ears. Cross-checking with the Delhi Police Crime Record Office didn't help either. However, the sleuth continued with the interrogation of the Tyagis as the officer had enough dope on them. The UP gangsters soon disclosed their companion Shyam Kishore's suspected links with D-company (the commonly used epithet for Mumbai's underworld headed by Dawood Ibrahim—a dreaded mafia don, now declared a global terrorist).

Apparently, Shyam Kishore, whose surname was Garikapatti, as we learnt later during his interrogation, had been tasked with the job of procuring weapons for Dawood's men for which he had contacted Amit Tyagi. It came to light that D's men were setting up a base in Delhi. After painstaking work, a flat in Gagan Vihar, east Delhi, was located and four other members of D-company, namely Subhash Singh Thakur, Bhai Thakur, Chandrakant Patil and Paresh Desai, were arrested. A large consignment of weapons and ammunition was discovered when their premises were searched.

Their arrest would set off a chain of incidents along a circuitous route eventually leading to my conversations with the 'Big Boss of Mumbai Gangland'. I will attempt to take readers through these disparate events as seamlessly as possible.

~

Since my last assignment before I had moved on deputation to the CBI was as DCP, Crime Branch, Delhi, Inspector Prithvi Singh and his superiors were aware that I was dealing with Dawood and his gang in my new job. They informed me of the arrests and, with the little knowledge that I had acquired of Mumbai's gangland, I realized the significance of the catch. The cases registered by the Delhi Police against the gangsters were under TADA. On a reference from us in the CBI, the TADA cases were transferred to the STF, CBI—a newly created branch tasked with investigating the serial bomb blasts in Mumbai in 1993 by the Government of India. Since the arrested men were linked to Dawood, the prime accused in the blasts case, the government considered the CBI better equipped to take a broader overview and tie up all loose ends.

On 8 August 1993 Subhash Singh Thakur, Bhai Thakur, Shyam Kishore Garikapatti, Chandra Kant Patil and Paresh Desai were handed over to us in the STF. We registered a case and began to interrogate them. They, particularly Subhash Singh Thakur and Bhai Thakur, were veritable storehouses of information on Dawood Ibrahim and the manner in which his gang functioned. But before I proceed further with this story, it is necessary to provide readers pen portraits of the five 'gentlemen' who were with us.

Subhash Singh Thakur, originally from a village called Nivada near Varanasi, was born in Mumbai in 1960. His father ran a small dairy farm in Khar. A chance encounter with Kalya Anthony, a local goon, made him take to crime in 1981. He committed several murders for Kalya Anthony and became a dreaded gangster. During an encounter with Inspector Fateh Singh Gaekwad of the Mumbai Crime Branch, he shot at the police officer and was injured in the return fire. He ran to a nearby cricket ground where Shyam Kishore Garikapatti was playing cricket. The injured Subhash Singh was taken to a hospital by Shyam Kishore and the two had been close friends and comrades-in-arms ever since.

Subhash Thakur's prowess as a ruthless killer soon attracted D-company's attention which brought him into the fold. He rose through the ranks quickly and became the key lieutenant of Sunil Sawant aka Sautya, Dawood's 'defence minister'. Shyam Kishore, a Central government employee's son, on account of his proximity with Subhash Thakur, also became an indispensable member of D-company's top 'hit' team.

Jayendra Thakur aka Bhai Thakur hailed from the Vasai–Virar area of Thane district bordering Mumbai. A local thug, who held sway over Vasai–Virar region with his ruthlessness and daredevilry, was contacted by Dawood to provide protection to his gang's consignments of contraband when they landed at the nearby coastline. In April 1991, a trawler carrying silver ingots smuggled by

D-company capsized in the shallow waters near a village called Wadrai in the area under Bhai Thakur's suzerainty. The local villagers looted the wrecked consignment. Dawood himself called Bhai Thakur to intervene and recover the robbed silver. The mobster unleashed nightlong terror on the village and beat up its residents mercilessly until he had recovered the stolen silver down to the last ingot. Three villagers lost their lives that night. However, no one went to the police to report the murders. Almost a year later, on 3 January 1992 the incident came to light and the police swung into action. Bhai Thakur had to flee to Dubai and seek refuge with Dawood. Thereafter, he was on the run and shuttled between Dubai, Kathmandu and Delhi with his friend Subhash Thakur until their arrest in Delhi on 23 July 1993.

Chandrakant Patil, a small-time property dealer from Vasai, prospered in his real estate business under Bhai Thakur's patronage. Patil acquired disputed properties and came on the radar of the local police on two occasions in 1987. He had been part of Bhai Thakur's army that had terrorized the villagers of Wadrai, killing three of them. He had been on the run ever since the incident came to light in January 1992. Illicit relations with a young prostitute, Rajani, of east Delhi, made him choose Delhi as his hiding place. He bought a flat in Gagan Vihar as a safe house for himself, not far from Ganesh Nagar Extension where he acquired another property for Rajani and her family. Occasionally, Bhai Thakur and Subhash Thakur used Patil's flat as a transit point and a hideout. It was here that they were eventually trapped by Delhi Police's Crime Branch.

Paresh Desai, the fifth mobster ensnared, was Bhai Thakur's driver and man Friday. He accompanied his master on all his missions, including the Wadrai rampage.

~

Their interrogation further revealed that D-company operated in the typical mould of an organized criminal group, with a don at the top, and a hierarchical structure of operatives under him. Since none of us in the STF had served in Mumbai, our knowledge of its underworld was either non-existent or at best rudimentary. Talking to these 'gentlemen' gave us invaluable insight into the workings of Dawood Ibrahim's gang and its 'leading lights'. Two names which figured often were Ahmed Mansoor (handling the gang's hawala business) and Manish Lala (D's 'law minister').

We succeeded in arresting Ahmed Mansoor from the Jama Masjid area of Delhi. Ahmed Mansoor had grown up with Dawood, and knew a lot about his formative years and his later life as well. Dawood's father was a constable and extremely strict with his seven children. When Dawood and his younger brother committed a mischief, they would be thrashed without mercy in full public view. The family lived in a small room in a crowded chawl, which seemed the end of the world to Dawood—he knew there was no future for him in those environs. Ahmed Mansoor also told us about Dawood's lavish lifestyle in Dubai, his fondness for *mujra*s (soirées musicale) and women, his keen interest in cricket and Bollywood and how his word was the law in Mumbai. Most disputes involving real estate, monetary matters, release dates of films by different Bollywood producers, casting of film stars, etc., were decided in his 'court' in Dubai. Almost all Bollywood personalities called on him to pay their obeisance. He had taken a special fancy to a film actress, whom he secretly married. The two reportedly have a son who is being brought up in Bengaluru by the film star's sister.

Mansoor narrated several anecdotes on how Dawood had built his Robin Hood image by helping people in distress. One of them was about an old Hindu widow living in a prime property on Napean Sea Road who was being troubled by her late husband's brothers. They had forcibly occupied a portion of her property and stationed a few local goons there. Having failed to get any help from the authorities, the hapless lady called Dawood's number in Dubai. To her good fortune, Dawood himself picked up the receiver and heard her tale of woe. He took her address and sent his men to her house. On realizing that the don himself had got involved in the matter and was on the widow's side, not only did the goons squatting on her property run for dear life but her brothers-in-law also withdrew.

Mansoor's interrogation and follow-up investigation led us to material on the linkages of East-West Airlines— India's first privately owned but now defunct airlines— with D-company and the nexus of the regional manager of the airlines with Dawood's men.

Further, the involvement of the then minister for power and a sitting MP in providing shelter to the gangsters came to light. On the court's warrants the minister, the MP and

the regional manager were arrested and sent to Tihar Jail
in Delhi.

On conclusion of the trial all eight accused were
sentenced to five years of rigorous imprisonment. They
appealed to the Supreme Court where the sentences of
Subhash Singh Thakur and Bhai Thakur were enhanced to
ten years. Enhancement of the sentence of an appellant by
the apex court, and, that too, by 100 per cent, is a rarity in
the history of the Indian judiciary. The sentences against
Shyam Kishore Garikapatti, Chandrakant Patil and Paresh
Desai remained unchanged, while the power minister, the
MP and the regional manager of East-West Airlines were
acquitted. The Supreme Court felt they did not know they
were giving shelter to or dealing with terrorists.

Ahmed Mansoor also provided information on Manish
Lala's proximity with D and his meteoric rise in D-company.
We succeeded in identifying several of Manish Lala's
properties in Mumbai, which were subsequently raided. The
Mumbai Police were taken aback by the interest the CBI
was taking in Manish Lala. They had hitherto not pursued
him with the same vigour with which other members of
Dawood's gang had been chased. He was an absconding
accused in the J.J. Hospital shootout case of 12 September
1992, a most sensational incident of gang warfare that had
sent shockwaves through India's commercial capital. Lala
was charged with sheltering Subhash Thakur and Shyam
Kishore Garikapatty after the J.J. Hospital shootout and
providing them other logistical support.

~

A word here on the J.J. Hospital shootout case to give an idea to the reader of the ferocity of internecine gang warfare in Mumbai of the late 1980s and '90s. A bitter gang rivalry between D and another mobster, Arun Gawli, had led to several killings on both sides. The victim of one such killing was Ismail Parkar, D's brother-in-law, who was shot dead on 26 July 1992 outside a hotel owned by him in the Nagpada area of Mumbai. One of the four assassins was identified by the police as Shailesh Haldankar, a member of Arun Gawli's gang. A month after Ismail Parkar's murder, Shailesh shot dead a Nagpada businessman but was caught by the local residents who beat him up mercilessly before the police arrived and arrested him. On account of his injuries, he was admitted to J.J. Hospital in Nagpada. He lay on a bed in Ward 18 of the hospital, guarded by armed policemen. On 12 September 1992 Dawood sent a team of twenty-four shooters, which stormed into the hospital and fired nearly 500 rounds. It was the first time that AK-47 was used in Mumbai's history of crime. The volley of fire killed Shailesh Haldankar and two policemen on the spot. Several others, including patients, their attendants and policemen, were grievously injured. Subhash Thakur and Shyam Kishore Garikapatti, two of the main perpetrators of the J.J. Hospital shootout, who had been evading arrest by the Mumbai Police since the incident, were now in our custody. During interrogation they too revealed Manish Lala's proximity with D and Manish's properties in Mumbai.

After the raids on his properties by joint teams of the CBI and the Mumbai Police, Manish Lala, then in Dubai, realized he was on the radars of the police and the CBI. He was always confident of dealing with India's legal system and taking it head-on. He surrendered before a Mumbai court on 7 January 1994, which remanded him to judicial custody and he was lodged in Arthur Road Jail in Mumbai.

~

In March 1993, barely six months after the J.J. Hospital shootout, a series of bomb blasts rocked the city of Mumbai (for more details, see the chapter 'Our Man in Dubai'). The Mumbai Police Crime Branch cracked the case, investigated it and filed their charge sheet in December 1993. A designated court was constituted under the provisions of TADA to try the case. In the interest of security, the special designated court was created within the jail premises itself to obviate the risk involved in taking large number of accused from prison to court on a daily basis.

Since the STF was put in charge of further investigation of the serial blasts, I visited the court on different occasions when important matters came up before it. Aware that Manish Lala was lodged in Arthur Road Jail itself, I decided to meet him in prison in the first week of June 1994. After obtaining due clearances, my meeting with D's confidant and legal adviser took place in the jail superintendent's office. I found Manish to be well spoken, suave and most unlike the other five members of D-company whom we had dealt with in July 1993. Towards the end of my brief questioning, he asked me to seek his remand in the TADA case against Subhash Singh Thakur, Bhai Thakur et al. for a longer interrogation session. He said he would not oppose CBI's remand application and would agree to be brought to Delhi. This sounded odd but he was persistent.

Sure enough, when we applied for his custody, we got it without any difficulty as there was no opposition from his side. He was brought to Delhi and his interrogation began. One day I asked my investigating officer to bring him to my office. My first question to him was why he had volunteered to be taken in custody in a TADA case unnecessarily. Although he had been mentioned by the other accused, he was legally not wanted by us in that case. Even after twenty years in the Indian Police Service, I wasn't prepared for the unusual response that came my way. He said, 'Sir, when I came to meet you in Arthur Road Jail, you offered me a chair and asked me to sit down. I have been to several police offices and met many police officers in the course of my work but never has anyone asked me to sit, leave alone take a chair. My meeting with you reassured me that in your custody, I would not be ill-treated. I decided to share with the CBI whatever was in my knowledge.'

Cast in a different mould with more brain than brawn, Manish Lala didn't seem to be a regular mobster. He was quite forthcoming, not only about his own life but about D-company as well. Born on 23 May 1952 in Mumbai in a well-off family, he was adopted by a Gujarati couple who had no issue of their own. His adoptive parents died when he was in his early teens. After that he made his living by doing odd jobs with export companies, hotels, architects and advocates. He worked with two eminent lawyers and realized that he had a flair for legal work.

By the time he was thirty, he had an office of his own at 75, Poddar Chamber in the Fort area of Mumbai. Sagir Ahmad, a subtenant of his, ran a travel agency. A client of Sagir's had a major monetary dispute with the travel agency and sought the intervention of Anees Ibrahim—Dawood Ibrahim's younger brother. It was a common phenomenon in Mumbai to have such disputes settled through the mafiosi for a fee. Anees Ibrahim sent his hoods to the travel agency. Sagir Ahmed was out on an errand then so the boys picked up Manish Lala instead and presented him before Anees. Manish explained that Sagir was his tenant and promised to tip off Anees as soon as Sagir came to office.

Manish, true to his word, informed Anees Ibrahim once Sagir was back. Anees rang up Sagir and presumably the dispute was settled to Anees's satisfaction. Street-smart as he was, Manish Lala gradually built on that chance meeting with the number two of D-company. He kept in touch with him and attended all the social events of Anees's extended family.

On 6 September 1983, Dawood got dreaded gangster Amirzada Nawab Khan of the rival Pathan gang killed in court. The hit was carried out by a rookie shooter, David Pardesi, to avenge the murder of D's elder brother Sabir, who had been gunned down by the Pathans in the wee hours of 12 February 1981 at a petrol pump in Prabhadevi, Mumbai. The Pathan gang and the Sabir–Dawood gang had been at war for some time to gain supremacy in Mumbai's underworld (see 'Ayeesa Kya?' for details). Despite a truce brokered between them by an elder don, Haji Mastan, the two gangs remained at each other's throats. Immediately after shooting Amirzada, the novice assassin David Pardesi was caught on the spot and disclosed to the police that he had pulled the trigger at the behest of D.

The Mumbai Police were now looking for Dawood who was on the run. Despite all his clout and contacts there was no let-up in the manhunt launched against him. Manish Lala once happened to be present with Anees when the matter was under discussion. With his knowledge and understanding of how the legal system worked, Manish offered to step in and help. He engaged a senior advocate, Shamrao Sawant, through whom he managed to get Dawood Ibrahim anticipatory bail, saving him from being arrested. The dons of D-company could not believe what Manish Lala had pulled off for them. In the process, Lala endeared himself to the first family of the Mumbai underworld for all time to come. In due course he would become the de facto 'law minister' of D-company and a close confidant of Dawood and Anees.

~

Manish Lala, during one of the interrogation sessions with me, mentioned that Dawood might be willing to give himself up to the CBI. He offered to speak with D and discuss the proposition and encourage him to return. Keeping my seniors in the loop, I allowed him to use my secret office phone to get in touch with Dawood. Unlisted and protected phone lines were provided those days to select officers for top-secret operations. I not only recorded the conversation but heard it over speakerphone as well with no one else present in my office except Lala.

Manish Lala first called Sunil Sawant aka Sautya (the 'defence minister' of D-company) who in turn contacted Iqbal (Dawood's younger brother). Iqbal brought Dawood on line using the conferencing facility. A fairly long telephone call between Manish Lala and Dawood Ibrahim ensued. After relating to D the sequence of events leading up to his being in CBI custody, Lala reassured Dawood that he himself had seen how fair and considerate the CBI was to him. Lala further told D it was time for him (Dawood) to come out in the open and present his case to the CBI. Dawood did not sound averse to the idea. Lala then asked him whether he would be willing to speak with the DIG in whose custody he had voluntarily come. Dawood agreed readily and thereafter followed long dialogues between the don and me on three different occasions: 10 June, 20 June and 22 June 1994.

My first conversation with him started on a rather awkward note. Maintaining my officiousness, I asked him: '*Haan batayiye, aap mujhe kuchh batana chahte hain, jaisa Manish ne mujhe kaha hai.*' (Yes, I understand from Manish that you have something to tell me. Please go ahead.)

The don spoke in a typical Mumbai accent, with confidence and an utter lack of fear. He made no attempt to please me, as is the wont of certain criminals when they are dealing with state authorities. He simply said: '*Saheb, iske pehle ki main kuchh bataoon, pehle aap batayiye ki aapko kya lagta hai ki maine Mumbai mein blast karwaye hain?*' (Sir, before I tell you anything, would you please tell me whether you too feel that I organized the blasts in Mumbai?)

'*Sawaal ka jawaab aap sawaal se de rahe hain. Mujhe kya lagta hai ye mayaney nahin rakhta. Agar aap kuchh kehna chahte hain to kahiye.*' (You are answering my question with a counter question. What I feel is of no consequence. If you have something to tell me, please go ahead.)

After this initial mind game, he went on to say the following.

Soon after the bomb blasts, when his name started appearing in the media as one of the prime suspects, he had expressed his desire to the then commissioner of police, Mumbai, to present his side of the story. But, regrettably, Dawood claimed, the then commissioner refused to talk to him.

D admitted that he had met Dawood Taklya and Tiger Memon (the two main accused in the serial blasts). However, that was in connection with a dispute between Tiger Memon and the smuggling syndicate of Haji Ahmed, Salim Sarang and Aslam Patni. According to Dawood Ibrahim, Dawood Taklya used to work for Tiger Memon but, of late, had started working for Haji Ahmed's syndicate, which had led to several disputes. He (Dawood) heard both sides and ruled that Taklya should resume working for Tiger, his first employer. He explained the reason behind his verdict to Taklya and Tiger: Taklya had worked with Tiger for a long time before he came in contact with Haji Ahmed. Therefore, it was only appropriate that he (Taklya) continue to work for his first boss (Tiger). After this decision, Tiger Memon had, in Taklya's presence, informed D that Taklya was extremely *mazhabi* (religious) and could do anything for the sake of Islam. D then patted Taklya on the back and told him to keep his religious fervour alive. Dawood Ibrahim said he had never expected that Tiger Memon would use Dawood Taklya to send arms, ammunition and explosives for subversive activities in Mumbai.

When I asked Dawood if he could deny Anees sending weapons to Sanjay Dutt, he confirmed that the film star had indeed been sent arms by his younger brother. However, that had nothing to do with the blasts. Sanjay Dutt had come in close contact with Anees Ibrahim during the shooting of the film *Yalgaar* in Dubai. The actor had requested Anees to send weapons to him for his own security and for the security of his family members in the wake of the communal riots in Mumbai. It was a fact that Anees had obliged Sanjay Dutt but it was not in his (D's) knowledge. Later, when D learnt that Anees had sent weapons to Sanjay Dutt without his knowledge and approval, he had beat up Anees black and blue. D said that by making this admission, he was only trying to convince me that he was being honest. He knew that in the process he had gone to the extent of implicating his own brother.

D also said that it could be verified with Taklya that during the meeting in Dubai, wherein allegedly he (D) had planned the serial blasts, he had in reality discussed a totally different issue. They had talked about a well that was supposed to be dug in Taklya's village with a donation from D. The contract had been given to one Sayyed Munim. Taklya complained to D that Sayyed Munim had misappropriated a part of the donation. D had promised to look into the matter and take action.

During one conversation he said: '*Saheb, mujhe yeh sab karna hota to mujhe hathiyar bhejne ki zaroorat nahi hoti. Hamare ladkon ke paas kaafi hathiyar pade hain.*' (Sir, if I had to do all this, I need not have sent any weapons. My boys have enough at hand.)

'*Kya aapke ladkon ke paas itna RDX bhi pada hai ki aap serial dhamake kara sakte hain?*' I asked him. (Do your boys have that much RDX to cause serial blasts?)

A flustered don fumbled for words for a moment and replied: '*Dekho, saheb, agar main yeh sab karta na to itni safai se karta ki police ke paas akkha saboot mere khilaf nahi milta. Aap ye baat samjho. Aap to CBI mein ho. Ek baat aur, main bhi apni poori family ko wahan se hata deta jaisa Tiger ne kiye la hai. Meri ma, meri behan, sab udhar Bambai mein hi baitha hai*'—thus evading my question on RDX. (Look, sir, if I had to carry out such an operation, I would have done it with such finesse that the police wouldn't have got a whit of evidence against me. You should appreciate this point since you are in the CBI. And, most importantly, I too would have moved my family members out as Tiger did. My mother and sisters are all there in Mumbai.)

In brief, what Dawood Ibrahim wanted to convey to me was that Tiger Memon had approached him (D) ostensibly in connection with his dispute with Haji Ahmed. During the meeting, Tiger had tricked Taklya into thinking that he (D) was part of the overall conspiracy behind sending consignments of weapons and explosives. He (D) had not been kept in the picture when the conspiracy was hatched.

Had he been involved, he would have executed the plan much more artfully as well as moved his family out of Mumbai, just as Tiger had done.

I knew all along that the alibis being presented by the don were pure wind. Enough irrefutable evidence existed in our case file, nailing his role behind the serial blasts. But I played along, hoping for, if nothing else, some information from him on other absconding members of his gang or Pakistan's ISI. With Manish Lala's persuasive skills to support me, a slim chance of convincing Dawood to return always remained.

Meanwhile, one of my superiors, for reasons best known to him, asked me to stop communicating with D. Perhaps my senior was wary of Indian intelligence agencies overhearing the ongoing dialogue and taking objection to my transgressing their turf. The unwritten code between federal agencies in India is that the CBI sticks to investigation while the intelligence agencies carry out covert operations. My superior had worked in one such organization for several years and perhaps felt such 'adventurism' was best left to the other agencies. Be that as it may, that was the end of my tête-à-tête with Dawood Ibrahim.

The CBI did not charge Manish Lala as there was no evidence against him in our case. He was returned to Arthur Road Jail and was soon out on bail as the Mumbai Police didn't charge him in the J.J. Hospital shootout case either.

With D-company in disarray and his big bosses Dawood and Anees hiding in Karachi, Manish was left with no one to give legal advice to. He distanced himself from the underworld and began dabbling in stocks. He created an office of sorts at 65, Old Oriental Building, M.G. Road, in Fort area of south Mumbai. Little did he know that he was on the radar of Chhota Rajan, friend-turned-foe of Dawood. Once Dawood's right hand and most trusted lieutenant, Rajan had become a thorn in the flesh of D-company's other ambitious bigwigs like Chhota Shakeel, Sunil Sawant and Sharad Shetty. Dawood's overdependence on Chhota Rajan had made him the object of their common envy. They teamed together to poison D's ears and gradually succeeded in alienating Rajan from him. Following the March 1993 serial blasts in Mumbai, D-company split broadly along communal lines and Rajan bid a bitter adieu to his old master. He took with him trusted boys of his own, who acted only on his orders, and formed his own breakaway gang. He took it upon himself to ferret out members of D-company and liquidate them one by one. Killing and counter killing by D-company and Rajan's gang continue till date. Manish Lala, although a Hindu, was perceived by Rajan to be a D acolyte. He too would fall victim to the ongoing internecine warfare.

On 4 June 1998, at about 6 p.m., three shooters of Chhota Rajan's gang, namely Venkatesh Reddy, Sanjay Wadkar and Kiran Dogre, pumped bullets into Manish Lala at his second-floor office in Old Oriental Building, killing him on the spot. Thus fell another important member of D-company to the interminable wars in Mumbai's underworld.

With the passage of time, several cases involving D-company kept coming to me and our paths crossed frequently—the last of this was during the spot-fixing case in the Indian Premier League (IPL) in 2013. The Delhi Police cracked a transnational multi-crore racket involving bookies, fixers, underworld and cricketers. I was the commissioner of police, Delhi, then and had a small but significant role to play in leading the operation. The backward linkages behind betting and spot-fixing in IPL-6 led to none other than Dawood (see 'Between Twenty-Two Yards' for details).

The don's involvement in the case made headlines globally. Unconfirmed news reports of Dawood fleeing from his lair in Clifton, Karachi, to some undisclosed location kept filtering in. However, there was no way for us in the Delhi Police to confirm or deny the information.

One day I received a call on my personal mobile in the last week of June 2013 from an 'unknown number'. It was in all probability the Don himself. He said: '*Kya, saheb, aap retire hone ja rahe ho. Ab to peechha chhod do.*' (What is this, sir? You are about to retire. Isn't it time you left me alone?) The caller hung up before I could respond. I smiled to myself bemusedly at the veiled threat reminding me of my impending retirement and the subsequent stripping of my security cover.

I made sure the charge sheet in the IPL spot-fixing case was filed before I retired. Mister D was named an absconding accused along with two of his associates based in Dubai/Karachi. Necessary follow-up steps such as issuance of the Interpol Red Notice, lookout notice and warrants of arrest from the trial court were taken despite knowing that similar measures in the past had been in vain. D continues to be safely ensconced in Pakistan with no chance of India getting him back. The Government of Pakistan; despite being given precise details of his place of hiding, routinely denies his presence in their country.

For the Government of India, on the other hand, the fact that the don continues to be under the patronage of the Government of Pakistan remains on the top of the agenda during all Indo-Pak talks. Giving up Dawood is a difficult demand for the Pakistan government to comply with since its intelligence agency, the ISI, stands to lose its credibility to engage Indians for terrorist activities in the future.

4

'Atithi Devo Bhawa'
Busting the 'Lapka Gang'

Television viewers in India will have often seen Bollywood film star Amir Khan in an ad campaign of the Government of India with the above tagline. Simply put, the Sanskrit mantra from the ancient Hindu scripture *Taittiriya Upanishad*, Sikshavalli 1.20, says 'guest is god'. It is part of a verse that lays down the Hindu code of conduct which places one's parents, teacher and guest on the same pedestal as god.

The word '*tithi*' means date; and '*atithi*' is one without a date—or appointment. In ancient times, it was not possible for a person to anticipate someone's date and time of arrival nor was it possible for the guest to communicate her travel details in advance. So, rather than be caught by surprise or be 'inconvenienced', our ancestors taught us to welcome *atithis* and treat them well, greet them and host them as one would host gods.

This culture prevails even today in rural India. As a child growing up in Bihar, I saw people getting offended if someone sought their approval or asked about convenience before visiting their place. Observing such formalities is considered a sign of distance in relationships. Friends and family are expected to simply arrive with the confidence that they will be welcomed and treated well.

Alas, this tradition—given the demands of modern life and exposure to other cultures—has not only degenerated into discouraging and shunning people who arrive at someone's doorstep without prior appointment but often ill-treating them as well. However, this is not a story of ordinary guests being subjected to maltreatment but a sordid account of the fate that may befall foreign visitors at some of the most sought-after tourist destinations of our country like Jaipur, Delhi, Agra, Varanasi, Udaipur, Khajuraho, etc.

Sometime in late 2001, my friend David Jones, then a senior detective in the Anti-Kidnap Unit of New Scotland Yard, UK, apprised me over telephone of several complaints that had reached his desk from different Commonwealth and European countries, giving vivid accounts of how low-budget tourists—mainly young white girls—had fallen prey to unscrupulous criminals during their visits to Jaipur, Delhi and Agra—the so called 'golden circuit of tourism' in north India. They were victims of cheating, forgery, robbery, abduction, extortion, molestation or even rape. On my request, Detective Jones forwarded a bunch of complaints and documents received from citizens of the UK, Australia, New Zealand, France, Germany, and so on,

who had suffered in a similar manner during their trips to
India.

At the time I was posted as joint director, Economic
Offences Wing of the CBI. I asked my DIG, B.K. Sharma,
to identify a competent team to carry out an analysis of
the documents received. DSP V.K. Shukla, under SP H.C.
Awasthy assisted by Inspector Ajay Bassi, was deputed
for the job. A common modus operandi adopted by the
miscreants to dupe young tourists emerged on examining
the documents. Members of a well-organized gang would
spot their potential victims among foreign tourists at railway
stations or bus stands with the help of autorickshaw or taxi
drivers, who would drive them to predetermined lodging
houses or budget hotels. The same drivers would offer to
take them sightseeing as per their (tourists') convenience.
After sightseeing or, sometimes even before it, they would
bring the tourists to jewellery shops run by members of said
gang. The shopkeeper would propose a deal in which they
(tourists) could make big and easy money. The proposal was
that the tourists buy jewellery or precious stones from their
shop and send them to their (tourists') own addresses back
home. The gangsters explained to them that by adopting
this method the high customs duty levied by the Indian
government on export of jewellery could be evaded. Once
the tourists reached home, they could sell the exported
material at huge profits and make big money. If the tourists
declined, as most did, they would be detained, forcibly
deprived of their passports, foreign exchange, credit cards
and subjected to extortion in various guises. Some of the
girls were molested and even raped. The tourists who went

along with the goons found themselves duped on reaching their home country, when the 'precious stones' turned out to be cheap glass. In Jaipur, the police commonly refer to criminals adopting this modus operandi as the 'Lapka Gang'. 'Lapka' is derived from the Hindi word 'lapakna', which means 'grabbing'.

The contents of these complaints made my blood boil. I asked DIG B.K. Sharma to initiate preliminary fieldwork. B.K. Sharma deputed Inspector Ajay Bassi to work on call printouts and telephone numbers sent by the New Scotland Yard and DSP Shukla to do the fieldwork. After painstaking analysis, Inspector Bassi zeroed in on two mobile numbers that had called most victims during their stay in India. Further inquiry revealed these numbers were no longer in use. However, the same handsets (located by their unique IMEI numbers) were still in use with new SIM cards. Based on the phone data of the two new numbers, one Liyaqat Ali aka Mike aka Ali was traced. Liyaqat was a habitual criminal of Jaipur involved in several cases of preying upon tourists. He was a history-sheeter of Jalupura Police Station, Jaipur. DSP V.K. Shukla collected Liyaqat Ali's dossier and the police record of his associates, and related material on miscreants using similar modus operandi in Jaipur and Delhi.

At this stage, I got back to David Jones and informed him of the developments. 'Dave, I now need a formal complaint from a victim who would be ready to travel to India to identify the culprits, make statements before the investigating officer [IO] and the court. She should be prepared to testify before the trial court when the case comes up for hearing.' His immediate response was: 'Well done, my friend! You have done great groundwork! But it is a tall order to locate the sort of person you require. No victim, to the best of my knowledge, wishes to return to India, ever. I will still do my best.'

The search for such a victim ended when the Anti-Kidnap Unit of the New Scotland Yard found Julie Clyde of South Australia. A thirty-year-old architecture student, Julie was married to a pension fund manager, J.K. Prudy. She had undergone a most horrific experience in November 2001 during her visit to India and was prepared to go to any lengths to bring her tormentors to book. She had her husband to support her in her quest for justice. A written complaint from her dated 24 January 2002 was received by the CBI through the Yard on 29 January, and a case on charges of outraging a woman's modesty, abduction, wrongful confinement, cheating and extortion was registered. Inspector Ajay Bassi was deputed as the IO of the case.

Julie's complaint, in brief, stated: A group of architecture students, including herself, from the University of Adelaide, Australia, had come on a study tour to the Bhuj area of Gujarat to see the damage caused by the earthquake to the buildings of the region. After three weeks of study tour, students were allowed some free time to travel across India. A group of six from among them went to Rajasthan. They reached Jaipur by bus on 15 November 2001 at five in the morning, after having visited Udaipur, Jodhpur and Jaisalmer. The entire group was taken to Evergreen Hotel at Chameliwala Market from the bus stand by autorickshaw drivers, who all seemed to have ganged up in persuading them to stay at that hotel. Julie and her friend Joan Doff, aged twenty-two, shared room 350 of the hotel.

The same day in the afternoon, Joan Doff, while returning to the hotel from a nearby post office, was accosted by a guy who introduced himself as Chiku. He tried to befriend her but was rebuffed. Later, in the evening when Joan was on her way back from the City Centre, the same Chiku met her and informed her that a member of her group of six had gone missing. He offered to assist her in looking for the 'missing girl', but Joan again turned down the offer.

Next morning, on 16 November, both Julie and Joan went to a cyber cafe located close to the hotel to check email. Chiku was there too. He offered to take them around Jaipur for sightseeing. This time the girls took the bait and accepted his offer. Chiku asked another friend of his called Noorie to bring a car in which they drove to Amer Fort, the main tourist attraction in Jaipur. After driving for ten minutes, the two miscreants stopped their car in a busy market, ostensibly to pick up a few items from their shop located close by. They invited the girls to see their shop and have tea with them. The girls accompanied them down a narrow and dark alleyway to an old building. They followed the goons up a circular staircase to a first-floor shop with no signboard or nameplate. It had a glass door with Lord Ganesh etched on it. The tourists were offered tea and shown some gems and stones. Meanwhile, another man called Mike came to the shop and proposed to the ladies that they join a scheme whereby they (the tourists) could earn some quick and big money. He told them the same cock-and-bull story about the customs duty on exports made by Indian nationals being prohibitive, and how visiting tourists could mail small parcels of jewellery or precious stones to themselves, and make huge profits on their sale by saving on exorbitant taxes.

The two girls declined the offer and said they were not interested. By this time the number of goons in the shop had increased to ten. The girls by then had already been in that shop for over six hours. It became clear to them that they were being held captive. To get out of the situation, they agreed to do as they were being told and attempt to escape as and when an opportunity came their way. They were asked to hand over their credit cards and passports to the goons who made out fake bills, prepared small parcels addressed to the tourists, forcibly took their signatures and withdrew huge amounts of money from their credit/debit cards.

Julie and Joan hoped they would now be allowed to go. However, only Joan was let off, with instructions to go the hotel, fetch Julie's and her own baggage. Joan was also instructed to leave a message for their other friends saying Julie and she were leaving for a bird sanctuary.

When Joan returned from the hotel, Julie and Joan were forced to get into a car and driven off to Delhi. Mike and Noorie drove by turns and reached Delhi past midnight. They went to the central post office (Gole Dak Khana) from where the parcels, prepared in Mike's Jaipur shop, were mailed to Julie and Joan, c/o Main Post Office, London.

They were then taken to Arpit Palace Hotel in Karol Bagh and confined in room 206. The next day

(17 November 2001), the two girls were taken from one jewellery shop to another. The people running the shops seemed to know Mike, Chiku and Noorie rather well. The shopkeepers, in collusion with the miscreants, stripped all the assets held on their credit cards under the guise of selling jewellery. In reality, no jewellery was delivered to them. All they got were receipts. Julie was made to call her husband Prudy in Australia and ask him to put more money in her account. Prudy could put only 4000 Australian dollars, which were immediately withdrawn by the miscreants. Similarly, Joan was forced to call her father, an executive in an oil company in London, and ask him to send 10,000 pounds by money transfer through Western Union. He sent 6000 pounds, which too were forcibly taken away by Mike.

Mike had been making sexual advances to Joan from the time they had left Jaipur. Once, he even pulled down her pants but Joan managed to ward him off with great difficulty. In a jewellery shop in Karol Bagh, where Mike had taken Joan, the shopkeeper tried to get extra friendly with her, passed lewd remarks and subjected her to several indignities.

On one of the occasions when Joan was away with Mike, Chiku was left to guard Julie in her hotel room. Chiku told Julie that he knew a special massage technique that would soothe her frayed nerves. He forced her to sit on the bed and started massaging the back of her neck and then fondling her breasts. He was about to sexually assault her when there was a knock on the door. Joan had returned with Mike and Julie was saved in the nick of time.

Eventually, in the early hours of 20 November 2001, the two girls were dropped at the international airport and forced to fly to London by Kuwait Airways, even though they had plans to return to Australia. Presumably, they were sent to London as the parcels prepared by the miscreants at Jaipur had been mailed to the Main Post Office of the British capital. In any case, it was part of the modus operandi of the gang to send its victims to a country other than the one to which they belonged.

On reaching London, Julie and Joan went to the Australian High Commission and reported what they had undergone in Jaipur and Delhi. The High Commission informed New Scotland Yard which recorded their statements. They also recovered the parcels from the Main Post Office, London. Subsequently, when examined by an expert, the 'precious stones' turned out to be made of glass. New Scotland Yard informed the CBI when they found Julie ready to pursue the matter in India.

~

On 12 March 2002 Julie came to Delhi accompanied by Detective Sergeant Anna Gooch and Detective Constable Stephen Goodhew of New Scotland Yard and gave a more detailed account of her travails. When the photographs of Liyaqat Ali and his associate Syed Asim Ali, both tracked down by IO Inspector Ajay Bassi on the basis of phone call details, were shown to Julie, she said they were not the culprits who had tormented her and Joan. However, Liyaqat, when questioned, disclosed that the 'Mike' we were looking for was a man by the name of Lalit Aggarwal. Both Lalit and he worked together in the 'Lapka Gang' and both shared the assumed name of 'Mike'. In August 2001, the gang had split and Lalit aka Mike, Mohammed Mobin aka Noorie and Sayyed Sadakat Ali aka Chiku had formed a separate gang. Every member of the 'Lapka Gang' had a criminal history and the Jaipur Police had their photographs and dossiers.

The following day (13 March 2002), Julie, escorted by the New Scotland Yard detectives and a CBI team led by Ajay Bassi, reached Jaipur. When the photograph of Lalit Aggarwal, obtained from the local police, was shown to her, she immediately identified him as Mike. Similarly, when the mugshots of Mohammad Mobin and Sadakat Ali were shown, she identified them as Noorie and Chiku respectively.

When taken around Jaipur, she retraced her friend Joan's and her movement from the bus stop to Evergreen Hotel, pointed out the cyber cafe near the hotel where they had met Chiku and their route to the first-floor shop where they had been detained for over seven hours before being driven to Delhi. IO Bassi recorded Julie's statement and recovered a large number of documents from the three premises connected with the case. However, as news of the CBI's involvement in the investigation of the case spread, Lalit Aggarwal aka Mike, Mohammad Mobin aka Noorie and Sadakat Ali aka Chiku escaped. Further investigation revealed that Mike had fled to Paris, Chiku to Germany and Noorie to Bangkok.

Julie was taken to Lalit Aggarwal's house in Jaipur where his Cielo car DL 1C F-XXXX was parked. She immediately identified it as the car in which Joan and she had been driven to Delhi. The IO seized the car. On a search of the house, useful documents connected with the case were recovered and seized.

When the joint team of New Scotland Yard and CBI returned to Delhi, Julie identified Arpit Palace Hotel in Karol Bagh, where they had been held captive, and the jewellery shops where they had been forcibly taken and robbed. The shopkeepers she identified were arrested.

Julie gave a statement to a judicial magistrate as well. She agreed to keep in touch with IO Bassi on email and promised to return to testify in court once the trial began. Her determination to get justice, come what may, was awe-inspiring. The British Police officers escorting Julie, and Julie herself, felt reassured that the CBI team was responsive and professionally up to the task.

On 2 April 2002, there was news that Noorie would appear before a Jaipur court in a case of the rape of an Australian girl in which Lalit aka Mike and he were the accused. A trap was laid by CBI officers and, as he emerged from the court complex, he was nabbed.

Since Joan Doff and Julie's husband were reluctant to come to India, DIG B.K. Sharma, who was supervising the case, was sent to Sydney in May 2002. He recorded their statements in the presence of Sudhir Kumar, consul in the Indian Consulate, and Jackie Carroll, an Australian Federal Police agent. B.K. Sharma also recorded a supplementary statement from Julie—the prime complainant—incorporating additional information required to fill up the gaps left in her earlier statements before the IO and the judicial magistrate.

Documentary evidence of all the transactions made by forcibly using the girls' credit cards was collected, including receipts issued by jewellers. Registers maintained in the relevant hotels in Jaipur and Delhi that contained entries pertaining to their stay alongside their captors were seized. Proof of purchase of Julie's and Joan's Kuwait Airways tickets to London was collected from a travel agent in Gole Market, New Delhi. Other members of the miscreants' support group who had facilitated the prime perpetrators in the commission of the crime were identified and arrested. Thus, the investigating team collected enough evidence to charge-sheet nine accused. A charge sheet in the case was filed on 5 June 2002. Six of the nine accused had been arrested but Mike, Chiku and one Afzal Baig, who had received and kept the robbed cash, were absconding.

Lalit Aggarwal aka Mike and Afzal Baig surrendered before the court of chief metropolitan magistrate on 3 October 2002. Their police remand for ten days was taken and they were questioned thoroughly. Following this, Sayyed Sadakat Ali aka Chiku surrendered on 13 October the same year. A supplementary charge sheet against the three was filed in December 2002.

~

True to her word, Julie returned to testify in court during trial. She reached Delhi on 13 April 2004 and stayed on till 2 May 2004. Besides her, Detective Sergeant Anna Gooch and Detective Constable Stephen Goodhew also deposed before the trial court. Julie handled her cross-examination with aplomb and confidence. She had done everything in her might to seek justice.

Over fifty witnesses have been examined in the case so far. Reportedly, the trial is in its final stages and hopefully the court's verdict should come by the end of 2015. If convicted, the accused will have the option of filing an appeal, first with the high court and then with the Supreme Court. It is anybody's guess when the final closure in the matter will happen.

Already more than thirteen years have gone by since Joan and Julie's horrific experiences during their trip to India. Julie's courage and determination to get justice are admirable. Regrettably, her friend Joan, Julie's husband and Joan's London-based father did not appear in the trial court to further strengthen the prosecution's case.

The wheels of the Indian justice system grind at their leisurely pace, as is their wont, given the huge number of cases to be dealt with and the dilatory tactics of defence counsels. Meanwhile, the members of 'Lapka Gang' whom we had arrested are all out on bail. Apparently, they have shifted their operational area for 'grabbing' young female tourists and robbing them to Goa, Pushkar and Kullu-Manali. God alone knows how many women have fallen prey to their vile ways by now.

Ironically, Bollywood superstar Amir Khan's sanctimonious message, on behalf of the Government of India to treat guests as gods, does not reach the people it is intended for.

5

'Ayeesa Kya?'
The unmaking of Latif

Most, who have lived in Gujarat during the '80s and '90s of the last century, will have heard of Abdul Latif. A gambler, bootlegger, kidnapper, extortionist, hired assassin and mobster par excellence, the mere mention of his name was enough to send shivers down the spine of businessmen, rival gang members and politicians. His notoriety spread beyond the borders of Gujarat, particularly to Rajasthan, Daman, Madhya Pradesh, Maharashtra, Delhi, Karachi and Dubai. He seemed beyond the reach of the law. *Latif: The King of Crime*, a movie based on his life, was released in August 2014. If Bollywood grapevine is to be believed, another biopic on him, named *Raees*, is also in the works. It has Shah Rukh Khan—no less—playing Abdul Latif, and Nawazuddin Siddiqui as a cop and is likely to hit theatres early 2016. The interest Bollywood is showing, more than eighteen years after Latif's death in a police encounter, will perhaps give an idea of his stature in the folklore of crime to contemporary readers who haven't yet heard of him.

Abdul Latif was born on 24 October 1951 to impoverished parents living in Kalupur, a Muslim ghetto in Ahmedabad. His father, Abdul Wahab Sheikh, was a tobacco seller bringing up seven children in a cramped hutment. Latif struggled to finish school and soon after began to help his father at his tobacco shop. He received two rupees every day from his father as remuneration. He often fought with his father for more money. At twenty, Latif got married and his financial requirements increased. His squabbles with his father over money became frequent and he decided to branch out on his own. Unable to find any respectable vocation, he took to crime in his early twenties. He began working with Allah Rakha, a bootlegger, who also ran a gambling den. Latif soon became an expert gambler himself and a card sharp.

Manzoor Ali, who ran a rival gambling den, was quick to recognize Latif's talent and asked him to join his gang. Latif became the supervisor of Manzoor's den on a monthly salary. After a couple of years, having been accused of pilferage of money, Latif left Ali's gambling den in acrimony and bitterness.

He then drifted into the trade of illicit liquor and joined a gang of liquor smugglers. Gujarat was—as it continues to be even today—a state under prohibition, where the illicit demand for alcohol had given rise to liquor mafias. Illicit liquor was brought from different parts of neighbouring

Rajasthan and sold at a premium. The trade required a vast and intricate chain of suppliers, transporters, distributors, retailers and the support of corrupt excise and police officers, as well as their political masters.

Latif cut his teeth in organized crime, grasping its basic concept of running a hierarchy of criminals, where every level of operatives played its allotted role, maintaining utmost secrecy and fair distribution of the loot among gang members. The glue that bound them was the quick gains they made regularly on account of the illicit demand that existed and the fear of severe retribution if they broke the omerta. Latif quickly established his supremacy, given his penchant for violence and bloodshed, and soon came to head an elaborate gang of his own. Several cases of murder, kidnapping for ransom and extortion were registered against him in different police stations across Gujarat. His ruthlessness and daredevilry were to make him a gangster difficult to pursue and apprehend.

Latif's first brush with the Mumbai underworld took place when he was introduced to Amin Khan Nawab Khan, Alam Khan Jangrez Khan of the Pathan gang of Mumbai by one Ramzan of Viramgam, Gujarat. The Pathans disclosed that following a quarrel with the Dawood Ibrahim gang over a consignment of gold, they had killed Dawood's elder brother, Sabir Ibrahim, in Mumbai in 1981. Ever since, the Pathans had been on the run. Latif gave them shelter in Ahmedabad and, unwittingly, became aligned with the Pathan gang headed by two brothers, Alamzeb and Amirzada.

In 1983, Alamzeb was returning by car to Ahmedabad from Surat with his associates Liyaqat Master and Iqbal

Bhupat. They had a chance encounter near Baroda with Dawood and his aides, who were travelling by car as well. One of Dawood's aides fired at Alamzeb but he escaped unhurt.

Latif himself would have a few encounters with Dawood. Detained in Sabarmati Central Jail, Ahmedabad, under COFEPOSA (an anti-smuggling law), Dawood was being produced in a Baroda court. He had won over the armed police team, headed by Sub-Inspector Bishnoi, which was tasked with escorting him from jail to court and back. During these trips the escort party allowed him, for a consideration, to visit a hotel off Narol Highway for relaxation and entertainment. One day Latif was tipped off about Dawood's movement. He, with his team, followed the vehicle in which Dawood and his close associates were travelling with Sub-Inspector Bishnoi. At Jamalpur, on account of a traffic jam, both cars had to stop. Liyaqat Master, Latif's hitman, got off the vehicle, fired several shots at Dawood, quickly climbed back inside and managed to flee from the spot with Latif. Dawood escaped unhurt but two of his associates were injured.

Thereafter, a bloody war ensued between the two gangs, with Latif on the Pathans' side. In September 1983, Dawood's hitman David Pardesi killed Amirzada in court in Mumbai. David would meet his nemesis in Ahmedabad some years later in the form of Latif's shooter Sharif Khan.

Thus a habitual recidivist who had cut his teeth on small-time gambling and bootlegging rose to script a story of an audacious and fierce underworld don. He began to exhibit ruthless control over the levers of his gangdom, which spread across India and beyond its borders as well. He had several run-ins with rival gangs and the law. Meanwhile, his bootlegging business and his gang activities continued to flourish. He built a Robin Hood type of image for himself in his community by helping the needy and the poor. In early 1987, lodged in jail, he contested the Ahmedabad Municipal elections from five wards and won in all five. Hugely popular in his community, Latif had become a role model for the younger lot. By the late 1980s, his ultimate ambition of becoming the Dawood Ibrahim of Gujarat had been realized in substantial measure.

Things, in fact, began to turn around in dramatic fashion and Latif's clout in the underworld soared. Now even Dawood thought it prudent to make peace with him. In November 1989 Latif received a message from Dawood to come to Dubai along with his cronies. A maulana administered an oath to Dawood and his men on one side and Latif's men on the other. All of them swore by the Holy Quran to be friends and work with each other. That was the coming together of two dreaded criminal gangs now ready to play complementary roles. Dawood advised Latif to quit the illicit liquor business and join him in the smuggling of gold and silver. Latif got into the gold trade with one Mamumiya Panjumiya, a notorious smuggler of Gujarat. In the interim, he also had to take on one Shahzada of Mumbai, who had become his arch-enemy. In a series of gun battles, several gangsters on both sides were killed. Abortive attempts on Latif's life kept him on guard and he never hesitated from taking murderous pre-emptive action.

Then came the infamous Radhika Gymkhana case, which would set a new benchmark in the history of crime in Gujarat. Suspecting one Hansraj Trivedi, an Ahmedabad-based bootlegger and owner of gambling dens, to have given shelter to hired killers sent by Latif's Mumbai rival Shahzada, Latif decided to take revenge on Trivedi. On 3 August 1992, acting on a tip-off, Latif sent a team of shooters to Radhika Gymkhana in the Odhav area of Ahmedabad to target Hansraj Trivedi, who was playing cards there with eight of his friends. The shooters, unable to indentify Trivedi for certain, called Latif on the phone and informed him of their problem. Not known to deal in half-measures, Latif played the hand he and his boys were dealt—he ordered his shooters to kill everyone present. With the ferocious and blood-curdling burst of an AK-47—the first time that a Kalashnikov was ever used in Gujarat——all nine people, including Trivedi, were killed. As the horrific story of the daylight slaughter at the gymkhana spread shock and terror across the nation, Latif's notoriety itself catapulted, immediately making him India's most-wanted criminal. For the super ambitious don from Gujarat, the nationwide attention he was receiving after the gymkhana episode was like being on top of a gangland pedestal—another infamous milestone crossed in a remorseless career.

But more was to follow. Following the Radhika Gymkhana episode, Latif was on the run. His team of shooters had been arrested and had disclosed to the police that it was Latif who had ordered the hit. With the police on his heels, in sheer desperation, Latif approached Hasan

Lala, a childhood friend and president of the Gujarat Youth Congress, for help. Lala expressed his inability to be of any assistance as a former Rajya Sabha MP, Rauf Waliullah, was gunning for Latif. Rauf would not allow any relief to be given to him. Reportedly, the former MP was going to publicly raise the issue of the deteriorating law and order situation under the then chief minister of Gujarat, Chimanbhai Patel, and the enormity of Latif's unchecked criminal activities. The insinuation clearly was that Latif enjoyed the chief minister's patronage. Lala suggested that Waliullah be eliminated first before expecting any powerful person to come forward to help Latif.

Meanwhile, Latif escaped to Dubai on the advice of Dawood Ibrahim and entered his protection. From Dubai, Latif ordered his trusted lieutenant Rasool Patti to kill Rauf Waliullah. On 9 October 1992 Hasan Lala tipped off Rasool Patti about the presence of Waliullah at a photocopying shop near the Town Hall, Railway Under Bridge, Ahmedabad. Rasool sent two shooters, Sajjad aka Danny and Mohammad aka Fighter, who gunned down Waliullah in broad daylight. The murder, perceived to be politically motivated, sent shock waves down the corridors of power. Under political pressure, the Rauf Waliullah case was transferred from the Gujarat Police to the CBI, and was handled by a branch with which I was not associated.

Latif, a dreaded household name in Gujarat, had, meanwhile, moved with Dawood to Karachi and was an honoured guest of Taufiq Jallianwala, a Karachi-based gold and silver smuggler. Taufiq was a partner of Dawood and Tiger Memon in their smuggling business and together they had planned and executed the Mumbai bomb blasts in 1993 (see 'Our Man in Dubai' for details). Latif, too, had played an important role in the conspiracy. He had received a consignment of arms and explosives that landed at Dighi Port in Maharashtra on 9 January 1993 and distributed it to other conspirators. The arms and ammunition that reached film star Sanjay Dutt, who is doing time at Yerwada Jail now, were part of this consignment.

When news of the Mumbai blasts came on the afternoon of 12 March 1993, Latif was with Dawood and Taufiq in Karachi and exchanged congratulatory messages with the two masterminds of the terror attack. He continued to stay in Pakistan and all law-enforcement and intelligence agencies in the country believed that Abdul Latif, the Dawood of Gujarat, was in hiding in Karachi, until one day the ATS of the Gujarat Police got a specific bit of information on him.

~

On 22 September 1995, K.N. Sharma, DIG (ATS) of Gujarat, informed me on the phone that Abdul Latif was calling on Ahmedabad telephone numbers 66346xx and 66337xx to extort over rupees fifty lakh from the subscriber of the two phones. Unable to pay the amount, the subscriber had got in touch with the ATS.

Those were the days when mobile phones had not arrived in India. Even otherwise, a call made on a landline phone from another landline, and that too from another city, was difficult to track. With the victim's consent and cooperation, the two telephones were monitored by the ATS, and with help from the Ahmedabad Telephone Authority, ATS came to the conclusion that the calls were being made through a D-TAX (digital telephone automatic exchange) located at Khurshid Lal Bhawan, Janpath, New Delhi. Kuldip Sharma, DIG (ATS), sought help from the STF of the CBI, of which I was then the DIG, to track down the calling number and, if successful, to organize an operation to nab Latif.

On the same day I directed H.C. Singh, SP (STF), and M.K. Bhat, DSP (STF), to visit the MTNL headquarters at Janpath, New Delhi. They met Sunil Saxena, DGM, Janpath D-TAX. Saxena, though extremely responsive and warm, explained that it was virtually impossible to track down the calling number in Delhi because of the complex steps involved:

(i)   The call must last for at least ten to twelve minutes for it to be tracked from the called number in Ahmedabad to the calling number in Delhi.

(ii) As and when the number in Ahmedabad got called in future by Latif, the local exchange to which it belonged (Naurangpur Exchange) had to be alerted.

(iii) The Naurangpur Exchange would then alert the Ahmedabad D-TAX, which in turn would track and tell whether the call had been routed to D-TAX 1 or D-TAX 2 in Delhi.

(iv) Even if the concerned D-TAX in Delhi was informed while the call was in progress, there were over thirty exchanges in the city from where the call could

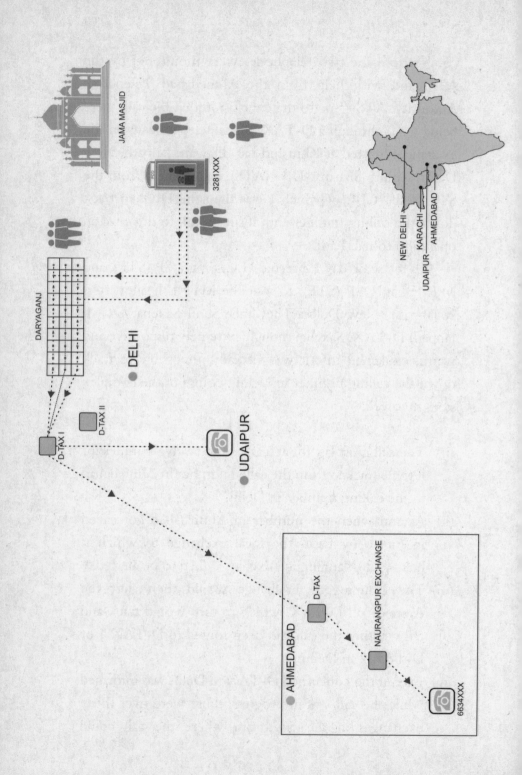

JAMA MASJID

DARYAGANJ

3281XXX

DELHI

D-TAX II

D-TAX I

UDAIPUR

AHMEDABAD

D-TAX

NAURANGPUR EXCHANGE

6634XXX

NEW DELHI

KARACHI

UDAIPUR

AHMEDABAD

originate. Moreover, some of the thirty exchanges were non-electronic. If the call originated through a non-electronic exchange, which was quite likely, there was no way the number could be traced further.

(v) It would be necessary that the Ahmedabad D-TAX through which the call was routed should inform D-TAX on a real-time basis as the call was in progress. And, Delhi D-TAX 1 and D-TAX 2 should be manned at the time the call was on so that D-TAX, Janpath, could inform the concerned exchange in Delhi on telephone, which would then make an effort to track down the number. Most automatic exchanges in Delhi were not manned after 9 p.m.

We took full cognizance of the practical problems in tracking down the number. However, I told Saxena that rather than not make an effort at all, we should take our chances and do whatever was possible. There was one thing that worked in our favour—the extortion calls made by Latif were generally between 7 p.m. and 10 p.m. Therefore, joint observation by the Gujarat ATS, STF of CBI and the telephone authorities of Ahmedabad and Delhi was required only for a few hours every day. In coordination with the ATS, officers were detailed on the two numbers in Ahmedabad, who were in wireless contact with their local Naurangpur Exchange, who in turn were in wireless contact with D-TAX, Ahmadabad. A team of STF was located in D-TAX 1 as well as in D-TAX 2 in Delhi between 7 p.m. to 10 p.m. on a daily basis. I kept my seniors in the CBI in the loop.

This arrangement continued without any success for several days. In the interim, Latif called Ahmedabad a few times but the calls lasted only a couple of minutes, so the calling number could not be traced. On 7 September 1995, to our good luck, a call made by him lasted for more than thirteen minutes during which the entire chain of communication set up between the Gujarat ATS, CBI STF and the telephone officials of the two cities moved like clockwork, and the calling number in Delhi was traced—3281xxx of the Daryaganj Exchange. The calling number was that of a PCO near Jama Masjid, a historical mosque in Old Delhi around which a congested and chaotic residential-cum-commercial area thrives.

Even though the calling number had been traced, I felt it was necessary to confirm that all earlier calls were also made from the same number. This was only possible by reading the digital data tapes of the Daryaganj Exchange. I was advised by Sunil Saxena, DGM of MTNL, Janpath, to get in touch with the GM (computers) of MTNL. When contacted, the GM (computers) acted indifferent and unhelpful. He wanted us to write a letter to him to which he would respond in a fortnight. All efforts made by my junior officers to explain the urgency of the matter failed. However, we were not about to give up that easily. He was given a mild rap on his knuckles and made to understand that declining a request from the CBI might not be the best thing for him to do. Consequently, the tapes from the Daryaganj Exchange reached the Computer Centre in Nehru Place, south Delhi, the very next day, where they were read electronically. It was confirmed that all earlier calls to Ahmedabad numbers were indeed made from the same PCO in Jama Masjid. Now we were hot on the trail of Abdul Latif. In all probability, he would use the same PCO again and, hopefully, be nabbed when he made the next extortion call to Ahmedabad.

Immediately, an officer from the Gujarat ATS, DSP A.K. Jadeja, was called. M.K. Bhat, DSP (CBI), and Jadeja together reached Churiwalan in the Jama Masjid area of Old Delhi, where the calling telephone number 3281xxx was located. They found it situated in an extremely congested by-lane and mounting any kind of watch on the PCO was quite out of the question. Also, conducting any raid in such a crowded area, without involving the local police, was not at all advisable.

On my request, Arun Bhagat, special director, CBI, spoke to T.R. Kakkar, the then officiating commissioner of police, Delhi, and requested him to extend help for a joint operation to be carried out by STF and the Gujarat Police. Kakkar asked us to get in touch with R. Tewari, additional commissioner of police (northern range), Delhi Police. Kuldip Sharma and I called on Tewari on 10 October 1995, who summoned P.N. Aggarwal, DCP (central), and Arun Kampani, ACP (Daryaganj), to his office. They were senior officers directly supervising the local police whose assistance we required.

A rough plan of action, basic and simple, prepared by us was given to the Delhi Police officers. The plan was: arrangements would be made with the help of MTNL authorities at the Daryaganj Exchange to monitor calls made from the PCO where the telephone 3281xxx was installed, between 6.30 p.m. and 10.30 p.m. every day. Two teams would be located with Motorola ultra-high frequency wireless sets at strategic points close to the PCO, and would maintain wireless contact with the officers based at the Telephone Exchange. When a call was placed to the known Ahmedabad number, an officer at the exchange familiar with Latif's voice would hopefully be able to identify and confirm whether the caller was Latif. A wireless message would then be sent from the Daryaganj Exchange to the two teams located at Churiwalan near the PCO, who would move in and nab Latif. The plan was accepted and approved by the officers of the Delhi Police.

K.N. Sharma and I then moved with Aggarwal and Arun Kampani to Aggarwal's office, also located in Daryaganj, not very far from the telephone exchange. Sunil Saxena, DGM, MTNL, Janpath, who had so far been extremely helpful, was requested to direct the in-charge of the Daryaganj Exchange to make the necessary arrangements for monitoring all the calls made from the PCO. Saxena spoke with Raju Sinha, divisional engineer, Daryaganj Exchange, and gave him clear instructions to assist us.

Meanwhile, Aggarwal and Arun Kampani assembled a team of twenty of their best officers and men drawn from various police stations of the district. A video film of a marriage attended by Abdul Latif and his cronies, namely Rauf, Sharif Khan, Rasool Patti, Sattar Battery and others, part of Gujarat Police's dossier on Latif, was shown repeatedly to all those present. The idea was to familiarize the police officers with the looks and mannerisms of Latif and his cronies. Audio tapes of the telephonic conversation between Abdul Latif and the called party in Ahmedabad were also played to the assembled officers and men so that everyone became familiar with Latif's voice. A comprehensive briefing of the plan was given to all those present and ideas, if any, were invited from those present. The final plan was drawn up with complete consensus and precision involving everyone as an important player.

Raju Sinha was requested to come over to the office of the DCP (central), where the entire plan was explained to him. Sinha, an intelligent and dynamic engineer, laid out, by the standards of the times, a sophisticated IT set-up in his office. However, he required a special gadget for listening to calls, which was only available with Malik, GM (vigilance), MTNL. I spoke to Malik who was kind enough to make the equipment available.

At 6.30 p.m. on 9 October 1995, a team comprising Kuldip Sharma, H.C. Singh, Arun Kampani, A.K. Jadeja and M.K. Bhat and I reached the office of Raju Sinha in Daryaganj. Sinha was ready with his telephone monitoring system comprising two computers linked to the two telephones installed in the PCO. The telephones were linked to special listening gadgets designed in such a way that neither the caller nor the person called would get any indication or hint that his conversation was being heard. Also, if we said anything into the mouthpiece, it would not be heard by either the caller or the called person. The gadget had a recording facility as well. Whenever any number was called from the two PCO numbers, the called number would be displayed on the video display unit of our computer, giving the name of the city called. One independent telephone line was kept free for the use of those of us sitting on watch. Sinha's set-up had another in-built facility. In the unlikely event of Latif using the PCO number to make a conference call with the Ahmedabad number, the calling number and its location would also show on the computer screen. A separate and dedicated team was available with us at the exchange itself that would move to that location. Thus, the possibility of Abdul Latif using another number in Delhi and conferencing through the PCO was also provided for. However, until 11 p.m. that evening there was no activity of any interest to us. Even though we dispersed without any positive development that evening, it was gratifying and reassuring to see that our arrangements were in perfect order and as good as they could possibly be.

I have delved deep into the technical arrangements, which by today's standards may seem rudimentary to law enforcement officers familiar with this trade, but it was truly state-of-the-art then. The use of computers and listening gadgets in the early 1990s was not as common as it is now. Investigators today, fortunately, have access to far better tools of technology for surveillance, but in those days it was actually a novelty to have the set-up created by Raju Sinha for our operation. Day 1 passed without any success.

The next day, arrangements were put in place by 6.30 p.m., exactly the way they were the previous day. We were in position at the exchange waiting to get lucky the second time. At about 8.30 p.m., a call was made from the PCO to a number in Udaipur, as was reflected on our computer. Since we were all expecting Latif to call

Ahmedabad, we did not take the conversation seriously in the beginning. It was only after a couple of minutes that Kuldip became suspicious that it could be Latif on the line. He gave me the headphone. Since I too had heard Latif's recorded conversations several times over, I confirmed Kuldip's suspicion. He took the headphone back from me and listened again, more carefully. As the conversation was in progress, he asked Arun Kampani to send a wireless message to Inspector Raj, ATS, Gujarat, to get closer to the PCO and report if he observed anything of interest. Kampani moved one of his two teams as close as possible to the PCO. Kuldip, meanwhile, still listening to the ongoing conversation, heard the expression 'Ayeesa kya?' (Is that so?), used typically by Latif, a fact known to Kuldip. Now Kuldip was absolutely sure that it was indeed Latif. Our teams were directed on the wireless to move in.

When Inspector Raj came close to the PCO he saw Latif face-to-face, sitting in the glass cabin. Raj gestured to the team closest to him to back him up. It was precisely then that Abdul Latif noticed the Gujarat Police officer and recognized him. He charged out of the booth. Inspector Raj blocked Latif and began to grapple with him. Meanwhile, a team led by the station house officer, Daryaganj, grabbed Latif and overpowered him at gunpoint. He was physically dragged out of the congested area, for over two furlongs, in full public view, to a police vehicle and driven to the office of the ACP, Daryaganj.

We at the exchange were oblivious of what had transpired at Jama Masjid. There had been no feedback from our officers on the ground which, we hoped, was a good sign. No news, in all probability, meant good news for us policemen. There was no point in waiting at the exchange any longer. As we prepared to leave, a handheld wireless set at the exchange came to life. In a message that was as garbled as baby talk, we deciphered that Latif had been caught and brought to the ACP's office.

We got there in no time. Abdul Latif Abdul Wahab Sheikh stood before us in flesh and blood. A Gujarat Police officer caught his jaw and forced his mouth open, revealing his set of stained teeth. A gold front tooth confirmed his identity. During the brief interrogation that followed, he admitted that he was indeed Latif.

When I called my special director, Arun Bhagat, his response said it all. 'Don't tell me you have got Latif?' he asked excitedly and incredulously. 'We have, sir,' I replied triumphantly. He came to Daryaganj Police Station immediately to see our precious catch for himself. Wanted in a number of heinous cases, it was taken for granted that Latif was hiding in Pakistan, enjoying the hospitality of Dawood et al. and the ISI, beyond the reach of the Indian law.

Kuldip informed his bosses and his chief minister, Keshubhai Patel. The catch meant the world to Gujarat. Kuldip had by then decided to take Latif to Ahmedabad the following morning by a flight that left in the early hours. The DGP, Gujarat, was keen that I too come along. He spoke with my special director and requested him to let me travel with the Gujarat Police team escorting Latif to Ahmedabad.

So there I was, having snatched only a few winks of sleep that night, with bleary eyes, on the 5.45 a.m. Indian

Airlines flight to Ahmedabad. With me was the triumphant
ATS team led by Kuldip Sharma escorting the elusive Latif,
whose time was finally up.

~

M.K. Sinha, DGP, Gujarat, the seniormost cop of the state,
was at Ahmedabad Airport to receive us. Netting Latif was
an exceptional event for Gujarat and the DGP's presence
at the airport was only befitting of the rare occasion. Warm
handshakes, hugs and congratulations were exchanged with
the DGP. Latif was driven to the city in a long cavalcade.

News of his arrest had still not broken and the city was
just about waking up for the day. After a couple of hours
the DGP addressed a press conference, for which I was
requested to remain present. When DIG (ATS) Kuldip
Sharma was asked to brief the media on the operational
details, he gave the CBI its due credit and I too featured
prominently in the local newspapers the following day.

I was put up in the VIP room of the circuit house,
which is normally reserved for the CM's official guests. I
was declared a state guest of sorts, or so it seemed. On the
invitation of Keshubhai Patel, Kuldip and I called on him
at his office in the afternoon. He got up from his chair
and greeted me with folded hands, a sign of his gratitude.
He said: 'DIG sahib, we will never be able to thank you
enough for what you have done for Gujarat.' I was touched
by his humility and sincerity.

A celebratory function at the Police Mess followed
in the evening. Most senior officers of the state based in

Ahmedabad and Gandhinagar were present. Along with
the Gujarat ATS officers I too was felicitated. Laudatory
speeches were made on how it was a red-letter day for
the Gujarat Police. As the ceremony was in progress,
messages came in that a 'victory procession' taken out by
the common people of the city to celebrate Latif's arrest
had been attacked with bricks and stones when it passed
through an area where Latif had once held sway. There
was a possibility of matters taking a communal turn. A few
senior officers in charge of the area, where the incident of
stone pelting had occurred, left the function hurriedly and
rushed to the spot. However, nothing untoward eventually
took place.

The following morning I was to take a flight back
to Delhi. After checking in at the airport I was waiting
in the departure lounge when a middle-aged uniformed
sub-inspector walked up to me and saluted me. He was
obviously an officer deployed with the airport security.
What he told me has remained with me until today. 'Sir,
you have no idea what you have done for us. Whenever
we would go to arrest a criminal, we would get mocked
and jeered at by the common people.' He continued,
'Invariably, petty criminals would say: "If you cops have
the guts, first go and arrest Latif and then come after us."
Sir, with the arrest of Latif, we can now walk with our
heads held high.' No other reward could be better than this
comment by a fellow police officer.

Talking of rewards, the Government of Gujarat was
gracious to recognize the contributions made by the Delhi
Police and the CBI. Every participant of the operation

received a letter of appreciation and handsome cash rewards. A formal ceremony was held at Gujarat Bhavan in Delhi to felicitate us. Even though he had not been in office at the time of the operation, the new chief minister of Gujarat, Suresh Mehta, especially flew in to Delhi to recognize the efforts of the two Delhi teams.

~

Latif was investigated for his role in several cases of murder and extortion, including the Rauf Waliullah case pending with the CBI. In the early hours of Saturday, 29 November 1997, two years after his arrest, he was shot dead by Gujarat Police at the Naroda railway crossing. Latif was fired upon by the police escort when he was apparently trying to escape after taking permission to relieve himself.

A testimony to the potential of police and civil cooperation, Latif's arrest showed what synergy can achieve. While the Gujarat Police provided the initial lead, the STF of the CBI, under my charge, followed it up with painstaking care and precision. On account of our personal contact with them, the telephone authorities, at the end of the day, provided excellent technical support. Displaying exemplary camaraderie, the Delhi Police proved to be a committed and capable comrade-in-arms. A senior officer of the Gujarat Police was there himself to identify the voice of the gangster and lead his team in Delhi. It was a dream operation that brought the curtain down on don Latif. May he rest in peace!

6

Our Man in Dubai
The CBI versus the ISI

It was the afternoon of 12 March 1993, much like any
other March afternoon in Mumbai.* The short-lived
winter in the commercial capital of India had receded and
summer was setting in. The city, which usually moves at
a frenetic pace, was taking a lunch break. Even though all
seemed well, the calm appeared a trifle strange. Generally
known for its cosmopolitan character and business-friendly
social and cultural ethos, the city had been ripped by two
bloody Hindu–Muslim riots in December 1992 and January
1993. The communal clashes had claimed 900 lives, mostly

---

* Disclaimer: This narrative is merely the story of the CBI's efforts to
arrest the absconders accused in the serial blasts that rocked Mumbai
on 12 March 1993. If at any stage I have betrayed traces of sympathy
towards the Memons or Yaqub, it may be seen as a case of the
Lima syndrome.

of Muslims. A sense of fear and uncertainty lay simmering under the tranquil surface.

Unlike the soothsayer, who warned Julius Caesar of the ides of March in the celebrated eponymous play by William Shakespeare, there was none to caution the city of Mumbai. None knew that within the next couple of hours catastrophe would strike.

Between 1.30 p.m. and 3.40 p.m., the city was rocked by a series of bomb blasts, leaving 257 dead, 713 injured and property worth lakhs of rupees destroyed. The targets were carefully selected to shock and awe the country. Some like the stock exchange building and the Air India building were government or semi-government establishments; some others were five-star hotels like Sea Rock at Bandra, Hotel Centaur at Juhu, Hotel Centaur at Santa Cruz; and other busy places with high footfalls like Zaveri Bazar, Katha Bazar, Century Bazar at Worli and Plaza Theatre were chosen to cause maximum fatalities and spread terror. Last but not least, a serious attempt was made to incite communal violence by lobbing hand grenades at a Hindu colony in Mahim and orchestrating a bomb explosion at a petrol pump adjacent to Shiv Sena Bhavan in Dadar, resulting in riots in which three lost their lives and several shops, homes and vehicles were destroyed.

Not only Mumbai but the entire country was stunned. Never before in the history of modern India had terror struck at this scale, with such ferocity and meticulous planning. Fortunately for India, the case was cracked by the Mumbai Police the same day with the discovery of a Maruti van MFC 1972 near the Siemens factory in Worli.

The vehicle lay abandoned and unclaimed. Seven AK-56 rifles, four hand grenades, fourteen AK-56 magazines and one timer pencil were seized from the van.

The duplicate registration book of the Maruti van found in its glove compartment revealed Rubina Memon, wife of Suleiman Memon, a resident of Al-Hussaini building in Mahim, as its owner. Searches conducted by the police on the premises found traces of RDX—a most lethal explosive material—in the garage, lift and flats belonging to the family of one Ibrahim Razaq Memon aka Tiger Memon, a notorious and hot-headed silver and gold smuggler of Mumbai.

(The gangster from Mahim had apparently acquired Tiger as his moniker after an incident—part of underworld folklore and of apocryphal origin—remembered by his contemporaries till date. It seems a customs officer seized a consignment of silver smuggled by Ibrahim Razaq Memon and had the temerity to purloin a part of it. Memon beat up the customs officer publicly and recovered the stolen slabs. Thereafter, out of 'reverence' and awe, his colleagues began to call him Tiger. On another occasion, as the story goes, his brother Yusuf, a timid youngster, was beaten up by goons residing in their neighbourhood. A vehicle driven by one of the goons there had splattered Yusuf with mud from a pothole. He was assaulted the moment he raised an objection. This happened barely fifty metres away from Mahim Police Station. The cops took both Yusuf and the local louts with them. Tiger reached the station as soon as he learnt of the incident and thrashed the assailants in the presence of the policemen on duty. He left the precincts taking Yusuf with him, and the police did not utter a word. This anecdote, again apocryphal, further reinforced Tiger's image of having a devil-may-care attitude towards governmental authority.)

Hidden on the premises inhabited by Tiger's joint family in Al-Hussaini building in Mahim were twenty-seven folded cardboard boxes. One of these bore the label 'Packsile Packages Limited, Lahore'. Another bore the marking 'Packers Packages Limited, Container Lahore P-12/90'. A third, recovered from the garage of the Memons, had its markings obliterated with white paint. Forensic examination later showed the markings to be of Wah Nobel Private Limited, Wah Cantonment, Islamabad, Pakistan. The investigations that followed revealed that the company was located at 12/92, G.T. Road, Wah Cantonment. It was engaged in the production of explosive substances like dynamite, RDX, safety fuses, detonators and blasting equipment. The company was, and may well be even now, a member of Rawalpindi Chamber of Commerce and Industry. Traces of RDX were found in the garage of the Memons.

As countless layers of the conspiracy behind this horrific crime unfolded one by one, much like an onion being peeled, it became clear that the triad of Dawood Ibrahim, Tiger Memon and Mohammad Dossa, infamous smugglers and underworld dons of Mumbai, was behind the blasts. They had used their extensive smuggling infrastructure and network of seafarers, couriers, landing agents, jetties, warehouses; the support of compromised customs and police officers; and local and offshore financiers, etc., for causing the blasts. Investigations would later show that the perfidious conspiracy of the three Mumbai smugglers was the brainchild of our 'friendly' western neighbour. But more on that later.

Dawood Ibrahim had fled Mumbai in mid-1980s to escape prosecution in numerous cases pending against him. He had made Dubai and Karachi his hideouts since then. Dossa escaped after the blasts while Tiger Memon fled to Dubai on the morning of 12 March.

The escape of Tiger Memon in the nick of time and the use of his premises and vehicles for keeping bombs were evidence enough of his complicity in the dastardly act of terror in his own city. The three were all declared absconding accused in the case and Interpol Red Notices were issued against them.

I was then posted as the DCP, Crime Branch, in the Delhi Police. Like other police officers of the country, I felt proud of the aplomb with which the Mumbai Police had solved the crime. Every bit of news connected with the investigation was followed by the Indian police fraternity with great interest. Little did I know that within months I myself would have lots to do with the case.

In June 1993, I moved on deputation from the Delhi Police to the CBI, as a DIG in the STF, a new unit of the bureau. Created in May 1993, the STF was to take over the Mumbai blasts case from the Detection of Crime Branch of the Mumbai Police. We waited for the first charge sheet to be filed by the Mumbai Police on the conclusion of their investigation before officially commencing ours. In December 1993, the Detection of Crime Branch,

Mumbai, then headed by JCP M.N. Singh with DCP Rakesh Maria (both later held the post of commissioner of police, Mumbai), filed their charge sheet and the STF formally took over the case. In the months to come we filed fourteen supplementary charge sheets, arrested twenty-nine absconding accused and tenaciously followed the case in court, which concluded in the conviction of 100 out of 123 accused. Nearly 800 witnesses were examined. However, this is neither the story of our investigation nor an account of how we prosecuted the case in court. It is the untold story of our operation to get ten members of Tiger Memon's immediate family, including three children, back to India from Dubai, in the face of serious attempts made by the ISI to foil our mission.

~

Yaqub, one of the twelve members of the Memon family declared absconders in the Mumbai blasts case, was arrested by the STF on 5 August 1994. He was interrogated at length and he made startling disclosures about his own conduct and that of his family members, before and after the blasts. Some of the revelations corresponded with what we already knew. Additionally, the documents recovered from his suitcase included Indian passports of his family members and his own, papers connected with properties in Pakistan, identity papers issued to the Memons by the Pakistani government, birth certificates issued by the Metropolitan Corporation, Karachi, school- and college-leaving certificates, microcassettes containing secret recordings of Yaqub's conversations with the Pakistani masterminds behind the blasts, video tapes with incriminating material against Pakistan, and so on. The evidence and information contained in these documents went on to fill the gaps and join the dots in our investigation. Pakistan's role in the conspiracy behind the blasts was established with documentary proof and by someone who had seen it all, first-hand. His disclosures and the material recovered from him were damning, not only for Pakistan and the ISI, but equally against the Memon family and Yaqub himself.

In the course of his custody with us, I spoke to Yaqub at length, often for hours without a break. He sat across from me at my office table, narrating the story of his life and the cataclysmic changes it had undergone in the wake of the blasts. He was a qualified chartered accountant and a member of a large and happy joint family, which originally hailed from Jamnagar district in Gujarat. His father, Abdul Razzaq Memon, ran a workshop named Famous Engineering and Welding in Mustafa Bazar, Byculla, Mumbai, which supplied machinery parts to Tata Oil Mills. His mother, Hanifa, was a simple homemaker. Yaqub had five brothers—Suleiman, Ibrahim, Ayub, Essa and Yusuf, all reasonably well educated and suitably engaged in different occupations. Three of them were married with children. Rahin, Yakub's twenty-year-old wife, was a charming young girl but the couple was till then childless.

Ibrahim Abdul Razzaq Memon, aka Tiger Memon, had studied up to the first year of college in Mumbai and started his career as a bank clerk in 1978. He slowly drifted into the smuggling of silver and gold with a large gang of committed members. Meanwhile, Yaqub had become a qualified chartered accountant and was making good money. He looked after Tiger's accounts as well and invested in several real estate ventures in Mumbai and Goa. In 1990, the family bought three flats, numbered 22, 25 and 26, and a garage in Al-Hussaini building at Mahim, a colony in the heart of Mumbai, largely inhabited by Muslims.

The Memons were the least affected by the December 1992 communal riots in Mumbai, following the demolition of Babri Masjid in Faizabad, Uttar Pradesh. However, the riots that followed, in January 1993, left the Memon family, much like the Muslim community of Mumbai at large, devastated. Yaqub Memon's office was completely burnt down and he had to recreate the income tax and sales tax files of his clients, piece by piece. He started operating from his residence. According to Yakub, he and his family lived in constant fear, not knowing what lay ahead for them.

~

The demolition of Babri Masjid, as is common knowledge, deeply hurt the religious sentiments of the Muslim community, not only in Mumbai but across India and even overseas. The communal riots that followed the demolition further aggravated the anti-Hindu and anti-establishment feelings among the minority community in India. A strong desire for revenge rose in the extremist and fundamentalist elements amidst them. The harmonious atmosphere in the country stood severely vitiated. The ISI of Pakistan sensed an invaluable opportunity to strike at India. They could use select Indian nationals from the minority community to execute their diabolical plans, aimed at causing terror attacks at an unprecedented scale; and who could be better partners than members of the Mumbai underworld? In any case, the riot-stricken Muslim community of the city was already looking towards the mafia dons of the commercial capital to seek vengeance on their behalf. The ISI seized the opportunity with both hands.

Taufiq Jallianwala and Syed Arif, two gold and silver smugglers of Karachi, were ISI's 'assets', whose services were always at its disposal. Their 'handlers' in the ISI conceived of a grand and vicious plan of hitting India with terror attacks at such major cities where the Muslim population was sizeable.

The plan was to train Muslim youth from cities like Mumbai, Chennai, Kolkata, Ahmedabad, Bengaluru, etc., in the handling of Kalashnikovs and improvised explosive devices (IEDs). On a day when a major Hindu festival like Ganesh Chaturthi or Dussehra was being celebrated and lakhs of Hindus congregated, major explosions would be caused, killing thousands of people, mostly belonging to the majority community. The masterminds behind the sinister conspiracy expected, and perhaps rightly so, that these bomb attacks and the resultant heavy casualties would lead to a severe backlash, wherein mobs of Hindus would march towards Muslim localities to take revenge. The Muslim youth, by then trained in Pakistani camps and equipped with automatic weapons, would open fire in self-defence, thereby killing more Hindus. This would further infuriate the majority community, and a civil war–like situation would emerge between the two communities, as anticipated by the ISI. The Hindu–Muslim divide in India would then be complete and irreversible, permanently destroying the country's social fabric, weakening the country like never before.

The ISI found the smuggling networks of Mumbai well suited to implementing their grand plan. Nothing could be better than the Indian smugglers' existing infrastructure, traditionally used to ferry gold and silver, and ship weapons and explosives instead. Also, several members of the smuggling syndicates were hardened criminals, ready to kill at their respective boss's command. Quite a few of them were young, sturdy and physically fit, capable of undergoing rigorous training for handling automatic weapons, and making and exploding bombs, etc. Fortunately for the ISI, Mumbai-based Indian smugglers Dawood Ibrahim, Tiger Memon and Mohammed Dossa were business partners with ISI's prized 'assets', Taufiq Jalianwala and Syed Arif. The ISI handlers shared their master plan with Taufiq and Syed and instructed them to bring Dawood et al. on board.

In pursuance of this grand plan, several conspiratorial meetings took place between the Karachi and Mumbai smugglers to thrash out the finer modalities of implementing the conspiracy. One such meeting was at White House, Dawood's Dubai residence. While Dawood, given his pre-eminent position in the Mumbai underworld, was the natural Big Boss of the operation, Tiger was made its chief executor. Three consignments of arms, ammunition and explosives were landed by the joint teams of Tiger and Mohammed Dossa in January and February 1993 at Dighi and Shekhadi on the western coast of India, not far from Mumbai. Vehicles were procured for making car bombs and men identified to place bombs with timer devices at predetermined targets. Every member of the implementation team, including Dawood and Tiger, was asked to wait till a final go-ahead from the ISI bosses was received. The ISI was waiting for a major Hindu festival and, in the interim, intended to train more young Muslim boys from other Indian cities and send additional supplies of weapons and explosive material.

~

There was an unexpected and accidental twist in the tale when Gul Mohammed, a Tiger acolyte, was arrested by the Crime Branch on 9 March 1993 in a case under different special acts of the state and Central governments. Gul aka Gullu, was privy to Tiger's plan as well as the preparatory work done by him for the final assault. Gullu's arrest made Tiger panic. He feared Gullu might spill the beans during interrogation. Tiger expected the Mumbai Crime Branch to be at his throat any moment and saw his hard work going up in smoke. He consulted Dawood over the phone, who in turn took other co-conspirators into confidence. They all decided not to wait any longer for their larger design of hitting at Mumbai as well

as at other metropolises in India. Tiger received the approval
he wanted for their 'common cause'.

Twelfth March was an auspicious day as per the
Islamic calendar. It was the day centuries ago when
Prophet Mohammed had launched Ghazwa-e-Badr
(the Battle of Badr), his holy war against rival Quraish
chieftains of Mecca. The Prophet's victory in the battle
had established Muslim supremacy in the region. Tiger
decided to make it his D-Day too. But, before waging
his own 'holy' war, Tiger had to make some crucial and
last-minute moves.

On 11 March 1993, Tiger's brother Yaqub flew to
Dubai with his wife, Rahin, and brothers Essa and Yusuf.
His parents, Abdul Razzaq and Hanifa, had left Mumbai
earlier, on 10 March, for the same destination. Tiger's
two other brothers, Ayub and Suleiman, both resident
visa holders of the UAE, were already in Dubai with their
families. Tiger reached Dubai on the morning of 12 March,
after instructing his men to strike in the afternoon of the
same day.

At about 4 p.m., the Memons heard the BBC breaking
news of Mumbai having been rocked by a series of bomb
blasts. Tiger began to jump with joy and was constantly
on the phone with his counterparts in Mumbai. Each call
brought news of one more bomb explosion and the rising
number of casualties.

The serial blasts in Mumbai drew worldwide attention.
Amidst the outrage in the international community, the
Pakistani establishment, particularly the ISI, realized it was
no longer safe for the Memons to stay on in Dubai. Tiger

left for Karachi on 14 March 1993. Yaqub followed, along with other family members. The tickets for all of them had already been booked. When the Pakistan International Airlines flight of 17 March landed in Karachi, the Memons were received and escorted out of the airport without any immigration formalities. Tiger was waiting outside in a Mistubishi Pajero. Armed personnel in plain clothes stood guarding him. The family was driven to a bungalow called Qasr-e-Rayaz that belonged to Taufiq Jalianwala, Tiger's smuggling partner based in Karachi. Armed guards kept watch and the family stepped out only for prayers at a nearby mosque. They stayed in the bungalow for about a week after which they were shifted to another bungalow at 25, Rufi Cottage, Gulshan-e-Iqbal, Karachi. There too they were under constant watch.

In April 1993, they were given passports issued at Islamabad under completely new Pakistani identities, much like what law enforcement agencies in many countries do in witness protection programmes. Several supporting documents like driving licences, fake educational degrees, property papers and birth certificates were issued to them. Clearly, the attempt by our 'friendly' neighbour was to create enough evidence to deny the presence of the Memons and the other perpetrators of the Mumbai carnage on their soil. Even if they were located and identified, the Government of Pakistan could claim they were from Pakistan, backed by these documents.

On 16 and 17 April, the entire family travelled to Bangkok in two groups. Two ISI officials, who had earlier received them at Karachi airport, accompanied them on the trip. On arrival they were received by officials from the Pakistan Embassy, presumably ISI agents seconded to the mission in Bangkok. They proceeded to a bungalow in the outskirts of the city on the Bangkok–Pattaya Highway. Their sudden move to Thailand was in the wake of growing international pressure on Pakistan to hand over the Memons to the Government of India. They returned to Karachi on 29 April to a new bungalow: D-58, Darakhshan Villa, Defence Housing Authority, Karachi.

According to Yaqub's account, their life was becoming increasingly complicated and unacceptable to them. The experience of calling each other by new names, living the life of captives, ridden with guilt and insecurity, hiding from the world in an enemy country, had together begun to take its toll. Most of the Memons, including Tiger's wife, Shabana, were inclined to return to India. Yaqub was at the head of this plan and took upon himself the role of leading the way for the rest. However, out of sheer naiveté, he thought that if he succeeded in collecting irrefutable evidence of the involvement of the ISI, Taufiq Jalianwala and Tiger Memon in the serial Mumbai blasts, the authorities in India would show leniency to his family members and him; and that the Memons may even be given a reprieve.

According to Yaqub, when Tiger learnt of their far-fetched plan, he was dismissive. He was also amused and scoffed at Yaqub. However, Yaqub and most members of the family were determined to return to Mumbai, disregarding Tiger's alarmist, albeit prophetic words of caution. The majority of Tiger's family was ready to face any consequence on their return to India, despite all that had happened, rather than spend the rest of their lives in an enemy country.

With the passage of time, Yaqub and the other Memons noticed that the surveillance over them was gradually diminishing. The armed guards were withdrawn and replaced by plainclothes men. They were no longer being followed by shadowy men when they stepped out of their safe house. Soon they found that they could move about town freely, without being pried upon.

Yaqub and his brothers Suleiman, Essa and Yusuf wanted to test the waters further by attempting to travel abroad. In early June 1994, Suleiman and Essa first left for Dubai, ostensibly in connection with business. On 20 June 1994 Yaqub travelled to Dubai and returned to Karachi within a week. At no stage were they stopped or checked. Clearly, their keepers' guard was down.

Yaqub contacted his trusted Mumbai-based cousin, codenamed 'Suresh' by us, who was most sceptical of the plan but reluctantly agreed to meet him on account of his Chacha jaan's (Abdul Razzaq Memon) persistent pleas. Yaqub and Suresh met twice for consultations. During both meetings, Suresh advised him to exercise self-restraint till he (Suresh) had obtained firm legal opinion supporting Yaqub's intended move. He required more time to consult trusted lawyers in Mumbai before Yaqub took the plunge. But Yaqub was adamant.

~

I am not privy to what transpired between his second meeting with his cousin and 5 August when Yaqub was arrested by the STF in Delhi. His arrest, a major breakthrough in the investigation of the 1993 serial blasts of Mumbai, made screaming headlines in the media and was hailed as a major achievement. The startling disclosures made by Yaqub during interrogation, and scrutiny of the documents seized from him, confirmed the devious and insidious role of Pakistan in the Mumbai terror attacks.

Yaqub disclosed that his family members, in the interim, would have fled Karachi and reached Dubai. When I asked him whether they would return to India if contacted, his reply was in the affirmative. However, they would have to be first traced in Dubai, persuaded and convinced that they would be given a fair trial. Yaqub said this difficult and risk-ridden task could only be performed by his cousin, whom he had met twice for consultations before his arrest. In his revelation lay hidden a golden opportunity for us, not only to bring back the fugitive Memons from Dubai, but also to catch several absconding accused in one go. I would not let this opportunity slip through my fingers in a hurry, I said to myself.

The plan we conceived was simple. Yaqub would be allowed to speak with his cousin Suresh over the phone to request him to come over to Delhi. Once in Delhi, Yaqub would be permitted to meet Suresh in person and urge him (Suresh) to proceed to Dubai, trace his (Yaqub's) family and persuade them to return to India.

Yaqub called Suresh from my office telephone. Suresh, who had heard the news of his cousin's sensational arrest and the media furore that had followed, was for a moment caught by surprise when he heard Yaqub's voice. Yaqub explained to him that he, by and large, was doing well in CBI custody. However, he was worried for the rest of the family. He (Yaqub) pleaded with his beloved cousin to come to Delhi and meet him.

Suresh, for obvious reasons, was most apprehensive of getting further involved in the matter. The idea of coming to the CBI office, meeting Yaqub, an accused in serious acts of terror, didn't quite appeal to him, to begin with. Following Yaqub's tearful conversation with him, I too spoke to Suresh and reassured him that neither he nor his family would come to any harm. Sensing his reluctance despite my assurances, I asked O.P. Chhatwal, my SP, then in Mumbai, to call him over to our office there and speak to him. On my SP's nudge, Suresh travelled to Delhi on 8 August, three days after Yaqub's arrest.

Yaqub succeeded in convincing him to undertake the mission, though Suresh had serious reservations initially. After all, he had his wife and children to look after. What if he were detained at any stage? How would his wife and children cope if something were to happen to him? But after extensive consultations with Yaqub, whom he loved dearly, he relented.

Once Suresh gave his consent, we requested our immediate boss, Joint Director S. Sen, to inform the director, CBI. We suggested that a meeting may be called to consider our plan of action and approve what we had in mind.

K. Vijaya Rama Rao, the then director of the CBI, convened a meeting the same day in his office in North Block, an imposing colonial-era building perched on Raisina Hill, New Delhi. It was attended by his trusted advisers, my immediate superiors, Satish Jha (my other SP in STF, Mumbai, and my second in command in the mission at hand) and me. Prophets of doom abound aplenty in the Indian police. Some of them were present at the meeting. They were not supportive of the idea in the least, each with his preposterous reservations. A few others, before voicing their opinions, waited to see how the director reacted.

Our argument was simple. Suresh, in any case, by his own admission, was a regular visitor to Dubai in connection with his business. He would arrange his own ticket, visa and lodging. On reaching Dubai, he would attempt to locate his relatives and, if traced, speak to them. If he succeeded in convincing them to return, we would take the operation to the next level, or we would abandon it. There was no risk for us whatsoever in this limited part of the operation. The director saw our point and gave us the go-ahead. The Doubting Thomases too nodded their heads in unison.

~

Suresh returned to Mumbai on 8 August itself and left for Dubai on 11 August after convincing his wife that all would be fine. He went straight to Al-Wasl Hotel, where the Memons stayed when in Dubai. To his utter disappointment, they were not there. Nonetheless, he checked in and began to look for them at their other haunts, only to be further dejected. Meanwhile, he got the eerie feeling that he was being trailed. He noticed a few suspicious characters sitting in the hotel lobby observing him. When he called me up and expressed his apprehension, I asked him to check out of Al-Wasl and move to a different hotel. He checked into Rex, Deira, on 19 August.

He was now scouring Dubai frantically, checking mosques, hospitals, shopping areas and so on, only to draw a blank. Meanwhile, with every passing day, our bosses in Delhi were getting impatient. Suresh was continuously reporting that he was being followed and he kept changing his hotels.

But there was one smart thing he did. Knowing that the Memons were fond of food from Delhi Darbar, a restaurant serving traditional Mughlai food at Al Khamara in Dubai, he would park himself there every evening. His patience and presence of mind were to pay dividends. On 21 August, he saw two of his cousins, Suleiman and Essa, come to Delhi Darbar to order takeaway—called 'parcel' in Mumbai's colloquial lingo—for the rest of the family.

When he met them, his cousins were ecstatic. Overwhelmed with emotion, they clung to him and wept. They took him where the remaining members of the Memon family were staying. Suresh learnt that within less than a week of their arrival in Dubai, Yaqub's wife Rahin had delivered a girl child, on 30 July. The newborn had been named Zubeida, which in Urdu means 'essence'.

The entire family had been through untold emotional highs and lows. The joy of Zubeida's arrival was preceded by the frightening realization that Yaqub was in serious trouble, the collective decision to surreptitiously slip out of Karachi and then Rahin's hospitalization on arrival in Dubai. Now, they had no idea what the future held for them; yet they were happy to be out of Pakistan. Reunion with their family's 'guardian angel' Suresh was reassuring, but they didn't know what to expect from him given the situation they were all in.

Suresh explained to his distressed family members that he had been sent by Yaqub to take them back to India, where, like him, they too would get a fair trial. He (Suresh) kept awake through the night of their reunion, trying to convince and persuade them to accompany him to India to face the law of their homeland. However, there was a small but serious problem. Rahin's passport had been deposited by the Memons at the Pakistani Consulate in Dubai through an agent, for the inclusion of her baby's name. The chances of getting it back were rather bleak as, by then, in all likelihood, the Pakistani authorities would have realized that it was the passport of one of the Memons trying to escape them.

As the day of 22 August broke, Suresh informed me of his success in finding his family members and also convincing them to travel with him to Delhi. However, he wanted a solution to Rahin's problem. I was elated that my plan had worked, if not in full, at least in ample measure. When I informed my bosses, the director wanted to know our further plan of action. I proposed that in the interest of expediency, the Memons should continue their travel to India on their Pakistani passports. Getting the Memons emergency Indian passports, with no arrival entry into Dubai, would make their exit complicated. Secondly, if they were given emergency passports by the Indian Consulate, it would have to be in their original names, which, in all probability, were on the wanted list of the Dubai immigration directorate, given the Interpol Red Notices against them. Giving them passports on fake identities was asking for too much of the Indian Mission. So the best and safest strategy was to get the ministry of external affairs to instruct our consulate in Dubai to give them visas on their Pakistani passports, without demur. Further, the consulate could be advised to facilitate their journey to Delhi. The bosses saw my point.

~

On the same day at 9 a.m., the director, CBI, on the advice of Joint Director S. Sen, presented me before Surendra Singh, the then Cabinet Secretary. The then Union Home Secretary and Special Secretary, ministry of external affairs (MEA), were also present for the meeting on the director's request (the officiating Foreign Secretary was out of station). After introducing me briefly to the bigwigs, he proudly announced, pointing at me, 'Gentlemen, this young man has something to tell you.'

I gave them a brief of the developments following Yakub's arrest and the outlines of our future plan of action. I requested them to instruct the Consul General of India in Dubai that when a man named Suresh approached him with seven Pakistani passports, they should be stamped with Indian visas without any ado. In the normal course, to get an Indian visa on a Pakistani passport, and vice versa, is a time-consuming and tedious process. I also explained to the top bureaucrats that giving them Emergency Indian passports had several inherent problems. My arguments were the same as those I had earlier put forth to my director. Everyone present saw my point and approved the plan. The Memons, holed up in Dubai, would travel to India on their Pakistani passports and would be arrested on arrival. The top bosses were convinced and also excited at the prospect of getting so many absconders back to face trial. The Cabinet Secretary asked Special Secretary, MEA, to do the needful.

The Special Secretary, I remember, had a severe back problem that morning. He took me to his office in South Block from the Cabinet Secretary's chamber, despite being in acute pain. He called up Prabhu Dayal, an Indian Foreign Service officer, then posted as the Consul General of India in Dubai, and virtually gave him carte blanche to comply with all my requests to him. He was informed that an important CBI operation was under way, which had the approval of the Government of India.

On reaching office, I called Prabhu, who knew me well. I informed him that someone called Suresh would meet him soon and present a few Pakistani passports. He should get Indian visas stamped on them post-haste. The Consul General understood that there was no need to ask further questions over the phone and assured me that all possible assistance would be provided.

Suresh met Prabhu Dayal at the Indian Consulate in Dubai the same day and submitted six passports. Suresh informed Prabhu of Rahin's situation. The Consul General offered a solution. Rahin could stay at one of his staffers' residence till her travel issues were resolved. The staffer was a married man and he and his wife had a small baby.

Suresh met the staffer and his wife and felt reassured that Rahin would be safe with them. He succeeded in persuading his relatives to leave Rahin behind and get out of Dubai at the earliest. He explained to them that they had little option as, sooner than later, the Pakistani authorities would trace them and, with Dubai's help, take them back to Karachi. They would then be subject to undue hardships for having hoodwinked them and for escaping from their 'custody'.

Simultaneously, Prabhu called me the same evening at about 8 p.m. (IST) to inform me that the passports had been serviced and returned to Suresh. He was waiting for Rahin's passport and had offered to look after her, in case the others agreed to leave her behind with her baby.

It was not difficult to comprehend how and why Suresh was being trailed, as he had reported. When news of Yaqub's arrest broke in the media, the ISI would have come to know that some members of the Memon family had fled Karachi. Possibly, Tiger Memon, to save his own skin, would have informed them. Cross-checking the immigration records at Karachi airport would have revealed that they had flown to Dubai. Yaqub's arrest in Delhi and his expected disclosures to the CBI would have severely embarrassed the ISI, denting their image in the eyes of the Pakistani government. They had to make amends by prompt damage control. They had to somehow get the Memons back to Pakistan and thwart their attempts, if any, to escape to India. The arrival of Rahin's passport at the Pakistani Consulate was further confirmation of the news they already had.

Suresh's shadowing by suspicious-looking men was thus becoming increasingly aggressive and obtrusive. He was beginning to crack under the pressure of being constantly followed and having to run from one hotel to the other. It took me considerable effort to keep him calm and pacify him over the phone. He requested me to arrange a car for him with a trustworthy driver, if I could. I turned to an old friend who had an office in Dubai. He directed his driver Shafi (now deceased), an Indian national, to report to Suresh. Shafi had driven me around on a few of my earlier visits to Dubai and knew that I worked for the Indian police. Before being deputed with Suresh, he had been briefed by my friend that Suresh was in Dubai on my behalf. That had charged Shafi up and he could sense that he was part of an important mission. Availability of a chauffeur-driven car bolstered Suresh's confidence. He, meanwhile, made a tentative booking on an Air India flight for himself and the family from Dubai to Delhi for 24 August.

But the worst was yet to come. Suresh went to the consulate to collect the money to pay for the return tickets (Pakistani passport holders coming to India must have return tickets). Suitable instructions to Prabhu had by then been given by the Special Secretary (MEA), on my request, to provide monetary support to Suresh. Suresh had become a familiar figure in the consulate and most, including Prabhu, took him to be a senior CBI officer deputed for the special covert mission. He was always accorded due respect and deference by the consulate staff. After completing his work he walked to the consulate parking, where Shafi was waiting for him in my friend's car. As they drove out of the parking lot they noticed a car tailing them. At the next crossing two more cars appeared from the side roads and began to follow Shafi's car. Shafi had spent over twenty-five years in Dubai and knew the city like the back of his hand. That it was an attempt by the baddies to put a spanner in the works of the Government of India was amply clear to Shafi. He drove leisurely and let them follow him, occasionally trying to shake them off, while Suresh sat panicking in the rear seat.

Suddenly, Shafi took a sharp turn and headed for a shopping mall where he dropped Suresh. He instructed Suresh to enter the mall and exit from the rear, where he would be waiting for him. The pursuers were now in a fix. Their quarry was inside the mall, but his car had left. Not knowing whether to follow the car or to go after the quarry, they decided to stay put, with a few of them entering the mall to look for Suresh. Meanwhile, Suresh had emerged from the rear exit, got into Shafi's car and driven to Air India's office to collect the tickets.

Little did he know that further surprises awaited him. To his utter shock, the Air India officials informed him that the bookings had been cancelled on the phone, ostensibly by one of the members of his family. On inquiry, his relatives denied having done any such thing. Now it was more than confirmed that he was indeed being trailed and every dirty trick in the book being adopted to thwart the Memons' return. Clearly, one of his pursuers, pretending to be a Memon, had called Air India and cancelled the booking. The news shook me and I decided to share it with my bosses, little realizing that I was committing a grave error.

For totally misplaced reasons the bosses went into a tizzy. They thought this was the beginning of a 'first-class diplomatic situation'. A high-level meeting was called by the director at his Tughlak Lane residence late at night. I was made to feel like a fool who had launched a far-fetched and ill-conceived misadventure, destined to ruin the fair name of the CBI. The director had long confabulations with his advisers and I was not allowed to speak. He decided to call up the Special Secretary in the MEA and inform him that the operation had been called off and he (the Special Secretary) should instruct his Consul General in Dubai to give shelter to the Memons in the consulate, arrange to give them emergency passports and organize their travel to Delhi.

The Special Secretary was terribly irked and dismissed the proposal outright. He said angrily: 'One moment you guys ask us to give the Memons Indian visas on Pakistani passports urgently, and the next moment you want us to give them boarding and lodging facilities in the mission. Our consulate is not geared up for such contingencies. I am sorry, I can't help you.'

When director disclosed the details of his conversation with the Special Secretary, his advisers looked at each other, not knowing how to respond. At that moment I decided to speak my mind. Addressing the director, I said: 'Sir, I don't understand why this panic has set in. Nothing has happened which would embarrass the government or us. We are only trying to get our own citizens back and, that too, not forcibly. They are absconders and ours is an attempt to bring them to book. I should be left alone and allowed to handle the situation.' Finding no other option, they decided to disperse and sleep over the problem. The parting jibe at me from one of director's worthy advisers was: 'Well! Had this operation succeeded, it would have been the greatest achievement ever of the CBI. But, alas, that was not to be.'

I returned home rather vexed and disappointed. I had come so close to success and had not quite made it. But I was determined not to give up and let the opportunity slip by in a hurry.

It is perhaps not an uncommon occurrence that when one sleeps over a problem, the solution sometimes hits like a bolt the next morning. After sleeping fitfully that night, when I woke up, an Indian Airlines newspaper advertisement announcing a direct flight from Sharjah to Delhi, begun several weeks earlier, flashed through my mind. I awoke my wife and shared with her the idea that had struck me. Why couldn't the Memons leave from Sharjah instead of Dubai? She asked me to first be sure of the fact that there indeed was such a flight. The Indian Airlines (it had not merged with Air India then) customer service, when called, confirmed that what I had seen was correct. And, more interestingly, the Air India flight from Dubai and the Indian Airlines flight from Sharjah both took off for Delhi within a few hours of each other. Thankfully, I was familiar with the topography of the two emirates of the UAE—Dubai and Sharjah—as I had visited them earlier during an investigation of the serial blasts, and knew they are minutes away from each other by car. I planned to make two sets of bookings for the Memon family: one from Dubai and the other from Sharjah. While the bookings from Dubai would be in their names as given on their Pakistani passports, we had to somehow ensure that the bookings from Sharjah remained a secret, lest the ISI played dirty again.

It was not even seven that morning when I called up the director and shared my idea with him. He quite liked it and asked me to go ahead. Perhaps, from the previous night's experience, he had realized the futility of involving too many advisers in the operation. He asked me to report to him directly and not share any information with intermediary officers. That suited me fine. That is how it should always be when an operation of this magnitude is under way. Fewer the levels of reporting and supervision, the better it is.

~

Here, a word about the CBI. It is primarily an anti-corruption body. Its core strength is the collection of intelligence concerning corruption in high places in the

Central government and its subsidiaries. Laying traps
for red-handed arrests of givers and takers of bribes,
investigating cases against public servants with assets
disproportionate to their known sources of income,
etc., are their forte. Investigating economic offences
and large-scale scams with intricate webs of financial
transactions, sometimes leading to highly placed bankers,
politicians and government officials, is its second area
of strength. In sheer comparative terms, investigating
what are referred to as 'special' crimes in CBI parlance,
such as cases of murder, suicide, bank robberies, terror,
etc., is the lowest priority. Most importantly, the culture
of conducting investigations of such cases, organizing
raids on dangerous felons, sitting on watch, conducting
surveillance, and so on, are generally not its cup of
tea. This is not a criticism but an honest admission,
as perceived by me during the nine years I worked in
the CBI. However, we should not take away from the
organization the credit for successfully investigating
countless cases of 'special' crimes. These include the
Rajiv Gandhi assassination case, the L.N. Mishra
murder case and lately the alleged murders of two sisters
in Badaun district of Uttar Pradesh. But what is truly
enviable and worth emulating by other police forces of
the country is the CBI's capacity to prosecute cases of
any variety in the court of law. Marshalling evidence
that can withstand judicial scrutiny is its USP.

I say all this in the context of the Memons' saga. The
mission I had embarked upon was something not up
the CBI's alley. It involved a huge risk of things going

horribly wrong, something my bosses were not ready for. Therefore, it was generally a hostile environment around us where, more or less, we were on our own.

The other question bothering a few readers may be: how is our country's CBI positioned vis-à-vis the ISI of Pakistan? The short answer is that there exists no equivalence and the two cannot be compared. The ISI is the Dirty Tricks Department of the Government of Pakistan, masquerading as an intelligence agency. It is largely preoccupied with subversive activities in India and Afghanistan. The CBI is purely an investigative agency and its Pakistani counterpart is perhaps the Federal Investigation Agency (FIA). Where the collection of intelligence from overseas is concerned we have our Research and Analysis Wing (R&AW). Yes, the CBI has in the past investigated several terror cases in which the ISI had a major role to play, the serial blasts in Mumbai in March 1993 being one of them. Now even that tenuous indirect linkage is a thing of the past with the creation of the National Investigation Agency (NIA). At present, cases of terror go to the NIA for investigation and never to the CBI.

~

Having reached a tacit pact with the director for a one-on-one communication, the immediate task at hand for me was to make a booking for the Memons from Sharjah to Delhi so that the ISI did not get wind of it. My plan was to take them out from Sharjah while keeping the bookings from Dubai alive. I decided to call

on A.M. Bhardwaj, Joint Secretary in the ministry of
civil aviation-cum-CMD of Indian Airlines. He was my
neighbour and a nice, affable man. I asked Satish Jha to
come with me. It was around ten in the morning when
we reached the Indian Airlines office at Patel Chowk.
When I began to share the outlines of the operation
with the chairman to make him feel involved, he said he
only wanted to know what was required of him. Having
served in the Indian Army before joining the IAS, he was
conscious of sharing information only on a need-to-know
basis. I said I wanted a booking for a group of absconders
on the Delhi-bound flight from Sharjah without their
names going up on the computer or flight manifest. He
called up the in-charge of Indian Airlines (operations)
and directed him to suitably instruct the airlines' Dubai
office. They (the Dubai office) were informed that a
person by the name of Suresh would approach them
to book seats for his family members. The reservations
made by him should be reflected in the airlines' database
with no names, and only a PNR number should show
on the computer. The operations manager was further
instructed that Suresh alone should be given the PNR
number and no one else. All other details could be taken
when the passengers reported for check-in.

The other issue to be resolved was the money required
for the second set of return air tickets from Sharjah to
Delhi. I felt approaching the MEA or my own bosses
would complicate and delay matters. With no time at my
disposal, I again turned to my friend in Dubai. He willingly
gave the required amount to Suresh, when Suresh met him

in his office on my advice. The money was, of course, later returned to my friend from government funds.

Things went as per plan, or so I thought. When Suresh approached the Indian Airlines office with the money, he was given a PNR number to be quoted at the check-in counter in Sharjah. Now Suresh was all set to leave for Delhi with his family members. He had been staying at the Claridges in Deira since 23 August. After packing up, he went to check out on the afternoon of 24 August, only to be told by the receptionist that his passport could not be returned to him. The hotel had received instructions from the Dubai government which had ordered that he stay put in Dubai. (In most Dubai hotels in the mid–1990s, passports were retained by hotel receptions and returned only while checking out, once all the hotel bills were cleared. I am not aware of the system now. However, the bit about the Dubai government's order was only a subterfuge.) Sure enough, when he looked around, he noticed the same set of hoods, who had been pursuing him all those days, sitting in the lobby looking menacingly in his direction.

Suresh called me up from his room in a state of utter panic, almost howling, accusing me of putting him in dire straits. He gave me the whole picture and for a moment I thought that the operation had fallen apart.

I called Consul General Prabhu Dayal and told him that Suresh was not being allowed to check out from the Claridges. Prabhu was by then at the end of his tether. Hitherto having met all my difficult demands, not once questioning what they were for, he asked me rather hotly, 'Neeraj, what *is* this all about?' I told him the whole story.

I said, 'Prabhu, these are the Memons wanted by us in the Mumbai blasts case and Suresh has to be helped in getting them back.' Prabhu asked me testily, 'What do you want me to do now?' I pleaded: 'Please go to the Claridges and tell the receptionist who you are. Also tell him you have received a complaint from an Indian national that he was being unnecessarily harassed, his passport was illegally retained by them and he was not being allowed to check out.' I also asked him to be prepared to proceed from the hotel with Suresh, straight to where the Memons were hiding, put them all in a vehicle and pretend as if he (Prabhu) was going to drop them at the Dubai International Airport. Somewhere on the way, he had to take a detour and proceed to Sharjah. He asked me, 'Does it have the Foreign Secretary's approval?' I confidently said, 'Yes,' but I was lying.

It must be acknowledged that Prabhu Dayal played his role brilliantly and saved the day for us. He drove to the hotel's porch in his official car, the tricolour fluttering in the breeze. Along with a number of the consulate staffers in tow, he stormed into the hotel lobby and walked straight to the reception. He disclosed his identity and demanded of the receptionist that Suresh's passport be released immediately and Suresh be allowed to check out. Taken by total surprise, the receptionist consulted his superiors and called up Suresh, who sat howling in his room. Profuse apologies were made to him and he was asked to come down with his baggage to check out.

When Suresh came to the reception, he was elated to see Prabhu and his officers whom he had got to know so well during his various visits to the consulate. To Suresh's relief, the ISI goons, seen sitting in the lobby earlier, had vanished. Prabhu then proceeded, with his entire entourage and Suresh, to the place where the Memons were waiting, all packed up. They were all bundled into an SUV of the consulate. Emotional goodbyes were exchanged between the family and Rahin, who was taken in another car to the consulate staffer's residence.

My guess is that the immediate objective of the ISI agents in Dubai was to somehow hassle the Memons to an extent that they did not leave for India. Clearly, they do not have any police powers of their own to stop or detain anybody in Dubai; so they had to stay at a distance and keep the Memons, particularly Suresh, on tenterhooks. I was sure that they (the ISI) had tied up with the immigration staff at the Dubai International Airport, where the Memons would be stopped from travelling to India on some specious grounds.

It was already late in the evening of 24 August 1994. Both Prabhu and Suresh had stopped communicating with me and I knew their silence augured well. It meant neither of them was in any difficulty and was, therefore, quiet.

I began to get calls from the Air India security staff deployed at the Dubai International Airport. They were police officers on deputation with Air India's security and vigilance branch, whom I had kept in the loop without giving any operational details. They informed me of unprecedented activity at the airport and they could sense that something big was in the offing. They further reported that senior officers from the immigration branch and the Pakistani Consulate were in animated discussions with each other near the Air India check-in counter, which had not yet started operating for its ensuing flight. I smiled to myself and thought: let the jokers wait at the Dubai airport while their quarries fly out from elsewhere.

As per plan, Prabhu's cavalcade moved towards the Dubai International Airport. There was no vehicle tailing them or even monitoring their movements. The pursuers had presumed that eventually the Memons would arrive there and be dealt with suitably.

The cavalcade, at a pre-planned spot, took a detour and casually proceeded towards the Sharjah International Airport. Prabhu parked his car at a safe distance from the terminal while his staffers helped Suresh, Suleiman, Essa and Yusuf (Tiger's brothers), Abdul Razzaq (Tiger's father), Hanifa (Tiger's mother), Rubina (Suleiman's wife), Ilyas (Suleiman's six-year-old son) and Aliya (Suleiman's nine-month-old daughter) to check in at the Indian Airlines counter. When Suresh disclosed the PNR number, the Memons and he were received and treated like special guests by the Indian Airlines staff. Things went off smoothly and they were now in the departure lounge, waiting to board. Prabhu did not leave Sharjah airport and kept a patient vigil sitting in his official car, while my heart pounded uncontrollably. We were so near success, yet not quite there.

It was well past midnight when I got a call from Prabhu that the flight had taken off and the Memons

were on board. I couldn't hold back my emotions and
started screaming with joy. I had the choicest expletives
for the ISI goons on my lips. The feeling can perhaps
be compared with what we Indians feel when we beat
Pakistan in an all-but-lost cricket match, on the last
ball when our final batsman hits a six and gets us home.
Imagine you are the batsman scoring the winning runs.
That is how I felt. Perhaps I felt even more euphoric. I
informed Satish Jha who was equally thrilled. I asked him
to be ready to come to the airport with me in the next
few hours.

~

Our job was not over yet. The Memons had to be
manoeuvred through the maze of arrival formalities at the
Delhi airport. The challenge was to prevent word of their
arrival and arrest from spreading, lest the media began to
hound us.

I called up the Delhi airport police and informed them
that a friend and I were coming to receive a few family
friends arriving from Sharjah. Inspector Gyan Chand, who
had once served with me in Delhi Traffic Police, was on
duty and was deputed to stay with me. Satish Jha and I
waited anxiously at the arrival lounge, right next to the air
bridge. When the flight landed, the first to emerge from the
air bridge were the Memons, as they had been upgraded
by the Indian Airlines staff at Sharjah. They were led by
Suresh who rushed and hugged me, howling like a child.
Behind him were the Memons in their traditional dress of

starched kurta–pyjama, the women in burqa and the men
sporting long beards. Inspector Gyan Chand, who held me
in high esteem, found it all very queer. Nonetheless, we
were all escorted to the chambers of the assistant foreigner
regional registration officer (AFRRO) and the passports of
the arriving passengers taken to the immigration counter.
As we waited for the passports to be returned, a junior
immigration officer came in and whispered something in
the AFRRO's ears. The officer scanned the Memons with
piercing eyes. He then said to me, 'Sorry, sir, we cannot let
them go. They are on our wanted list and lookout notices
against them are pending.'

I realized that the time had come to call off the charade
and tell the immigration officer the truth. I said, 'They
are members of the Memon family wanted in the Mumbai
blasts case. They have arrived in Delhi at the culmination
of a CBI operation, which has the approval and blessings
of the Government of India.' The AFRRO, though very
polite, would have none of it. I asked him, 'Whom would
you like me to speak to so that you are given the necessary
orders to let them come with us?' He said, 'Sir, either
my special director or Joint Secretary (foreigners) V.S.
Ailawadi.'

I did not know the special director in charge of
immigration personally but had heard of his reputation of
being obstructive and negative. Fortunately for me, I had
met Ailawadi—the then Joint Secretary (foreigners) in the
ministry of home affairs, looking after the immigration
department—only a couple of evenings earlier at a senior
colleague's residence. I had, in fact, casually asked him a

hypothetical question that if people with Pakistani passports were to land in Delhi as part of a CBI operation, could I ask him for help should there be a last-minute hitch? The positive and helpful man that he is, he had said, 'Of course!'

All members of the Memon family, SP Satish Jha and assorted immigration officials packed in that little immigration office were watching this last-minute drama unfold. It was not yet nine in the morning. I called up Ailawadi's residence. His gracious wife, Aarti, answered. She said, 'VS has left for office early because it is his last day as Joint Secretary (foreigners). He has gone to wind up and hand over charge before he takes up his new assignment.'

My heart began to pound. What if he had already handed over charge? What if the news of him no longer being Joint Secretary (foreigners) came to the notice of the AFRRO? I called up Ailawadi's office and luckily got to speak to him. Giving a reference of our earlier conversation, I informed him that several wanted accused in the Mumbai blasts case had been brought to Delhi by the CBI against heavy odds, but the AFRRO was not letting us take them out of the airport. Most bureaucrats in Ailawadi's place would have said that they had been transferred out and were no longer in a position to help. Instead, he asked me to hand over the receiver to the immigration officer. When asked by the Joint Secretary what the problem was, the AFRRO informed him that the passengers the CBI officers wanted the charge of figured on the wanted list. Ailawadi's instructions to the immigration officer were loud and clear. After all, the officers who had come to receive the passengers were from the CBI, the investigating agency of the case. It was because they were wanted that the CBI officers were at the airport to arrest them. Why should Immigration have a problem? The AFRRO should take a written request from the CBI officers and let them take the Memons with them, he instructed.

With a trembling hand, I wrote out an application mentioning their real names, their assumed identities, the Pakistani passport details, etc., requesting the AFRRO to let them come with us. He reluctantly acquiesced, now that he had a document to fall back on and his Joint Secretary's instructions, in case he was ever faulted.

I was later to learn that when the special director of immigration came to know about the entire episode, he was terribly annoyed with the AFRRO. He felt the Memons should not have been allowed to leave without his consent. 'Delhi Immigration missed the opportunity of showing the world that it was they who had caught the Memons before handing them over to the CBI. We could have claimed the huge reward money announced for their arrest as well,' he shouted at his subordinate officer. But, alas, the birds had flown!

The Memons were formally arrested as they emerged from the air terminal by DSP I.S. Saroha, the then IO of the case. The nature of the operation leading to the arrest was such that the IO, much like other members of the STF, had not been kept privy to what had been going on thus far.

~

There was one last thing which remained to be done and that was to get Yaqub's wife and daughter back. News of the arrest of the Memons had broken and the media went into overdrive. Various theories were doing the rounds, including one that a deal had been struck between the CBI and the Memons. The CBI director had to angrily tell the press that there had been no such deal. The fact that details of the operation were kept under wraps only added to the wild speculations.

Truth be told, there was no deal whatsoever with either Yaqub or the other Memons. No assurances were given to any of them at any stage. All claims of the Memons having been lured to return with promises of a lenient view being taken are bogus. I say this with all the sincerity at my command.

Coming back to Rahin and her baby Zubeida, no workable strategy could be worked out. There was even a talk of smuggling them out by the sea route. But these were all fancy ideas given the delicate dictates of international diplomacy.

The director took a call and decided that Rahin should come out in the open and make an official declaration to the Indian Consulate that her husband and other family members were in India and in custody. That she was herself an absconding accused and would like to return to her country and face trial. And so, the Indian Mission in Dubai should help her. She did as she was told.

An emergency passport was provided to her by the Indian Consulate with her child's name endorsed on it. Her tickets were procured and Dubai authorities kept informed. There was no cloak-and-dagger game to be played this time. The consulate made a formal request to the immigration authorities of Dubai to let her leave, which was acceded to. I attribute the change in Dubai's attitude to the widespread media reports following Memons' return.

It was 5 September 1994. All was set for Rahin and her baby daughter's departure by Air India. After bidding a tearful goodbye to the family of the consulate staffer, who had given her and her month-old-baby shelter and care, Rahin, accompanied by Indian Consulate staff, arrived at the Dubai International Airport. She hoped to see her husband Yaqub and other family members in the next few hours. That was all that mattered to her at that moment.

But unexpected twists and turns are inherent to such tales. It was, I clearly remember, a Friday afternoon. I got a call that Rahin was at the airport but had been denied immigration clearance for departure as her name figured on the Interpol Red Notice list. This was the Red Notice that had been issued after the Mumbai blasts case. I was in my office when the news came. The only person I could turn to was my colleague Ravi Sharma, posted at the Interpol headquarters in Lyons, France. I called him in sheer desperation.

His phone rang incessantly with no response. My last glimmer of hope was fading. I tried again, and this time after a few rings he answered. After hearing out my rather unreasonable request to get Rahin's name off the Interpol Red Notice list pronto, Ravi responded, 'Do you realize it's the beginning of a weekend and the

Interpol headquarters is already closing? My family is waiting outside in our car. We are off for a skiing holiday. How do you expect me to help you?' I said, 'Ravi, the job has to be done. We have come this far and it can't get deferred because of this notice.' Very reluctantly, he asked me to send him a fax with a formal request, which I promptly did. It is to Ravi's credit that he delayed his family's departure and got the Interpol to withdraw the Red Notice immediately.

When I conveyed this news to our consulate officials, who in turn informed the Dubai Immigration, the immigration officials looked at their computer screen in sheer disbelief. Suddenly Rahin's name had disappeared from the Red list. She was allowed to leave. She and her daughter were the last passengers to board the Indian Airlines flight leaving for Delhi.

She was arrested by the IO on arrival. Nonetheless, she was over the moon on meeting Yaqub, who wept with joy seeing his month-old daughter for the first time.

My responsibility of making the operation a success was more or less over. The mission had succeeded and I couldn't believe what we had pulled off. The support I had received from my colleagues, superiors and several agencies, chiefly the ministry of external affairs and the Indian Airlines, goes to show that when there is unity of purpose and synergy between various wings of the government, wonders can be achieved.

After me, there were able officers to follow up on further investigation, submit a supplementary charge sheet and then prosecute the case in the designated court. My team in Mumbai, led by SP O.P. Chhatwal, pursued the prosecution of the case diligently for over two decades and continues to do so even today. The trial of several other absconding accused of the case, like Abu Salem, Ejaz Pathan, Mustafa Dossa aka Majnu, Tahir 'Taklya', Feroze, Riaz Siddique, Karimulla, arrested subsequently one by one, continues till today. The CBI till date relies on the in-depth knowledge of the mammoth case Chhatwal (retired long since) has and his prosecuting acumen. A few others who served in the STF at that time also chip in now and then.

The evidence on record against Yaqub and some of his family members was overwhelming and irrefutable. Yaqub was charged with offences of criminal conspiracy behind the terror attack on Mumbai. He was tried for arranging funds, air tickets for co-conspirators to travel to Pakistan for arms training, motor vehicles for making car bombs and for the use of the Memons' premises for the storage of arms, ammunition and explosive material.

The wheels of justice rolled slowly but surely to their inexorable conclusion. Twenty years down the line, after a protracted trial, Yaqub was sentenced to death in 2007; his father, Abdul Razzaq, died in custody; Rubina, Essa and Yusuf were awarded life sentences. Rahin, Suleiman and Yaqub's mother, Hanifa, were, however, acquitted.

The main perpetrator of the crime, namely Tiger Memon, as per intelligence inputs, leads a merry life with his wife and children in Karachi, as do his brother Ayub and Ayub's family. Reportedly, both Tiger and Ayub are engaged in flourishing and diverse business ventures, including real estate. Once in a while, we hear of Tiger planning terror attacks in India in tandem with groups like Lashkar-e-Taiba.

Yaqub was hanged on 30 July 2015, amidst raging controversies and considerable media furore.

7

The Return Gift

The arrest and deportation of
Roshan Ansari

The year 2002 brought me a bag of mixed fortunes. Aftab Ansari and Raju Anadkat, two of the most wanted gangsters of India, were deported from Dubai on 10 February 2002. It was the successful culmination of a long and arduous joint police operation in which I had the privilege of playing a significant role. It was a moment of great triumph and jubilation, both for the CBI and me. I was on cloud nine with a euphoria whose fragrance lingers till today.

Plenty of follow-up action was required and I was fully engrossed in getting the interrogation reports of the deportees prepared. The huge database of information that emerged during their interrogations had to be collated from diverse sources and disseminated to various agencies.

In the middle of all this, in less than a fortnight, an order reached me that I was transferred back to the Delhi Police, my parent police force.

The sudden move caught me totally off guard. Even though I had already completed my tenure of deputation, the director had indicated he wanted to retain me a bit longer. He and I, in a matter of just over two years that we had worked together, had come very close to each other professionally. I liked his non-interfering approach and his unconditional support in operational matters. And, my guess is, he too had become fond of me because my team showed results that brought laurels to the CBI. However, I had felt a slight change in his attitude towards me ever since a senior officer had joined the organization a couple of months before. I suspect the new entrant was not particularly pleased with the director's fondness for me and was working on him slowly, but surely, to distance him from me.

Nevertheless, taken aback by the order, I went to meet the director in the false hope that I would be asked to continue while he took up the matter with the government. To my utter surprise, he asked me rather matter-of-factly to hand over. All he said by way of goodbye was: 'Neeraj, your tenure in the CBI has not been an ordinary one. But it is time for us to part.'

The message was loud and clear. Despite feeling hurt and pained at the cussedness of it all, I wound up, as soon as I could, and left. No formal farewell, no emotional goodbyes from the organization I had served devotedly for nearly nine years, arguably the most productive part of my police career.

I later learnt that there was much more to it than met the eye. An economic offender—also a public servant— was behind my sudden transfer. He had been booked by my team in 1999 and eventually charge-sheeted in two cases in 2002. The white-collar criminal was extremely well networked with the powers that be and ensured I was given no further extension. Perhaps, my director would have stood his ground and ensured my retention, but my guess is that the newcomer to the CBI, whom I have mentioned above, realized it was time for him to strike. Presumably, he advised the director that it wouldn't be in his (director's) best interests to hold on to me any further. Be that as it may, I was happy to be back in the Delhi Police, where again I continued my work against terror and organized crime.

In March 2002, after rejoining the Delhi Police, I thought of taking a much-needed break. The formal posting order assigning me to a particular position was yet to come from the Government of Delhi. I took leave for a few days and travelled with my wife to Dubai—my favourite hunting ground—on vacation. Coincidentally, it was the twenty-fifth anniversary of our marriage, and the trip was a gift to my wife.

My friends in the Dubai Police laid out the red carpet for us and two officials—Brig. A and Maj. M—who had assisted us in getting Aftab Ansari and Raju Anadkat back, went out of their way to look after us. Our ambassador, K.C. Singh, was equally kind to us and at his hospitable best. The memory of an evening he and his gracious wife hosted for us at the beautiful Emirates Golf Club is still fresh in our minds. We returned home in less than a week after a most memorable holiday.

I was beginning to just about settle down in the Delhi Police in my new job as joint commissioner of police (special branch) when a call from the Dubai Police was to involve me yet again in a CBI operation. On 2 April 2002, Maj. M of the Dubai Police called up to tell me that a woman of Indian origin, namely Roshan Ansari, married to a Dubai Sheikh, had escaped to Mumbai from Dubai, after murdering her grown-up stepdaughter, Muna Ahmed. Apparently, the stepmother and stepdaughter had a running feud with each other that was getting intolerable for Roshan. On 1 April 2002, the lady could take it no more and, in a fit of rage, killed the young girl. She buried the dead body in the storeroom of the victim's house with the help of three Indian expatriates and a Bangladeshi national.

The murder made headlines in the Dubai media and the Dubai Police were under tremendous pressure to arrest the accused. They had succeeded in nabbing the three Indians and the Bangladeshi but the prime accused, Roshan Ansari, had made good her escape by fleeing to her country of origin. The Dubai authorities wanted the Indian police to arrest and send her back. They expected, and naturally so, that the good deed they had done for the Indian police in nabbing and handing over Aftab and Raju would be reciprocated by us without delay.

I didn't have the heart to tell Maj. M that I was no longer in the CBI. Call it the burden of obligation I personally carried or the moral responsibility I felt, all I said to the caller was: 'Please mail me the details and I will get going.' Within minutes an email was in my inbox with all details connected with the murder.

The fugitive, Roshan A.S. Ansari, whose parents lived in Ghatkopar (West), a communally sensitive area of Mumbai, was married to a Dubai national, A. Hamid M. Kabanji, and had a daughter, Hind Kabanji, by him. This was Kabanji's second marriage. He had a twenty-year-old daughter named Muna Ahmed by his first wife. Roshan had flown out of Dubai with her five-year-old daughter, Hind, by Air India flight AI 700 on the evening of 1 April 2002, the day of the murder. Both mother and daughter were UAE passport holders whose details were mentioned in the mail.

I called up the director of the CBI and apprised him of the phone call and the request made by the Dubai Police. I needed further instructions. After a pause, all he said nonchalantly was: 'Yaar, why don't you do it yourself? Everyone in the CBI will listen to you and do what you want done. If anyone doesn't, please let me know.' He hung up, leaving me in a quandary. I was left holding the baby, but felt immensely pleased with the trust and confidence reposed in me by the director, even after I had left the CBI.

I turned to DIG Virendra Singh, posted in the Mumbai Economic Offences Wing of the CBI. He had served with me during my last assignment in the CBI before my return to the Delhi Police. I was then joint director of EOW-2 with branches in all four metropolitan cities. An Indian Revenue Service officer of the 1985 batch, Virendra came on deputation to the CBI as an SP. His initial years in the CBI were rather rough as he couldn't get along with his boss. When I took charge of EOW-2, I found in him a sincere, clear-headed, upright and hardworking officer. Having worked as his supervisory officer, I can say with confidence that he has far superior police instincts and investigative acumen than most IPS officers I have come across in my long career. Today, back in the Income Tax Department, he continues to do excellent work and holds an important post.

I forwarded the email I had received from Dubai to Virendra and asked him to contact Maj. M of the Dubai Police for any further details. Virendra set out on the task immediately by forming a dedicated team under DSP D.S. Shukla. The team commenced the mission first with the verification of the address of Roshan Ansari's parents at Ghatkopar (W). The obvious thing to do was to ascertain if she was hiding with her parents. This required keeping the given address under surveillance and making local inquiries in the neighbourhood. But that was easier said than done.

Maru Miyan Chawl, near Pankhe Shah Baba Dargah on Lal Bahadur Shastri Marg, Ghatkopar (W), where Roshan's parents reportedly resided, is a communally sensitive area. It is thickly populated with shanties and houses built cheek by jowl, each eager to devour the other, set amidst a labyrinth of narrow lanes and by-lanes.

The Dubai Police had provided a landline number, +91-22-5002xxx, installed at the residence of Roshan's parents. The location of the house, the landline number, etc., had to be verified and confirmed. It was just not possible for any outsider to go into the area without being spotted by local residents, who guarded their turf fiercely. The CBI team, therefore, had to tread with caution and adopt out-of-the-box methodologies. D.S. Shukla got hold of the local telephone lineman and accompanied him to the premises under the ruse of inspecting the telephone. They found the premises, got to meet Roshan's mother and confirmed that the landline was indeed the right number. Also, quite expectedly, the fugitive was not there.

With prior authorization, the said telephone was put under surveillance. For days, no calls from Roshan were received and neither was any conversation about her overheard. Clearly, she was taking all precautions to evade us.

The Dubai Police, meanwhile, was getting restive. Both Virendra and I received numerous calls from them, eager to know the progress made by us. Roshan's husband, Kabanji, was building immense pressure on the local authorities to arrest the murderess of his grown-up daughter. He helped the police recover Roshan's diary from her residence in Dubai. It had a Bangalore (now known as Bengaluru) address scrawled on it. Virendra requested Pratap Reddy, an SP posted at the CBI office in Bangalore, to verify the address. Reddy was hesitant as the area was communally sensitive and required assistance from the local police.

The UAE, of which Dubai is a part, has a consulate in Mumbai. A senior official of the consulate visited Virendra's office to impress upon him the significance of getting Roshan quickly as it was in the best interest of healthy diplomatic relations between the UAE and India.

Virendra assured him that all possible efforts were under way. Anxiety levels in the ministry of external affairs, ministry of home affairs and the CBI were getting higher, even though it was early days. Both Virendra and I were feeling the heat already.

Meanwhile, the Dubai authorities had put the telephones of Roshan's contacts, relatives and well-wishers under technical surveillance. On one such number, a call was received from two Bangalore numbers whose last three digits were not displayed on the monitor of Dubai Police's tapping equipment. A woman calling herself Saira, who, according to the Dubai authorities, was none other than Roshan, had made those calls. I asked Virendra to proceed to Bangalore as further follow-up would require contact at senior levels. Virendra, in turn, suggested I get a deportation order from the ministry of home affairs, which might come handy if Roshan were located.

On 11 April 2002 I paid a visit to the office of Joint Secretary (Foreigners) in Khan Market, New Delhi. In a manner of speaking, I had no locus in the matter as I was no longer with the CBI and had nothing in writing asking me to participate in the operation. But, sometimes, one comes across positive-minded officers in the government who want things to get done and don't raise unnecessary bureaucratic issues. I was asked by the officer concerned to make a request in writing which I did. I got the deportation order in just about fifteen minutes as I waited in the Joint Secretary's office. I faxed a copy to Virendra immediately.

Virendra proceeded to Bangalore and established contact with senior officials of the local police, seeking assistance to locate the address where 'Saira' resided. After showing considerable reluctance, the Bangalore Police provided their support—even assigning women police officers for the operation—to the CBI team. On reaching the given address, a woman called Saira was found residing there, but it was not Roshan. She admitted that she was distantly related to Roshan but knew nothing of her whereabouts. Local inquiries confirmed her statement and the CBI team had no option but to retreat. It was a bit of a setback but Virendra soldiered on.

He contacted the general manager of Bharat Sanchar Nigam Limited (BSNL—Government of India's telephone department), the seniormost officer of the department in Bangalore. His request to him (let us call him Mr BSNL) was to track the Bangalore number calling Dubai's numbers provided by the Dubai Police. Virendra gave the time at which the calls were made and their duration.

Mr BSNL initially dilly-dallied, saying that backward tracing was not possible. Virendra retorted: 'If forward tracing is possible, so should backward tracing.' It was 9.30 at night and the BSNL officer said, 'We shall consider your request tomorrow morning.' Virendra hung up after cautioning him: 'Look, this is an operation involving national security. I have no problem waiting till tomorrow morning, but if an untoward incident takes place at night, the responsibility will be yours.'

The veiled threat, albeit a subterfuge, worked and put the fear of God in Mr BSNL who called Virendra back in ten minutes. 'I have put three of my best engineers on the job who are reaching the switch-room immediately and will commence work. I have given them your number and they will call you as soon as they trace the calling number,' said a chastened Mr BSNL.

At about four the following morning, Virendra received a call from the switch-room that the number had been traced. Virendra further requested for details of all the calls immediately before and after the call to Dubai was made. Three Mumbai landline numbers figured in the call details. On further investigation, of the three only one was found of relevance to the ongoing operation. It was a number installed in Ghatkopar (W). This number too was taken to be intercepted.

Meanwhile, someone on Saira's behalf called Roshan's parents from Bangalore on their landline and informed them that the police had come calling, looking for Roshan. The caller also said that it was good that Roshan had left Bangalore with her cousin Babu much before the police reached her (Saira's) house.

Virendra was keeping me informed of all developments. The pressure from the Dubai Police was mounting, but all we could do was keep them in the loop and ask them to be patient. At a personal level, I got news that my father had taken seriously ill. On 22 April I left Delhi and reached Patna, my home town, to look after my ailing father. God bless mobile phones—I could continue to remain in touch with Virendra, even as I sat by my father's bedside in the hospital, and speak to him whenever he needed to consult me.

It was already over twenty days of our being informed of Roshan Ansari's escape to India from Dubai. Given that

Aftab Ansari had been arrested within a day of our request and deported within ten days, we were not faring too well. But we did not lose heart and kept pursuing all possible leads.

The Mumbai landline number, which had been figured out after examining the call details of the Bangalore number, turned out to be that of Roshan's maternal uncle. Roshan was calling this number frequently, using different SIM cards. She travelled to Goa, then Hyderabad, followed by small towns in Maharashtra. All along, we were keeping a tab on her movements using technical data but failed to nab her as her stay at any one place was always very brief. She knew she was being trailed and, so, kept running from place to place with her five-year-old daughter, escorted by her cousin Babu.

Finally, a call was received on her maternal uncle's phone that she had run out of money and had no option but to return to Mumbai. Roshan requested him to make some independent and safe arrangements for her stay in Mumbai. She didn't wish to risk staying at her parents' house in Ghatkopar (W).

The following morning her uncle received a call that she had arrived in Mumbai. Her uncle asked her to reach Vashi Bridge where his son would meet her. He would take her to the place where the arrangements for her stay had been made. Our team was in no position to reach the rendezvous point in such a short while, given the distance between where they were located and Vashi. However, now that she was in Mumbai, it was that much closer for us to monitor her movements; and logistics were that much easier to manage.

Here the police instincts of DSP Shukla came to the fore. He guessed that Roshan's mother would definitely attempt to meet Roshan. He had seen the mother when he had gone to verify Roshan's Ghatkopar address with a telephone lineman. Two teams were formed, one located at Ghatkopar and the other at Vashi station. Whenever the Ghatkopar team saw a woman matching her description, they would follow her all the way to Vashi station. However, the team stationed at the only exit point at the station could not spot her. This exercise continued for three to four days with no success.

Meanwhile, Roshan called her brother's mobile from her mobile on 2 May. Her brother was a barely fifteen years old. We could ascertain the location of her mobile to be in Mumbra, another thickly populated and congested area, dotted with slums and shanty towns. Mumbra is a part of the Thane commissionerate neighbouring Mumbai. Searching her or, for that matter, anyone in Mumbra without knowing the exact address was more difficult than looking for the proverbial needle in a haystack. We waited for Roshan to make one more false move.

She called her brother's mobile, already under our observation, the very next day from a public telephone booth. From the call details of her brother's mobile, we immediately came to know the number of the public booth. The booth, however, was not where the records of the telephone department showed it to be installed. Somehow, with the intervention of senior telephone officials, the local lineman—the lynchpin of the telephone department— was located. It was he who had installed the telephone at a diverted location, presumably for a consideration. It required a bit of intimidation by us, holding the threat of CBI action against his wrongdoing, before he took us to the booth. The public telephone booth was immediately brought under our watch, a most risky task in such a congested and close-knit locality. It is to the credit of our officers that they kept the place under surveillance in the face of all odds.

A woman in burqa, matching the height and build of Roshan, was spotted approaching the telephone booth in the evening of 4 May. It was already dark but ASI A.R. Raut of the CBI, keeping watch over the booth, spotted her from a distance and followed her. As expected, she came to the telephone booth and stood in the small queue of people waiting for their turn to make a call. ASI Raut quietly stood behind her, as if he too wanted to make a call. When her turn came, she lifted her veil and began dialling. The ASI could steal a good look at her, which matched Roshan's photographs mailed by the Dubai Police. When she had finished her call, she began to walk back in the same direction from where she had emerged. Raut trailed her discreetly without arousing her suspicion. She went into a chawl, which the inspector took note of and immediately called the mobile of Inspector U.K. Morey, the seniormost officer at the spot. Morey informed DSP Shukla who rushed to Mumbra.

It was a Sunday evening and Virendra had taken his family for a quiet dinner to Khyber, a popular Mughlai restaurant, located at Kala Ghoda, south Mumbai. His mobile rang and it was DSP Shukla on the line. He said

Roshan's location in Mumbra had been ascertained and it was time to move in. Virendra had to give up on his family outing and rush. He asked Shukla to hold his horses as it was not prudent for the CBI to raid Roshan's premises without the local police.

Inspector Morey met the officer-in-charge of Mumbra Police Station who was far from cooperative. He wanted to know how and why the CBI team had ventured into his jurisdiction without his knowledge. Shukla informed Virendra, still on his way to Mumbra, of the reluctance on the part of local police to help. Virendra, in turn, called up a senior police official supervising the area. Shockingly, he too sang the same tune as the officer-in-charge of the police station. Virendra had to tell him that it was better if he took a positive decision in the matter at his own level. In case he didn't, Virendra would have to bring the matter to the notice of the CBI director. The obvious consequence would be the director calling up the Thane commissioner of police, who would then instruct the local police to do exactly what they ought to be doing themselves. Fortunately, good sense prevailed on the senior police officer and he instructed the officer-in-charge to provide local support to the CBI team immediately.

A joint team of the Mumbra Police and the CBI headed by Inspector Morey raided the chawl, which Roshan had been seen entering. Roshan was apprehended and taken out after some resistance from her and her family members. Lady Inspector Jyotsna Raasam of the CBI and a couple of lady constables from the Mumbra Police Station had to deal with her firmly as she denied being Roshan. When she was shown her photograph received from Dubai and other documentation, she gave in. Soon she and her five-year-old daughter were driven out of the sensitive area of Mumbra in a CBI vehicle.

It was past midnight when Virendra informed me that Roshan had been apprehended. I asked him to proceed to the international terminal straightaway. We had to try to put her and her daughter on the first flight to Dubai to face legal action there. Taking her to our office or any police premises was fraught with risks. Soon a lawyer would appear on the scene, with her family members and well-wishers in tow, to raise a hue and cry. Also, I decided not to wake up the CBI bigwigs lest they got into legalities and official formalities. The best strategy was to serve everyone a fait accompli. We had a deportation order from the Government of India and that was good enough to empower us to send her off. I told Virendra that if there was any flak later, I would take full responsibility.

The CBI team with Roshan and her daughter were on their way to the airport. Roshan had calmed down and confessed that she had indeed murdered her stepdaughter and fled Dubai. Luckily for us, an Emirates flight was scheduled to leave Mumbai for Dubai at five in the morning. We had two major problems at hand: passports and tickets. The passports of Roshan and her daughter were not recovered. Virendra was in touch with the immigration authorities at the airport to find a way out. In the meantime, Roshan disclosed to the CBI team that she had hidden them at her uncle's place in Ghatkopar (W).

Immediately, DSP Shukla left for Ghatkopar with a small team and succeeded in locating her uncle's place in the dead of night and recovering the passports. With one issue behind the team, the next big problem was to arrange tickets for her and her daughter. I called up Brig. A of Dubai. I was aware that he was associated with Emirates airlines security and could help. When I phoned him, he was in London. My call woke him up from sleep. He assured me that the tickets would be arranged and the Emirates airlines staff at Mumbai would extend every possible help.

In the interim, Virendra and Maj. M of Dubai Police had been in touch with each other. Maj. M of the Dubai Police requested Virendra to come with Roshan to Dubai and be his guest. But, Virendra politely declined. Lady Inspector Jyotsna Raasam, who had heard this conversation between Virendra and Maj. M, volunteered to escort Roshan to Dubai. When asked whether she had a passport, she replied in the affirmative and said it was lying at her home in Andheri, not very far from the air terminal. She was asked to rush home in a CBI vehicle and get it as soon as was possible. Dubai was informed of her escorting the fugitive, and her ticket was also arranged by them immediately over the phone. By the time Inspector Jyotsna Raasam returned with her passport, it was time for the Emirates flight to leave. However, it waited until the lady inspector returned and was on board with the fugitive and her daughter.

Virendra stayed on at the airport until the flight had taken off. It was a miracle how so many complex issues had been resolved in such a short while. A small crowd

of Roshan's relatives and well-wishers had meanwhile collected outside the terminal building and begun to raise slogans against the police. They had no clue it was the CBI that had packed off Roshan to Dubai. Virendra asked the airport police to deal with them.

I received news of Roshan's safe arrival at Dubai International Airport, duly escorted by Inspector Jyotsna Raasam at about 7.30 a.m. (IST) on 5 May 2002. Interestingly, Brig. Khalfan Khalfan Abdulla, Director General, Department of Criminal Investigations, Dubai Police, was himself present at Dubai Airport to receive Roshan and Inspector Raasam. A formal handing over–receiving was done before the Dubai Police took charge of the fugitive.

Now that it was no longer too early to call the director, I phoned and informed him of all that had transpired the previous night. There was no immediate reaction from the other end. Quite understandably, he would have been a trifle upset that we had neither informed him of her arrest nor of our decision to deport her. We had also sent a female CBI officer abroad without keeping him in the picture, which was something against all official propriety. But, it is to his credit that he didn't say a word to express his displeasure. At the same time, he was not effusive in his praise of what we had quietly and swiftly achieved. Virendra informed me later that he too was never ticked off on any score by the director. In fact, during the next quarterly meeting of senior CBI officers, the director praised Virendra and his team for the Roshan Ansari operation in everyone's presence.

The deportation of Roshan Ansari made headlines in Dubai papers. Inspector Raasam was interviewed by leading dailies and quoted extensively. She handled the questions extremely well by holding forth on the difficulty level of the operation and on how we had not spared any effort in nabbing the murderess.

I received several calls from our Dubai colleagues, expressing their gratitude. The ministry of external affairs was equally pleased as we had succeeded in demonstrating our commitment to mutual cooperation on law enforcement with the UAE. Ambassador K.C. Singh was quoted in Dubai newspapers, hailing the deportation as a milestone in the diplomatic relations between India and the UAE.

Happily, following the deportation of Roshan Ansari, Dubai reciprocated by arresting and deporting to India several absconders in the Mumbai bomb blasts case, like Ejaz Pathan, Mustafa Dossa aka Majnu, Tahir 'Taklya' Merchant, etc. Ravindra Rastogi, an absconding accused in a white-collar crime, involving fraud in claiming duty drawback, was arrested and sent to Mumbai by the Dubai Police. Viji Wahid, another economic offender wanted in a CBI case, was summarily deported. My sense is that it is most unlikely that these arrests and deportations would have happened had we not succeeded in tracing Roshan and sending her back to Dubai. In a manner of speaking, her deportation became the turning point in Indo-UAE cooperation in matters connected with law enforcement.

Later, we came to know that Roshan was tried for murder and sentenced to fifteen years of imprisonment by a Dubai court.

The CBI team which had participated in the operation was rewarded handsomely by the director. Both Virendra and I received letters of appreciation. That successful operation holds a special place in my memory as I was considered worthy of leading it even though I was no longer on the rolls of the CBI. But the bulk of the credit goes to Virendra Singh, who demonstrated exceptional perseverance and police skills, despite not being a career police officer. Equally, for the exceptional fieldwork done during this operation, involving surveillance, searches and arrest in extremely sensitive and hostile terrain, the team headed by DSP D.S. Shukla deserves hearty commendation and accolades from all who appreciate quality police work.

8

Devil Wears Khadi
The unmasking of Romesh Sharma

It was sometime in the summer of 1998 when Suparna Sharma, a young reporter from the *Indian Express*, walked into my office at Yashwant Place, located in the diplomatic area of New Delhi. I was then a DIG in the STF of the CBI. She had visited me a couple of times earlier as well for news stories on the Mumbai underworld of which I had gained some knowledge while investigating the Mumbai bomb blasts case of 1993. But on this occasion, it was she who had information to give me. Little did I know that her input would lead to the undoing of, arguably, one of the most important members of the Mumbai underworld, a man who, behind the veneer of a Delhi-based politician, covertly provided succour and support to the notorious Dawood Ibrahim gang. He stood out as a notorious example of how perfect a matrimonial alliance there could be between the political world and the underworld. The political hat he wore ensured that it was always going to be tough for investigators like us to prove his criminal nexus.

The intrepid Suparna told me that she had gone to interview one Romesh Sharma at his farm in Chhatarpur in south Delhi as someone had given her a few incriminating documents about his activities. While walking in, she had noticed a helicopter parked in the lawns of the farm. She thought it rather unusual and, therefore, took the trouble of sounding me out.

I had vaguely heard of Romesh Sharma during my stint as the DCP, south Delhi, between 1989 and 1992. He lived at Mayfair Garden, not very far from my office, and was reportedly a dubious character. However, the local police had never received a formal complaint against him. In the garb of a neta, he made sure that he kept the cops at bay. But I was totally ignorant that since my days as DCP the man had grown big and now owned a sprawling farm in Chhatarpur with a helicopter parked in its lawns. Surely, one could have a Mercedes or a Ferrari parked in one's farm, but keeping a helicopter was out of the ordinary and warranted an investigation. The reporter also gave me the landline numbers of Romesh, both of the farm and his Mayfair residence.

I shared the information on the helicopter with O.P. Chhatwal, my SP in the STF. Between the two of us, it was decided to depute an officer to visit the farm and verify the information. Inspector Hassan of the STF, who was put on the job, did well to trace the farm and peep in through a crevice in its compound wall. To his utter disbelief he did find a helicopter parked inside. However, he returned without taking note of any distinguishing mark on the helicopter. Chhatwal sent Hassan back to complete the job. On his second visit he came back to report that the aircraft had 'VT-EAP' inscribed on it.

Meanwhile, by a happy coincidence, Inspector Ishwar Singh of the Crime Branch of Delhi Police came to call on me. He had worked with me as a sub-inspector in South district where he had carried out a few extraordinary investigations. Later, as an inspector in the Crime Branch, he became quite a celebrated officer when he uncovered the match-fixing scandal in international cricket involving the South African team (see 'Between Twenty-Two Yards' for details). Since procedures for taking phones under technical surveillance were rather complicated and time consuming in the CBI, I shared Romesh Sharma's numbers with Inspector Singh. Aware of Sharma's criminal profile, he took these numbers under lawful interception, based on my 'source' information, and began listening to his conversations.

Around the same time, as a follow-up to our investigation into the helicopter affair, Chhatwal contacted the Airports Authority of India to ascertain the ownership details of the chopper. Records showed that it was initially registered in the name of one H. Suresh Rao, a resident of Mumbai and the sole proprietor of Pushpak Aviation Pvt. Ltd. Subsequently, the registration had been transferred to Romesh Sharma in 1996. But what raised our suspicion was the selling price of the helicopter, which was a mere 40,000 rupees.

The Airports Authority of India records also revealed the address of Suresh Rao in Mumbai and his telephone number. Chhatwal flew to Mumbai and called Suresh Rao to our STF office located close to the Sachivalaya (Secretariat) of the Maharashtra government. Suresh, to begin with, was most apprehensive when Chhatwal began to question him about his helicopter. He thought it was Romesh Sharma's latest ploy to use the CBI to get at him. But when he realized that the CBI officer had come to listen to his travails at the hands of his tormentor, he broke down. It was the first time any government agency was ready to give him a patient hearing. He had the following story to narrate.

His company Pushpak Aviation was in the business of renting out helicopters. One of his helicopters had been hired for campaigning by Romesh Sharma who was contesting the parliamentary elections in 1996 from the Phulpur constituency of Uttar Pradesh. He told Rao that he couldn't possibly disclose to the authorities that he had hired the helicopter and incurred the heavy expenditure involved, on account of the restrictions on campaign expenses imposed by the Election Commission of India. He cleverly urged Rao to prepare documents to show as if the aircraft had been sold to him much before the elections. Sharma assured Rao that the sale documents would be destroyed soon after the elections were over and the helicopter returned to him. Rao thought he was poised to make a killing as the assured hiring of the helicopter for the entire duration of the elections was going to fetch him a neat sum of money. Driven by avarice and taken in

by Sharma's sweet talk, Rao prepared the sale documents
and executed a predated memorandum of understanding as
though he had sold the helicopter for Rs 40,000 to Sharma
on 24 February 1996.

On 26 March the same year, the helicopter was sent to
Phulpur where it was used for electioneering by Sharma. It
did not come as a surprise to anyone (except perhaps to his
underworld henchmen, political funders and close allies)
that Sharma lost the elections badly. After all, he was more
of a fly-by-night operator than a grass-roots politician, and
the electorate generally know which side of the toast to
butter on voting day. Rao directed his employees deployed
with the helicopter to bring it back to Mumbai. But Sharma,
on 11 May 1996, forcibly took possession of the helicopter,
made Rao's technicians desmantle it, and loaded it on to a
truck. When a few of Rao's employees present at the spot
protested, they were intimidated and even assaulted. The
truck was driven from Phulpur to his farm in Chhatarpur.
On arrival, it was reassembled and parked in the front lawns
where it was seen by the reporter. H. Suresh Rao, as he
told us later, telephoned Sharma several times to protest
and ask for the chopper's return, but Sharma refused to
take his calls. Rao then came to Delhi but could meet
Sharma with great difficulty after numerous attempts, only
to be thrashed mercilessly and warned of dire consequences
if Rao bothered him ever again.

On the orders of Sardar Joginder Singh (a former CBI
chief), all officers in the CBI of the rank of DIG and above,
were provided with laptops, a novelty at that time. Suresh
Rao and Rakesh Gupta, a Delhi-based friend of his, informed

us that Rao was not the only person who had been forcibly deprived of his prized possession. There were many others, in Mumbai and Delhi, whose properties had been grabbed by Romesh Sharma. The laptop, meanwhile, became one of my closest companions. I loved to tinker with it, and soon became an expert in making PowerPoint presentations, something that was considered a novelty in the police department in those days. I prepared a presentation on Sharma and regularly updated it with the bits of intelligence inputs that kept trickling in, including pictures of the properties grabbed by him and other information given by Suresh Rao, Gupta and others. However, I could not get an opportunity to share my presentation with my director, T.N. Mishra, on account of his hectic schedule in Delhi and his frequent tours outside.

Fortunately, a delegation of CBI officers headed by Director Mishra, which included me, was visiting Mumbai in September 1998, to share with the chief justice of the Mumbai High Court the concerns of the CBI about the slow pace of trial in the Mumbai bomb blasts case. On my request, the director took some time out to see my presentation on Romesh Sharma, at the end of which he felt that, though we had adequate material to move against Sharma, we should tread with utmost caution. Mishra had earlier served in the Special Protection Group (the Indian counterpart of the Secret Service of the US) and had often seen Sharma with political bigwigs and sometimes at a former prime minister's residence as well. His advice was to get some current and conclusive material against Sharma, which would keep political hurdles and interference at bay, should we decide to search his premises or arrest him.

Lady Luck came smiling soon after, when Inspector Ishwar Singh caught Romesh Sharma on tape speaking with Abu Salem, a close associate of a notorious don of the Mumbai underworld, Dawood Ibrahim. Both Abu and Dawood were wanted in the Mumbai bomb blasts case. They were both absconding but kept the wheels of their nefarious activities in India rolling through remote control from Dubai and Karachi.

Of the various illicit rackets being run by Sharma in cahoots with the underworld, particularly with Abu Salem, were extortion and arbitration of disputes for a fee. In the course of the technical surveillance on Sharma, Inspector Ishwar Singh overheard him settling a dispute between Anand Jain of Reliance Group and Rajendra Banthia, a Mumbai-based stockbroker. On another occasion, Sharma had mediated the ransom of a leading businessman of Gujarat when he was kidnapped by the Babloo Srivastava gang. The hostage had to part not only with the negotiated ransom amount for his freedom, but also a heavy 'arbitration' fee to Sharma. However, what clinched the issue in our favour was the intercept of a conversation between Romesh Sharma and Abu Salem, wherein they were caught discussing a property dispute between a certain Ramesh Malik, owner of a property in Chirag Enclave in south Delhi, and his cousin Ashok Malik, a retired corporate executive.

It is not uncommon that when the cup of sins of an evil force runs over, destiny conspires in its own mysterious ways to bring about its doom. I have seen this happen with desperate offenders oftentimes in my career as a police officer. By a most fortuitous coincidence, I received a call from a senior colleague working as Special Secretary in the ministry of home affairs, who gave me an overseas number to check whether it belonged to someone called Abu Salem. My database on the Mumbai underworld, collated since 1993, the year the STF of the CBI took over the investigation of the Mumbai bomb blasts, revealed that indeed the number was Abu Salem's. When I rang back the Special Secretary confirming the information, he asked me to come over immediately to the North Block, an imposing office complex on Raisina Hill in Lutyens's Delhi, which houses ministries of finance, home, and personnel and training. There I was asked to accompany the Special Secretary to meet Arvind Varma, Secretary, department of personnel and training. Ramesh Malik, who apparently had known Varma for long, had informed him that he had received a threatening call on his landline from someone asking him to write off his property in Chirag Enclave in favour of his cousin Ashok Malik. The caller had left his mobile number and had disclosed his identity as Abu Salem.

Malik, who was genuinely ignorant of anyone called Salem, asked, 'Salem who?' 'Ask your thana in-charge or your commissioner of police, you so-and-so, and they would tell you who Salem is,' came the terse reply.

Now that I had confirmed to both Varma and the Special Secretary that the caller was no fake but a dangerous gangster, they wanted me to help Ramesh Malik. It was obvious that his cousin Ashok Malik wanted a quick settlement of the property dispute in his own favour and had contacted Abu Salem directly or through someone easily accessible, who was closely linked with the underworld. Chances of the latter were clearly higher.

Since my senior colleagues expected me to provide immediate relief to Ramesh Malik, I immediately put an inspector from my team, based in Mumbai, on the job. He had it conveyed to Abu Salem, through a circuitous route of informants and contacts, that his DIG had learnt of the threat calls made by him to Ramesh Malik and that it was in Salem's interest to lay off.

Much to Ramesh's relief, Salem called him to say: 'Malik sahib, you never told me that you knew such senior people in the CBI and the government like Neeraj Kumar. You can rest assured that you have nothing to fear from me. On the contrary, if you need any help, please let me know.'

It is only later that I learnt that Ramesh Malik's telephone was under the observation of the local police as well, which too had jumped into the fray. Apparently, Malik had reported the matter to V.N. Singh, commissioner of Delhi Police, who had directed the concerned police station to look into Malik's complaint. The conversation between Salem and Ramesh Malik, which mentioned me by name, was recorded by the local police. (The intercept was given a vicious twist in the days to come to get at me, as subsequent events were to show. But more on that later.)

When we received the intercepted conversation between Romesh Sharma and Abu Salem, courtesy Inspector Ishwar Singh, we played it to Director T.N.

Mishra, who then felt reassured that the decks were clear for us to move in on Romesh Sharma. Salem's involvement in the Malik family affair was known to me. No one in authority—political or bureaucratic—would dare to intervene or interfere on behalf of a person conspiring with the underworld. However, the director rightly advised us that the cause of action by us should be an event more contemporary and immediate than the complaint given by H. Suresh Rao, of his having been forcibly deprived of his helicopter in 1996.

Suresh Rao was called to our office in Delhi from his city of residence, Mumbai. As per a premeditated plan conceived by us, he was to meet Sharma at his Mayfair residence and again ask him to return the helicopter. In all likelihood, given his track record as an irascible and violent person, Sharma would refuse and resort to some strong-arm response. Rao was then to lodge a report in the local police station at Hauz Khas, which would register a case and we would have it transferred to the CBI. The plan was approved by our seniors and shared with the local police officers who decided to cooperate with us.

On 20 October 1998, Suresh Rao, accompanied by his friend Rakesh Gupta, SP O.P. Chhatwal and I visited the office of the DCP, South district. While I waited in the office of Adl DCP, Chhatwal proceeded to Sharma's Mayfair Garden residence with Rao and Gupta. Rao went in, as Chhatwal and Gupta stood on watch outside at a safe distance. Very soon they saw Sharma dragging Rao out by the scruff of his neck, bundling him in Sharma's car and driving off. Chhatwal tailed the car discreetly and saw it drive into 11, Mahadev Road, a sprawling government bungalow in the heart of the city.

Chhatwal and Gupta returned to the DCP's office where I sat waiting. The then DCP, South, after a few minutes of jittery nerves fearing the worst, directed Inspector Jasbir Malik of South District to proceed to Sharma's 11, Mahadev Road office to rescue Rao. Meanwhile, I walked into Sharma's Mayfair Garden residence with other CBI officers and the local police. His assorted domestic staff, alarmed by the arrival of the police in such large numbers, dared not offer any resistance. We began to search the premises and found the house had secret doors and escape routes, much like we see in Bollywood movies. It also had a full-fledged gymnasium. Among other incriminating evidence were animal skins and a surfeit of expensive imported liquor bottles. But what were worth their weight in gold for us were numerous property papers hidden under the mattress of his bed. To my most pleasant surprise, they included the property papers of Ramesh Malik's house in south Delhi as well. Ramesh had rented out his house to his first cousin Ashok Malik on company lease. Ashok worked for a corporate house as a top-level manager. However, when Ashok retired, the company would naturally not extend the lease. Ashok then wanted Ramesh to sell the property to him which was not acceptable to Ramesh. As subsequent investigation by the local police revealed, Ashok approached Romesh Sharma to twist his cousin's arm so that Ramesh sold the house to Ashok.

As the search was in progress, I saw Romesh Sharma arrive outside his house and come charging in. Strongly built with a muscular body, toned over the years with weight training in his private gym, he was like a raging bull. He angrily demanded of the uniformed police officers as to what was going on. He was directed to speak with me, the man behind the raid. He approached me as a ferocious and hungry carnivore would its prey. In that brief moment I had to react and the reaction came naturally to me. Here was a monster of a man, with overwhelming evidence of his crimes strewn all over, attempting to browbeat the police. I gave him a tight slap, perhaps the tightest I could muster, and, lo and behold, the man was on the floor. Dragging him to his first-floor bedroom I showed him all the property papers recovered from under his mattress. The man realized his game was up and the next second he was at my feet, begging for mercy.

He was then taken to Hauz Khas Police Station where a case was registered on the complaint of H. Suresh Rao, relating to the helicopter matter. Romesh Sharma was arrested.

~

Expectedly, the arrest made the headlines. In the police, perhaps as in other spheres of life, a common human foible is to take credit for a piece of good work which in fact belongs to someone else. In my thirty-seven years of police service, I have come across a number of colleagues who, leave alone giving credit to the rightful and deserving person/s, specialize in stealing it for themselves brazenly and shamelessly. Following the arrest, a certain senior colleague, who had returned to mainstream policing only recently after a long hiatus, and anxious to announce his arrival with a bang, went on a huge media overdrive to corner the accolades for himself. However, many in the government and the media knew the truth and reported that it was primarily a CBI operation led by me.

This was enough to infuriate the man. On seeing my name in the print and electronic media, he was livid. He sought time from the then Union home minister and played out the tape-recorded intercept between Ramesh Malik and Abu Salem. His intention was to insinuate a nexus between Salem and me! That Abu Salem had backed off in the Malik brothers' dispute, on account of my intervention, was evidence enough to suggest a link between me and the underworld—this was the hypothesis put forward by my esteemed senior colleague.

I received a message from the director's office, who had been apprised of the contents of the tape by the home minister, to reach his office the following morning. The director asked me what it was all about. He obviously didn't know about the Ramesh Malik–Ashok Malik affair. I narrated the whole story, but somehow the director did not seem to quite comprehend the full import of what I was saying. Gopal Achari, the special director and my immediate senior, who was also present in the director's office, came to my rescue. 'If Neeraj's name can put the fear of God in a gangster, we should be proud of him instead of reading anything suspicious. After all, what are police officers for,' said Achari. The director seemed a bit reassured but said that we were all wanted at the home minister's residence in Pandara Park. So there I was, present before the home minister, being made to feel like a gangster myself. Fortunately, the minister heard the entire story patiently and was satisfied that the impression my jealous and opportunistic colleague sought to create was totally false.

But, there was more to come. With Romesh Sharma's disclosures, many big names from politics, industry and some from the bureaucracy, along with their skeletons, came tumbling out of the closets. Several feathers were ruffled and powerful people began to gun for me. Complaints, innuendos and allegations were recklessly flung at me from different quarters. Meanwhile, as a follow-up to Romesh Sharma's arrest, a top industrial house of the country was to be investigated. I was asked by the director to keep myself out of these investigations. What followed in a couple of days became a source of great embarrassment for the CBI, perhaps one of the biggest in its history.

The residence and offices of the industrialist's family were to be raided in Mumbai. Quite curiously, and much to the disgrace of the CBI, the *Asian Age* ran banner headlines on the impending raid scheduled for later the same day. Obviously, the entire search operation proved to be futile and hugely embarrassing, drawing adverse media attention and making a mockery of the CBI. I am sure my bosses rued their decision and realized somewhere that it was not the smartest step to have pulled me out of the case. The director lost face and was soon relieved of his charge.

My team, in the meanwhile, put together a comprehensive note on the contacts of Romesh Sharma in high places. This report only confirmed what the N.N. Vohra Committee, appointed by the Government of India in 1993 to probe the criminal–police–bureaucrat–business nexus, had brought out.

One of the many revelations in the interrogation of Romesh Sharma was the proximity of the underworld with a major political party in the country, whose prominent members were either operating on behalf of mobsters or had close financial links with them. It so happened that an ACP of the Delhi Police Crime Branch was keeping certain telephone numbers of Chhota Shakeel, Dawood Ibrahim's right-hand man, under lawful interception. A call originating from a senior leader of the aforesaid political party to Chhota Shakeel was intercepted in which the caller told Shakeel that 'Netaji', the party's leader, had informed him that I had met him (Netaji) and tipped him off that I had been tasked by the government of the day to keep a tab on him. Even though this information, prima facie, was preposterous, when the ACP shared it with his seniors, one of them, not on the friendliest of terms with me, found it extremely useful in framing me. He asked the ACP to prepare a transcript and to doctor it in such a way that I got into serious trouble. The ACP declined to distort the transcript and submitted a true reproduction. Even so, my 'friend' shot off a letter to the Union Home Secretary with a copy of the taped conversation and its transcript suggesting that I had links with the underworld. It was déjà vu for me. I had gone through the same experience only a couple of months before. I was again summoned to the director's office and once again Gopal Achari, the special director, came to my rescue. He explained to the director that the conversation was between two criminals and could not be taken on face value. Secondly, the contents of the intercept were patently preposterous and deserved to be junked. Firstly, I had not been asked by the government to keep an eye on the political leader. Secondly, even if it were so, why would I inform the concerned politician that I was keeping him under surveillance? Apparently, the director explained the situation to the Union Home Secretary and requested him to outright reject the insinuation made by my colleague in the Delhi Police. The then director of the Intelligence Bureau, who too was tasked to give his opinion on the tape, was firmly of the same view, as any sane person would be. Mercifully, the matter was given the burial it deserved.

The two attempts made at maligning me by two senior colleagues, one out of sheer envy and the other to settle old scores, are perhaps the saddest incidents of my life as a police officer. They say one should never underestimate the power of jealousy, or that of spite, to destroy.

While, on the one hand, working in tandem with officers of sister police agencies and getting results on account of the resultant synergy can be a most gratifying experience, the vengeful and debilitating mindsets of a handful of malicious colleagues can really pull you down. Even though, by God's grace, I came out of the two vicious attacks on my integrity unscathed, they left deep scars on my psyche.

~

Meanwhile, investigations into the affairs of Sharma revealed his meteoric rise from a humble background to becoming one of the most influential over-ground members of the underworld. Apart from having a close nexus with politicians of all hues, he had floated his own political party, contested elections and had aligned himself, from time to time, with the high and mighty of Indian politics.

Hailing from Agrasen Nagar in Phoolpur district, close to Allahabad, in Uttar Pradesh, he came to Delhi and made a living selling handkerchiefs on the footpaths of Sadar Bazar. In 1972, he moved to Mumbai and became close to Varadarajan Mudaliar, popularly known as Vardhabhai, who then ruled the underworld, and became his key aide. Through the underworld nexus, Sharma developed a huge interest in the real estate business spread across the western suburbs of Mumbai. His modus operandi was to identify disputed properties and buy the share of one of the claimants, thereby getting access to the premises. Then, using his underworld connections, he would make the other claimants vacate the property and take possession of the entire premises. One of the properties acquired with the help of Varadarajan Mudaliar's gang is located at Survey No. 5xx in Mumbai. It is a huge plot of priceless land, located by the sea, near Hotel Sun and Sand. Our inquiry showed that it originally belonged to one S.J. Almedia, who had leased it to Nanubhai Zaveri in 1947–48. In 1980, Romesh Sharma, with the help of Varadarajan, grabbed the plot by making forged documents showing its sale for Rs 21 lakh from one Leon J. Allams (nephew of

S.J. Almedia), who had inherited only 1/25th of the property. Allams, who possessed the letter of administration in respect of the property, had sold the same for Rs 45 lakh to Tanvir Mohammad Hussain Merchant, Swat Chand Bafna, Moti Lal Deerachand Doshi and Pukhraj Pirchand Doshi in 1989. As per another agreement of October 1993, the property stood in the physical possession of Romesh Sharma and the title of the property vested in the names of the four persons named above. During field inquiries, I visited the plot spread over several acres, with a commanding view of the Arabian Sea. The invaluable piece of land has at least two dozen palm trees and must be worth thousands of crores now.

Our field inquiries further revealed that using strong-arm tactics Sharma had earlier grabbed R-371, Jai Mata Kutir, Gandhigram Kutir, Juhu; Sant Sadan Bungalow No. 10, Union Bank, Pali Hills, Bandra; and Flat No. 307, Sundar Mahal, next to Ambassador Hotel, Church Gate— all prime properties in Mumbai worth hundreds of crores put together.

He moved to Delhi as he soon realized that acquiring a political persona coupled with his underworld links would make him a force to reckon with. He hopped from one political party to another, aligned himself with one leader one day and another the next, eventually creating his own All India Bharatiya Congress Party (AIBCP), from whose office on Mahadev Road Suresh Rao had been rescued and Sharma picked up by the police on 20 October 1998.

During his stay in Delhi he grabbed properties that included C-30, Mayfair Garden; C-28 (basement), Mayfair

Garden; S–41, Panchsheel Park; C–31, Hauz Khas; Jai Mata
Di Farms (where H. Suresh Rao's robbed helicopter was
parked); and the first floor of B–121, Sarvodaya Enclave.
The stories behind the forcible occupation of each one
of these properties were both bizarre and fascinating, and
would run into several pages. The ease with which he
grabbed them is a telling comment on our feeble system.
Readers can get a fair idea of the eventual ineffectiveness
of our legal system through the fact that Sharma is now
a free man, having served his sentence of fourteen years,
and continues to be the proud owner of these priceless
pieces of real estate, enjoying the riches they generate.
None of the genuine owners has come forward to lodge a
complaint because of the fear of the underworld. Even if
anyone had, Section 102 of the Criminal Procedure Code
empowers the police to seize only movable properties and
not immovable ones! The police can seize wristwatches,
jewellery, motor cars, weapons, etc., but not real estate,
which may have been acquired with the proceeds of crime
or have been forcibly grabbed. Incidentally, a proposal
was moved by us in the CBI in 1999 to the ministry of
home affairs to amend the law in the wake of this case.
Our proposal, though accepted in principle, lies dormant
in a government file somewhere in the labyrinths of the
bureaucratic system and is yet to see the light of day.

One of the distinct traits Romesh Sharma revealed
during our investigation was his insatiable lust for women.
Besides exploiting them sexually, he would use them
to entertain and oblige powerful people in politics and
government, in cahoots with the chief liaison man of a top

corporate house. We rescued several girls, barely in their twenties, held captive in some of his properties. However, neither they nor their parents were interested in lodging complaints with the police and taking legal action against him.

I came to know that a certain respectable woman from an affluent background was employed in Sharma's staff. He was exploiting her sexually on a regular basis. One evening, her grown-up daughter came to pick her up when Sharma's lustful eye fell on the young girl. He sent the mother on an errand and, while she was away, raped the daughter.

With great difficulty I traced the woman and knocked on the door of the south Delhi flat where she lived. She opened the door and when I introduced myself she said, rather dramatically, 'I knew you would come.' She had closely followed the news reports on Sharma's arrest and could guess that I had become aware of the unseemly events involving Sharma and her. But she flatly refused to lodge a report. 'I don't wish to ruin my daughter's life,' she said, anguish and pain embedded deep in her voice. Right then the doorbell rang and in walked her daughter, a petite and good-looking girl, perhaps back from work. She exchanged pleasantries with me and went into her room. Her mother asked me, rather mockingly, 'After seeing her, do you still want me to lodge a report with you? She is getting married in a couple of months.' It became clear to me that Romesh Sharma spared no efforts in unsettling his victims mentally, pulverizing their psyche to an extent that they could no longer muster the courage to speak out against him and his dubious ways. The woman I met was one such victim. I got her message loud and clear. I had no choice but to leave.

Romesh Sharma was sentenced to fourteen years of imprisonment in the helicopter case investigated by us. All credit for the successful prosecution goes to O.P. Chhatwal, my SP, who followed up the case relentlessly up to the highest court of appeal. Sometime in early 2012, when I was posted as DGP (prisons), Delhi, I visited the Rohini Jail under my charge for inspection. As I was leaving the prison premises, lo and behold, Romesh Sharma stood before me with folded hands, dressed in his usual attire of dhoti, kurta, Nehru jacket and Gandhi topi, with a big red tilak on his forehead. 'How are you doing, panditji?' I inquired. 'My prison sentence is coming to an end and I will be released soon,' he said triumphantly. 'Good for you, panditji. My good wishes,' were my parting words.

Sure enough, he was soon a free man. On the ensuing Diwali, a respectable woman, who introduced herself as the granddaughter of one of the greatest Hindi poets, called on me at my residence. I welcomed her warmly as I hold the poet in great esteem. She said, 'I have come on behalf of Romesh Sharma to pay you his respects and convey his good wishes.' I was astounded and had to explain to her at great length who Romesh Sharma was and why she should keep away from him. She left hurriedly, rather perplexed. Romesh Sharma had inveigled one more unsuspecting woman. The artful conman was back to his old tricks.

9

Salim, the Disposable
Tracing absconder Salim Kurla

On 20 January 1995 it was past 10.30 p.m. Inspector Raman Tyagi of the STF of the CBI, based in Mumbai, was still at work. He was busy completing the reply to a tricky matter coming up the following day in the trial court for the Mumbai serial bomb blasts case of 12 March 1993. He was just about beginning to wind up for the day when his office phone rang. He thought it was his wife again, asking him what time he would reach home. For a moment he thought he would be better off not taking the call. But, though a trifle vexed, fortuitously, he picked up the receiver.

'*Aadaab*, Inspector sahib,' the caller greeted him. Raman recognized the voice immediately. It was his mole in the D-company.

'*Haan, bolo, kya khabar hai* (Yes, tell me what news you have for me),' Raman asked impatiently.

'*Aapke kaam ki khabar hai, Inspector sahib. Salim Kurla ka phone number mil gaya hai. Woh Hyderabad mein hai* (I have useful news for you. I have got Salim Kurla's number. He is in Hyderabad),' the caller said.

'*Achcha, aur bhi kuchh hai ki bas phone number?* (Good. Besides his phone number, do you have any other information?)' inquired the inspector.

'*Nahin, aur kuchh nahi hai. Aap Hyderabad pahuncho, wahaan apna koi number de dena. Salim se baat karke main aapko confirm kar doonga ki woh wahaan hai ki nahin. Aap taiyyari kar ke rakhna. Idhar apun nakki karega, udhar aap raid maar dena* (No, there is nothing more. You should reach Hyderabad and give me a number. First, I will call Salim and if he is available on the number I am giving you, I will let you know. You should, meanwhile, locate the address where his phone is installed and keep a team ready close by. You raid the premises as soon as I confirm to you that he is there),' said the mole conspiratorially.

Raman noted down the number. Since the informer had never given an incorrect input in the past, Inspector Raman Tyagi thought it fit to inform his superior Satish Jha, SP, STF, Mumbai, immediately. The SP instructed the inspector to discuss the matter in detail the following day.

~

Dawood Ibrahim, son of a head constable of Mumbai Police, had slowly but steadily become the uncrowned king of the Mumbai underworld in the 1980s and '90s. Other contemporary dons like Haji Mastan, Karim Lala et al. had aged, invested their ill-gotten wealth in legitimate businesses and retired to comfortable lives, free of worries of raids by the police and customs departments. However, with numerous criminal cases pending against him and countless enemies baying for his blood, Dawood jumped bail and escaped to Dubai sometime in the mid-1980s. He continued to run the affairs of his gang by remote, through a well-structured hierarchy of trusted lieutenants who lived in Mumbai and its suburbs. His number two in the gang was his younger brother Anees Ibrahim, an impulsive, ill-tempered and abusive mobster who was in and out of Mumbai.

His well-organized crime syndicate, often referred to as D-company, with interests in smuggling of gold and silver, extortion, arbitration of disputes, hawala, contract killings, real estate, financing of films, betting in cricket, etc., held sway over the crime scene of Mumbai. All was going well till his and his gang's involvement in the serial bomb blasts of 1993 surfaced (see 'Our Man in Dubai' for more). Dawood had to run from Dubai to Karachi, where he presently stays, in Defence Colony, Clifton, under the protection of the ISI.

Both Dawood and his brother Anees are accused in the blasts case as are many of his gang members and associates, including Salim Kurla. Salim Bismillah Khan, a resident of Kurla, was given the moniker Salim Kurla by D-company to differentiate him from several other Salims in the gang. This is a common practice in the underworld where several gangsters share the same first name. For instance, D-company has Chhota Shakeel, Lambu Shakeel, Salim

Kutta, Salim Tempo and the protagonist of this story, Salim Kurla.

Salim, besides being an extortionist and a hatchet man in the gang, was immensely interested in Bollywood and often visited film sets. His intimate knowledge of film personalities also helped his gang in identifying soft targets for extortion and aspiring starlets for carnal pleasure. Salim himself was an inveterate womanizer and married thrice before fate intervened.

Salim, as part of the larger conspiracy behind the March 1993 blasts, sent four of his acolytes—Usman Khan, Sayyad Issaq, Sheikh Ibrahim and Mohammad Haneef—to Pakistan for training in the handling of weapons and explosives. They underwent a four-day intensive training camp organized by the ISI in the jungles near Islamabad. Interestingly, on the day of the blasts, Salim Kurla and Sayyad Issaq were in the lock-up of the Mumbai Police Crime Branch. They had been arrested in a case of extortion where a Gujarati businessman was the victim. Later, during the investigation of the serial blasts, all his four associates were arrested and sentenced to six years of rigorous imprisonment. However, Salim Kurla fled and the CBI announced a reward of Rs 2 lakh for his arrest.

Rajendra Sadashiv Nikalje aka Chhota Rajan, born to Maharashtrian parents, also belonged to an impoverished background, and grew up in the lower-middle-class locality of Tilak Nagar in Chembur, central Mumbai. Rajan started his criminal career as a black marketeer of cinema tickets at Shankar movie theatre in the late 1970s. He came in contact with Rajan Nayar aka Bada Rajan who was a bootlegger.

He took over Bada Rajan's gang after the latter's murder
by a rival gang. He soon teamed up with Dawood Ibrahim
and became one of his main lieutenants. He joined Dawood
in Dubai and operated under his suzerainty until the gang
broke up broadly on communal lines in the wake of the
Mumbai blasts. With this backgrounder, let us get back to
the main story.

At about eleven on 21 January 1995, the morning after
Raman had received his mole's call, Satish Jha called me up.
I was DIG of the STF then, based in Delhi. He gave me the
details of the intelligence input and sought further instructions.
He had already ascertained the address of the premises where
the landline number given by the mole was installed, with the
help of J.V. Ramudu, the then zonal DCP (now the police
chief of Andhra Pradesh) in Hyderabad. I asked Satish to
proceed by the first available flight to Hyderabad along with
Inspector Raman Tyagi. The SP wanted one more trusted
officer, namely Inspector D.K. Pardesi, to accompany him. I
asked him to go ahead and informed him that I too would try
to reach Hyderabad the same evening.

Satish and his officers, inspectors Raman Tyagi and
D.K. Pardesi, reached Hyderabad that evening by eight
and I reached by nine-thirty. We were booked to stay at
the Andhra Pradesh Police Officers' Mess at Masab Tank,
near Banjara Hills. However, I chose to drive straight to
the office of the ACP, Begumpet, Secunderabad—the twin
city of Hyderabad, then the capital of undivided Andhra
Pradesh. The CBI officer who came to receive me at the
airport informed me that my colleagues from Mumbai
were waiting for me there.

By the time I reached the rendezvous point, Raman and Pardesi had recced the ground-floor flat of K.R. Tyagi, where the target phone was installed. The CBI inspectors discreetly noted the location of the premises. Raman had then informed his mole that his senior officers and he himself (Raman) were in Hyderabad. The phone number of the ACP's office, our makeshift base camp located not far from the flat, had also been shared with the informer. The team headed by Satish Jha had done everything that was required to be done as part of the plan hatched by the informer. We all waited anxiously in the ACP's office for the final go-ahead from the mole.

To our complete horror, after a brief hiatus, Raman appeared with a long face before Satish Jha and me. He reported: 'Sir, my informer called. There was a change of heart among the big bosses in the gang. They tipped off Salim Kurla, saying, "*Doctor saab aa rahen hain. Nikal lo.* (A police team is on its way. Leave quickly.)"' The mole was not answering his phone thereafter.

Raman stood before us, dejected and embarrassed. I lost my cool and upbraided him for the poor quality of the information he had gathered. What did he mean by 'change of heart'? Raman offered an explanation: apparently, Dawood and his younger brother Anees had gotten tired of Salim Kurla's frequent demands for money to sustain his family and himself. Occasionally, they had hinted to him that he was better off on his own, but since Salim was on the run it was difficult for him to generate any income.

In the cruel world of the mafiosi, someone close today can become disposable the next day, particularly when a gang member becomes a liability. Salim Kurla, a trusted and loyal aide, who had played a role in the conspiracy behind the serial blasts in Mumbai, had, with passage of time, become an irritant with his persistent demands for more and more money. That was the time the two brothers—Dawood Ibrahim and Anees Ibrahim—asked their trusted aide (Raman's mole) to tip off the police and have Kurla arrested. However, as the impending raid and Kurla's nemesis drew closer, the two brother dons had second thoughts. They fondly recalled the risks Salim had taken in the past in their service. They also thought of Salim's wife and three children. Anees himself called up Salim and asked him to run, as quickly as he could. Salim had left the same morning and, presumably, would have by then travelled hundreds of miles away.

Besides being deeply disappointed, other mundane but serious worries haunted me. I could foresee the problems that awaited me back in Delhi. I had verbally given my approval to Satish Jha for the air travel of Raman Tyagi and D.K. Pardesi, who were not entitled to fly. As per official norms, as a DIG, I was not authorized to do so. At the time of giving the go-ahead to Satish Jha for his officers' air travel, I was reasonably sure that the operation would succeed, in which case there would be no difficulty in getting the necessary approvals from my bosses post facto. But the operation had failed even before it had begun. Raman had to hear all this and much more from me, spoken in not the most pleasant of tones. With drooping shoulders and head bowed, he stood before us, crestfallen and guilt-ridden. I rubbed it in by letting him know that I had left important tasks in Delhi and travelled unnecessarily to Hyderabad, thanks to his half-baked intelligence input.

Having given adequate vent to my disappointment and anguish, I now had to decide what to do next. Left with practically no option but to wind up, forget all about Salim Kurla and return to the Hyderabad Police Mess to retire for the day, Satish and I began our long drive back.

I clearly remember that drive in a CBI car, with Satish and me in the rear seat. It started rather gloomily, with an uneasy silence enveloping us. I looked out of my car window and Satish stared into the darkness from his side, as we drove from Begumpet towards the Police Mess. I was still in a foul mood and, I suppose, Satish was equally cut up.

Out of the blue, in the midst of despair and distress, a thought crossed my mind. Our boys had seen the premises where the landline was installed. Why not at least go and see it. Right then, as if some sort of telepathy was at play, Satish spoke up: 'Sir, what do we lose by visiting the flat where Salim Kurla was hiding?' It was one of those moments when two people sitting together are struck by a common epiphany, but are hesitant to voice it first. I told Satish he had stolen the words from my mouth.

We asked our driver to stop. Raman, who was in a vehicle following us, walked up to our car. Satish instructed him to lead us to the recced flat.

Inspectors Raman Tyagi and D.K. Pardesi piloted us to a four-storeyed residential building in the middle of a vast swathe of land covered in darkness. A few houses—some complete, some under construction—dotted the dark landscape, while a street light or two flickered and blinked laboriously, struggling to fight for survival. Quite clearly, it was another of those unplanned and unauthorized colonies that sprout up in the suburbs of most Indian cities.

We stopped our vehicles at a distance from the house where Salim Kurla had resided before escaping, and began to walk stealthily towards it. As we came closer, we found to our surprise the doors of the ground-floor flat wide open. A brightly lit room appeared before us with loud Hindi film music playing from a stereo system. There was no one in the room. We walked in and found ourselves in the middle of a large and reasonably well-furnished living room. After a few shouts of '*Koi hai?* (Is someone there?),' a ten-year-old boy appeared. Strangely, he was unimpressed on seeing us. We asked him for his parents, who too emerged from an adjoining room almost simultaneously, most unfazed by the presence of so many strangers. When we introduced ourselves as CBI officers, they asked us to sit down, and offered refreshments. We politely declined. On being asked whether the landline number 8131xx was installed in their house, their response was in the affirmative. When asked if any outsider used the phone occasionally, they again said yes. They further disclosed that the occupant of the second-floor flat, namely Ahmad, used their phone once in a while. Inspector Raman Tyagi showed the photograph of Salim Kurla to the flat owner, K.R. Tyagi, who confirmed that it was indeed the same person.

When we went up to the second floor, we found a huge lock hanging at the door. Tyagi and family, the occupants of the ground floor, informed that Ahmad sahib, as Salim

Kurla was known to them, had left the same morning with his wife and three children in a Fiat. They gave us the car's registration number, colour and other description. As a routine response, we asked the Hyderabad Police officers, accompanying us as support staff, to broadcast the details over police wireless. Nothing further was left to be done at the spot. Satish and I decided to leave for the Police Mess. As we were about to depart, the young boy, pointing to a two-wheeler parked in the open, right outside the house, said, 'Uncle, yeh scooter unhi ka hai (This scooter is his).' Salim had left his scooter behind as he could not have possibly driven both his car and the two-wheeler. We paused for a moment and, out of sheer police instinct, decided to leave inspectors Tyagi and Pardesi behind. Though it was most improbable, hypothetically there was still a slim chance that Salim might return to pick up his scooter. The inspectors and Sub-Inspector V. Rao of Hyderabad Police stayed back close to the apartment building to keep watch, just in case our intuition was right.

On reaching my room in the Police Mess I had a quick shower before getting into my sleeping suit. But for some snacks eaten at the ACP's office, I had gone without dinner. It was sleep that I needed the most, after a disappointing and distressing evening. It was already well past midnight. I switched off the room's light and lay down. Just as my head was about to hit the pillow, there was a knock on the door. I thought it must be a kind soul from the mess staff who had come to ask if I needed something to eat. After switching on the light, I opened the door, only to find inspectors Raman Tyagi and Pardesi with a tall, well-built man, looking a bit familiar, sandwiched between them. Raman lost no time in informing me that the person with them was none other than Salim Kurla!

I quickly changed and went down to the mess lounge to speak to Raman, Pardesi and Salim. Meanwhile, Satish had been given the good news and he too joined us. Raman narrated the sequence of events leading to Salim's arrest thus:

Soon after our departure from that house, CBI inspector Raman Tyagi along with Pardesi and Sub-Inspector Rao of Hyderabad Police waited patiently, keeping an eye on the scooter. They spotted an autorickshaw approach the area and stop at a distance. After a few minutes, the headlight was switched off and a tall figure emerged from the passenger seat of the three-wheeler. He stood tentatively, silhouetted against the faint light in the area, looked around a bit, and began to walk towards the building under the cover of darkness. The police officers hid behind the bushes on the side of the *kaccha* road leading up to the house. As the tall figure came within their reach, the cops emerged from their hiding and surrounded him. They frisked him to make sure he wasn't armed. On being asked who he was, he first said he was Firoze Ahmed Pasha. But when shown his photograph, he admitted that he was indeed Salim Kurla. As we had anticipated intuitively, he had come that late to pick up his scooter. When asked about the whereabouts of his family, he refused to reveal any details. The officers slowly walked him to the autorickshaw that had ferried him to the place. The driver, Syed Yusuf, when questioned, informed them that he had picked up Salim from near Hotel Heritage, Sindhi Colony, Secunderabad.

Our happiness knew no bounds. An operation gone awry had worked out successfully at the end only because we had kept control over our senses and responded to our police instinct when it mattered most. Oftentimes, some police actions, seemingly mindless and defying rationality, bear fruit and bring results. Had Satish and I not thought of visiting the premises when all seemed lost; had we not left Raman and Pardesi behind to respond to the outside chance of Salim returning to pick up his scooter; had the two CBI inspectors and the Hyderabad sub-inspector not acted as able policemen, the operation was a goner. That we salvaged it from the brink of failure was part luck and part professional acumen in the face of adversity. More importantly, we had not failed to respond to our gut feel, intuition and police instinct.

There was still some work to be done, which included searches of Salim's hotel room and his flat. We asked our officers to complete the remaining tasks before day broke.

At 2.45 a.m. the CBI team reached Hotel Heritage and found Salim's wife, Rizwana, with their three children in Room 437. Rizwana had the key to the flat from where they had fled that morning. Quickly, searches of the hotel room and the flat were made in the presence of independent witnesses. However, nothing of interest emerged. Salim's Fiat and scooter were seized and deposited at Begumpet Police Station.

Salim Kurla was produced before the magistrate, 11th Court, Secunderabad, on 22 January 1995 and his transit

(or journey) remand obtained to enable us to produce him
before the special court trying the serial bomb blasts case
in Mumbai. He was taken by the 4.30 p.m. Indian Airlines
flight to Mumbai. During the flight, Salim Kurla was seated
between Raman and Pardesi. A well-known film actor was
also on board and saw Salim. Unaware that he was in CBI
custody, he smiled and waved at Salim. Apparently, the
two had met on several occasions earlier and knew each
other rather well. During his interrogation, Salim disclosed
he had extorted Rs 5 lakh from another Bollywood star
who was all the rage then. After interrogation he was sent
to judicial custody, pending the ongoing trial of the case.

On 28 May 1997, after more than two years of
judicial custody, Salim Kurla was granted interim bail on
health grounds. His bail petition mentioned uncontrolled
diabetes, hypertension and backache as his ailments. He
often got admitted to hospitals to create documentary proof
of his protracted illness as a ruse to get his bail extended.
Reportedly, he had resumed extortion and other criminal
activities during this period.

Meanwhile, internecine gang warfare between
Dawood Ibrahim and Chhota Rajan had reached its peak.
The Dawood gang, traditionally of 'secular' composition,
where loyalty and performance mattered and not religion,
had, after the serial blasts, split vertically on communal
lines. Chhota Rajan had become the self-styled leader of
the Hindu gangsters, who had either been expelled by
the D-company bosses or had left on their own. The two
factions were targeting each other's men one by one. Rajan
had already got Manish Lala (Dawood's legal adviser),

Thakiyuddeen Wahid (of East-West Airlines, suspected to be a front company of Dawood), Mirza Dilshad Beg (a Nepal-based mobster turned politician close to Dawood), Irfan Goga (a Dubai-based Dawood associate), etc., killed. Further, Chhota Rajan had vowed to kill every accused in the serial blasts one by one.

At 11.30 a.m. on 21 April 1998, Salim lay on a hospital bed in Ward 1 of Belle Vue Nursing Home on Virar Desai Road, Andheri (West) in Mumbai. A group of eleven assailants entered the nursing home. An advance reconnaissance had identified the exact location of the target they were determined to do away with. Members of the hit team positioned themselves strategically inside the hospital to meet any last-minute contigencies. Five of them barged into Ward 1 and shot Salim Kurla eight times before he slumped dead in his hospital bed. His driver, Arif Cablewala, attending on him, received four bullets and succumbed to his injuries a little later.

Thus, Salim became the first victim of Rajan's bloody campaign. The others to follow were Mohammad Jindran, Hanif Kadawala, Rafiq Madi (who survived the attack miraculously), Mohammad Shakeel, Majid Khan (brother of accused Yeda Yaqub) and Akbar Abu Sama Khan. The killing spree would have continued but for a near fatal attack on Chhota Rajan himself in Bangkok on 15 September 2000, masterminded by Dawood's right-hand man, Chhota Shakeel.

Scott Adams, the famous American writer, cartoonist and creator of Dilbert comic strip, once observed: 'When times are bad, gloves come off and employers are less nice.

People become disposable.' Salim Kurla had outlived his
utility and D-company had fallen on relatively bad times
compared to their heyday when their writ ran large in
Mumbai. Salim had become dispensable, destined to be
cast aside by his bosses and meet a bloody end.

10

'Baitha hai, sir, baitha hai!'
The netting of the
Punjab CM's assassin

The Delhi Golf Club, located in the heart of Delhi on 220 acres of prime real estate, comprises an eighteen-hole Asian PGA Tour 'A' course and a shorter nine-hole 'B' course. The 'B' course is mostly used by beginners and executives anxious for a quick round of golf before they get to work in the morning. It was a Sunday afternoon in September 1995—hot and humid—when I, a struggling rookie of the sport (I firmly believe that my struggling days are yet to be left behind!), having hacked through the first eight holes of the *chhota* (small) course, stood on the tee box of the ninth, a par three. I noticed beyond the green and close to the clubhouse a group of three men watching me intently from the far end. I wondered what had brought them to the rather exclusive, forested and lush precincts of the club. As I got close to the green, I recognized one of them. He was an inspector who had served with me during two of my assignments in the Delhi Police, before I had moved to the CBI on deputation in 1993.

My first assignment in the CBI was as DIG in its STF. I had offices in Mumbai and Delhi, both headed by officers of the rank of SP. The investigation of the serial blasts, perhaps the most horrific and audacious act of terror in India's history till then, would keep me flitting between the two cities for most part of the year. Even though our primary mandate was the serial terror attacks, we had inexorably been drawn into various other cases, mainly connected with terror. This is the story of one such case.

I finished playing the hole and went up to the officer. He said he had an important bit of information for me. As we strolled together to the car park, he disclosed that he had an input on the whereabouts of Jagtar Singh Tara, one of the infamous assassins of Sardar Beant Singh, the former chief minister of Punjab credited for having dealt a body blow to terrorism in his state. The CM had been assassinated on 31 August, barely a couple of weeks earlier. The two people accompanying him were his informers, who were absolutely sure of the veracity of their tip-off. As per the information, the terrorist was likely to be found either in his rented apartment in the semi-urbanized village of Arjun Nagar, near Safdarjung Enclave in south Delhi, or at a gurdwara in Adhchini Village, again in south Delhi.

The inspector said his informers had decided that they would themselves go in advance to his (Tara's) hideouts, confirm his presence and let us know. However, they cautioned me that Tara could be armed with an AK-56 rifle and definitely had a cyanide pill on him. Further, the operation to nab Tara had to be conducted urgently, positively by the next day, before he disappeared.

A brief chat with them was enough to convince me that the information was indeed reliable and needed to be acted upon post-haste. But before getting into action, I wanted to know why hadn't they or the inspector gone to the Special Cell, the counterterrorism wing of the Delhi Police or the Chandigarh Police. Their answer was simple: 'We don't trust them. We would rather let the information die its natural death than share it with them.' The answer told me it was rather late in the day to persuade them to approach the local police. The informers, it turned out, had shared the intelligence inputs with the inspector on the condition that it would be passed on to an agency that would handle it with finesse, and after safeguarding their interests. They were apprehensive that if they approached the local police or any officer not of their confidence, they themselves could come to grief. Since they knew the inspector well, who knew me personally, they had approached him, who in turn had brought them to me.

That left me with no option but to get going. After all, the case was of utmost significance, both from a national and international perspective, with a direct bearing on the internal security of the country. The chief minister of Punjab, during his tenure, had taken a hard line on the Sikh terrorists in his state. He had given a free hand to his police chief, K.P.S. Gill, and supported him to the hilt in his relentless campaign against terrorism. The common perception was that during the CM's tenure, widespread human rights violations were committed and many innocent civilians killed in cold blood in the name of fighting terror. Radical elements in the Sikh community had for long been baying for the blood of both the CM and the DGP.

At 5.10 p.m. on 31 August 1995, the CM came down from his second-floor office in the Punjab and Haryana Secretariat in Chandigarh. He was about to get inside his official car parked in the VIP porch, when a suicide bomber dressed in police uniform, later identified as Dilawar Singh, managed to sneak close to the car and blow himself up. The CM and seventeen others were killed instantly. Those grievously injured in the suicide bomb attack numbered fifteen.

As subsequent investigations revealed, the assassination was the culmination of a sinister conspiracy hatched by the masterminds of Babbar Khalsa International (BKI) based in Pakistan, Germany, the UK and the USA. Founded in 1978, the BKI took the name Babbar Khalsa from the Babbar Akali movement of 1920 which was against British colonial rule. The modern-day Babbar Khalsa was created as a result of the bloody clash on 13 April 1978 between mainstream followers of Sikhism and the reformist Nirankari sect. The killing of thirteen Sikhs in the armed clash and the failure of the legal system to bring the guilty to book gave rise to militancy among the fundamentalist elements in the Sikh community. This resulted first in the birth of the Babbar Khalsa in India, and later its international wing the BKI. In the wake of the Khalistani movement fighting for an independent state of Khalistan to be carved out of

India, the BKI assumed a pre-eminent role in fighting the Indian establishment. The militant group was determined to avenge the deaths of innumerable Sikhs perceived to have been killed in fake encounters by the police, with the tacit approval of Sardar Beant Singh, the then CM of Punjab.

As there was no time to lose, I drove straight to the residence of Arun Bhagat, special director, CBI, my immediate boss. The assassination case had been transferred to the CBI from the Chandigarh Police on the day of the incident itself, and was being handled by another branch of the organization, again under Bhagat. By a curious coincidence, soon after the case came to the agency, Director K. Vijaya Rama Rao, in a meeting held in his North Block office in Delhi, spoke to three officers, including me. Even though none of us was formally connected with the investigation of the case, the director felt we could make some contribution in cracking it. He added that the CBI faced a tremendous challenge with the case, unsolved until then, and it was the duty of each officer to contribute to its resolution. We were asked to keep our eyes and ears open, deploy sources and collect intelligence connected with the crime. Providence willed it that within days of this meeting I was to become the medium for an important contribution.

Bhagat heard me out patiently at his Bapa Nagar residence. At the end of the conversation, most nonchalantly, he asked me to go ahead and nab the culprit. 'Sir, but to carry out an operation to arrest a terrorist of a Sikh militant group, I would need adequate armed backup. The man also carries a cyanide pill,' I protested. 'Oh! Never mind. I know you can manage on your own. Just go ahead and do it,' he said brushing my misgivings aside.

While I found his confidence in me rather flattering, prudence and discretion clearly demanded a far more comprehensive and professional response. I had expected that the special director would involve the branch investigating the case and discuss the operation with the director. But his trust seemed so absolute that he wanted me to go ahead on my own. That left me at a complete loss on how to proceed further. After all, here was a chance to apprehend one of the most dreaded and wanted men in India; but with no backup in place it felt a bit like trying to go after a man-eating predator with an air gun. No amount of bravado and back-patting can replace the very real prospect of taking on a cold-blooded assassin without a crack team of armed and combat-ready commandos in place.

And yet necessity and desperation can bring out the best in men. I knew then that I had to go with what I had, play the hand I had been dealt. It was already 7 p.m. or so when I returned home. I rang up Satish Jha, my SP based in Mumbai, and asked him to rush to Delhi by air with his support staff to report to me the following morning. He immediately realized that an important operation was in the offing and didn't make any queries on the phone. He had collaborated with me on several similar missions in the past. However, I thought to myself, the presence of three or four trusted men under Satish was not going to suffice. Clearly, I needed more trusted hands with courage, grit and, most importantly, unfailing loyalty to me to go on this dangerous mission. Where was I to find such people and how? Here was a situation where I had pucca information on the whereabouts of an armed terrorist wanted in a sensational act of terror and I was expected to get him with my own limited resources without involving any other agency. How would I do it? Would I be able to live up to the expectations of my boss? Was it not a most foolhardy mission to begin with? Why couldn't I assertively tell my boss that I couldn't do it alone?

Sleep that night played truant. My mind was racked by fears of all kinds, not knowing what lay in store for us the next day—success or failure, life or death. It is only when faced with such situations that we turn to God and his Grace. I caught a few winks of sleep with a prayer on my lips.

Satish Jha, with three of his trusted officers, namely Raman Tyagi, D.K. Pardesi and Anil Nair, took the 6 a.m. flight from Mumbai and drove straight to my residence from the Delhi airport. It was about nine in the morning when they reached me. I shared the information with him and the other officers. Enthused and excited with the precision of the tip-off, they assured me that together we could pull it off. They felt that if the man was spotted and identified, they could overpower him before he reacted with his weapon.

But Satish and his boys could, at best, cover one of the two places where our quarry was likely to be found. I decided they would be deployed at the gurdwara. I gave them a vehicle and asked them to reach Adhchini where

I would meet them with one of the two informers. They left my residence quite charged and upbeat, giving me considerable reassurance and positive energy. However, the fact remained I still needed equally trusted and confident men for the other venue. While the police is easily pilloried in the media when things do not go as per plans, little does the fourth estate know of the reality of some of our operations, as the details are never shared in national interest. Who in his right senses would ever believe what we were out to do? Most may even say that it would have been best to call off the operation, instead of attempting something so daring and risking so many lives.

As I sat with a cup of tea on the lawn of my residence, wondering how to cover the other place, Constable Dharambir Singh, originally of the Delhi Police, then on deputation to the CBI as my security aide, arrived for duty. 'If I point out a man and say that he is an armed terrorist, will you be able to overpower and disarm him?' I inquired hesitantly, aware I was expecting a bit too much. 'Sure, sir. Why not? I can do it,' he responded confidently. He never once asked for an armed backup. I thought to myself we now have one more trusted hand for the mission. Surender Singh, a tall and wiry young constable provided to me by the Delhi Police for security at my residence, reported for duty next. I put the same question to him and got the same answer. 'That makes it two,' I said to myself, 'almost like clutching at straws in order to keep from drowning.' By a happy coincidence, ASI Anchal Singh of the Delhi Traffic Police came to pay me a courtesy call. He had been on my personal staff in the

Delhi Police for many years, always by my side in trying times, most notably during the anti-Sikh riots of 1984. He is the sort of subordinate officer a senior could go to war with. I asked him if he was willing to participate in a counter-terror operation commencing shortly. He too responded positively, though he had a condition. He did not intend to inform his superiors as they would never give him the go-ahead. After all, why should a Delhi Police officer get involved in a CBI operation whose details had not been shared with his seniors? The matter would have to be cleared by none less than the commissioner of police himself. So, Anchal Singh wanted his participation to be kept confidential, informal and unofficial. Since he was in his uniform, I gave him a long and loose white shirt, fitting his tall and broad frame, and asked him to change. These developments were gradually making me more confident and reassured. I quickly got ready and reached my office at Yashwant Place, Chanakyapuri, with the three Delhi Police personnel. I picked up H.C. Singh, SP, STF, ASI Hawa Singh and two other CBI men from the office for the operation. They were asked to proceed to a pre-decided point in Safdarjang Enclave with one of the two informers and wait for me.

I first visited Adhchini Village, where the other informer and Satish Jha with his team were waiting. The gurdwara was recced by us discreetly and it was decided that the man, if spotted and identified, would be picked up not from inside the holy place for obvious reasons, but at a safe distance away. Those were the days when mobile phones had not yet arrived in India. To make matters more difficult, the CBI, primarily an anti-corruption agency, had no wireless network of its own. Thus, there was no way the team under Satish Jha could stay in touch with me as I intended to head the other team to be deployed in Arjun Nagar. So I left Satish and his three officers in a government jeep, after wishing them godspeed and the best of luck.

The other informer and I then reached Arjun Nagar, an unplanned, haphazard, semi-pucca residential area with houses packed close to each other. He pointed out a ground-floor apartment in a congested by-lane to be kept under watch. It was possibly the terrorist's place of stay from where he could surface. The area was such that it seemed impossible to find a location from where to mount a watch. With great difficulty, we found an open plot of land with a four-foot-high boundary wall close to the entrance to the lane. I collected my Team-2 and we all sat in the open ground hiding behind its low walls.

It was the first time that I was sitting on watch myself, dressed in casuals, that too in the open and in broad daylight. After an hour or so, I could feel that my Delhi SP, a career CBI officer not given to such adventures, was getting a bit uncomfortable with this onerous duty assigned to him. He requested me to allow him to leave as he had some important files to attend to! Now, it wasn't even a nifty little ruse. Positive energy and confidence were the need of the hour. Those who lacked either were not going to be of any help. Even though we were woefully short of men, I let him go as there was no point in having someone on the surveillance and operation team who was unwilling and whose body language belied his discomfiture.

We waited all day, with no food or water, crouching under the low boundary wall. The harsh September sun beat down on us relentlessly and the humidity enervated us. Still we waited patiently, our eyes scanning the area for a tall and strapping young Sikh. The wait stretched on for several hours before people in the neighborhood began to notice us and found our presence on the empty plot highly suspicious. We could see them whispering to each other and a small group of people began to collect close by. It was already 5 p.m. when I decided that before one of the onlookers dialled 100 and a scene was created with the arrival of the local police, it was better to call off the watch. My officers were asked to wind up and leave. As we walked to our vehicles parked at some distance, the informer appeared out of nowhere and requested me to check out one more place. By then I was quite exasperated and furious. 'You can keep your information to yourself. Don't waste our time,' I shouted angrily at him. Our patience had clearly been tested.

'Sir, please believe me and let us check out one more place,' he pleaded with folded hands. Most reluctantly, I agreed to follow him. He took us to a different part of Safdarjung Enclave and left us at a safe distance. He went to check out another place where he thought the terrorist could possibly be hiding. He returned soon, trembling like a leaf, soaked in perspiration, fear writ large on his face. He murmured, almost inaudibly, '*Baitha hai, sir, baitha hai* (He is sitting there, sir, he is actually there)!' We broke up into ones and twos. He guided us stealthily and took us to a small single-storey municipal market built in the shape of a U. He disappeared after giving us the name of a travel agency located in the market where, according to him, our quarry sat.

The travel agency was nowhere to be seen in the U-shaped market. It seemed like yet another red herring. Just then Constable Dharambir Singh noticed an independent toilet block at one end of the U-shaped market. Between the toilet block and the adjacent tip of the U, there was a narrow and inconspicuous passage. It could easily be missed by anyone not familiar with the topography of the place. Dharambir felt there might be shops at the rear of the building accessible through the passage. I asked ASI Anchal Singh and Dharambir to go in advance and check. They came back in no time to confirm that indeed there were shops at the rear and one of them was the office of the travel agency we were looking for.

Four of us approached the shop discreetly and found that the glass exterior of the shop was tinted and opaque. A decision in such situations defies logic and thought. In all my years of policing at different levels, across sundry assignments, I'd never been confronted with a more perilous and bone-chilling situation. This was it, the moment of truth. Across the tinted glass lay life. Or its eternal companion, death. My decision to come to this point without a commando unit, without weapons and bulletproof jackets, without cordoning off the entire area, without taking some local residents into confidence, could all backfire, literally, within a matter of seconds. All our combined heroism could blow up in our face. The danger was just too large and imminent, and it was now only metres away. In the next few moments we could well be contributing a glorious chapter to India's counterterrorism history and be front-paged next day. Or we could ourselves become history. As we began to take our next few steps, life and death hung on a balance. Which way would it tilt?

ASI Anchal Singh, Constable Dharambir Singh, Constable Surinder Singh and I barged into the shop almost spontaneously, each on his own yet together as a team. We were half expecting the men inside to be sitting with Kalashnikov rifles, ready to fire a burst. Instead, to our surprise, and relief, we found a tall, turbaned Sikh youngster sprawled leisurely in an executive chair. Alongside sat another person, a *mona* (a Sikh without a turban), equally relaxed. They were caught totally unawares and we overpowered them in no time. The man in the turban, when questioned, admitted that he was indeed Jagtar Singh Tara. His body search revealed a cyanide pill hidden in his turban but, fortunately, there was no weapon on either of them. Having realized that their game was up, Jagtar Singh Tara and his companion offered no resistance. They said they they would come with us willingly. We brought the two of them to our vehicles and drove them to the STF office located in Yashwant Place, Chanakyapuri. It was still not dark and quite a few bystanders saw us taking the two young men away. Later, we came to know of a call received at the Delhi Police control room reporting the abduction of two youngsters by unidentified persons.

As if our last few hours were not mentally draining enough, there was yet another twist remaining to this tale. En route to our office, the official Ambassador car carrying

TOWARDS JNU

AFRICA AVENUE

OUTER RING ROAD

SAFDARJUNG ENCL AVE

TOWARDS AIRPORT

RK TENNIS
ACADEMY

DEER PARK

IIT DELHI

SAFDARJUNG
DEVELOPMENT AREA

GREEN PARK GURDWARA

GREEN PARK MAIN

AUROBINDO MARG

ADCHINI GURDWARA

SARVODAYA ENCLAVE

TOWARDS NEHRU PLACE

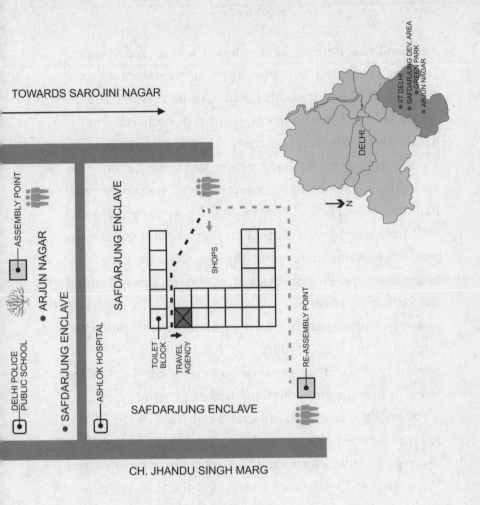

TOWARDS SAROJINI NAGAR

ASSEMBLY POINT

DELHI POLICE PUBLIC SCHOOL

ARJUN NAGAR

SAFDARJUNG ENCLAVE

ASHLOK HOSPITAL

SAFDARJUNG ENCLAVE

TOILET BLOCK

TRAVEL AGENCY

SHOPS

RE-ASSEMBLY POINT

SAFDARJUNG ENCLAVE

CH. JHANDU SINGH MARG

N

DELHI

IIT DELHI
SAFDARJUNG DEV. AREA
GREEN PARK
ARJUN NAGAR

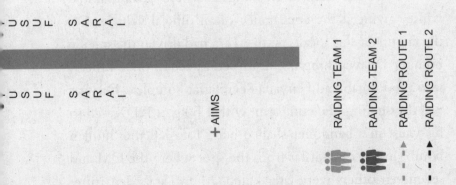

U S U F   S A R A I

U S U F   S A R A I

+ AIIMS

RAIDING TEAM 1

RAIDING TEAM 2

RAIDING ROUTE 1

RAIDING ROUTE 2

Tara and the four of us developed a snag and stopped. Imagine the scene: four so-called CBI sleuths stranded in the middle of a busy south Delhi road in a ramshackle car with a Babbar Khalsa terrorist, the first to be arrested in the Sardar Beant Singh assassination case! It took some time for the vehicle to be fixed before we were on our way again. Each one of those minutes spent waiting seemed like an hour. The tall assassin and his accomplice could well have overpowered us. Why they did not make their move confounds me even to this day. Perhaps they were under the impression that an armed convoy was just round the corner to cover us, and hence decided to capitulate passively. Fortunately, we were soon in the safe confines of our office, and sighs of relief rent the air. Director Rao and Special Director Bhagat arrived on hearing the news of the arrest in no time and complimented us generously.

A brief interrogation of Jagtar Singh Tara disclosed that his accomplice Jagtar Singh Hawara and he had bought a silver-grey Ambassador car DBA 9598 from the Paschim Vihar area of Delhi. Tara had signed the delivery papers disguising himself as one Basant Singh. He had first driven it to Patiala and then to Chandigarh where it was painted white, giving it the appearance of an official vehicle. On the fateful day, at about 3 p.m., Tara had driven the suicide bomber Dilawar Singh, a dismissed Special Police officer, into the Punjab and Haryana Secretariat complex. Dilawar was dressed in police uniform, with 1.5 kg of RDX tied to his waist in a bandolier-shaped belt. Tara left the 'human bomb' in the car not far from the spot where the CM and seventeen others were later killed. After Tara's departure,

Dilawar Singh was joined by Balwant Singh Rajoana, a serving police constable. Rajoana was a standby suicide bomber. So confident were the conspirators of the eventual success of their plan that they did not even bother to affix a fake number plate to the car.

Tara disclosed that the man sitting with him in the travel agency office at the time of his arrest was in no way connected with the crime. But his co-conspirator, namely Jagtar Singh Hawara of the Babbar Khalsa, could be in Nandgram, near Ghaziabad in Uttar Pradesh. Immediately, the assistance of the Special Cell of the Delhi Police was taken and a nightlong search operation launched. I was so fatigued by then that I slept in one of the flats in Nandgram despite the excitement of the operation under way, which was now headed by Satish Jha. Unfortunately, we could not find Hawara as he had left much before our arrival. We handed over Jagtar Singh Tara to the branch investigating the case. He was then formally arrested.

Subsequent investigations led to the arrest of eight others, including Hawara and Rajoana. In all, thirteen accused were named in the CBI charge sheet, three of whom, namely Wadhawa Singh, Mahal Singh and Jagroop Singh, are still in hiding in Pakistan.

Nine years after their arrest, on the night of 21 January 2004, Jagtar Singh Tara, Jagtar Singh Hawara and Paramjit Singh Bheora, all undertrials in the assassination case, escaped from the Burail Model Jail. They dug a ninety-four-foot-long tunnel with a weightlifting rod. The tunnel went beneath three walled security rings. It was their third attempt to escape from the jail, the earlier attempts being in 1997 and 2002. Forty bags of excavated earth and debris were found hidden behind the cell's cupboards. Taps installed in the cell were kept running to drown the sound of digging. Complicity of the prison staff was suspected, leading to the arrest of the jail superintendent and six other staffers, including the deputy and assistant superintendents. The audacious escape had brought to naught the good work done in arresting and prosecuting the dreaded terrorists—or so it seemed. Within two years, Hawara and Bheora were apprehended, but Tara remained elusive. On conclusion of the trial in the assassination case, Balwant Singh Rajoana was sentenced to death while others, except one, were awarded life imprisonment.

On 6 January 2015, as I sat watching TV, the news of Jagtar Singh Tara's arrest in an eastern province of Thailand, after more than ten years of his audacious escape from prison, flashed on the ticker. Full-blown stories began to appear soon after, as more details came in. The following day the newspapers were replete with front-page reports on Tara's recapture. When news on him last came in, he had not only been extradited to India but also sentenced to life imprisonment.

It has now been twenty years since we arrested Tara in Delhi. Today every little detail of the operation feels so surreal, as if it never happened. I still reminisce rather bemusedly at my decision to go unarmed after a Babbar Khalsa terrorist, with only a handful of trusted men. Had anything gone wrong and if Jagtar Singh Tara were indeed carrying his Kalashnikov, as was the initial information, the result could have been catastrophic for all of us. If, on the other hand, he had escaped from our clutches, it would have been hugely and unpardonably embarrassing. The police fraternity, particularly from my own organization, would have scoffed at us. The operation, labelled as amateurish, reminiscent of the antics of Keystone Cops, could have become a laughing stock for a long time to come! That we managed to pull it off was yet another blessing from God, rewarding us for our sincere and courageous efforts.

11

Between Twenty-Two Yards
Tracing 'MK', the pioneer of
match-fixing in cricket

In November 1999, Inspector Ishwar Singh of Delhi Police Crime Branch was investigating an extortion case registered at Desh Bandhu Gupta Road Police Station, in which an exporter of Indian handicrafts and garments was receiving threatening calls from Dubai. The extortion calls, as reported by the complainant, came from mobile numbers +971-50-6799xxx and +971-50-6796xxx. Almost as a matter of routine, the inspector wanted to know if any Delhi number was in touch with the calling numbers. His analysis disclosed 98100xx411 to be one such number. It was registered in the name of Krishan Kumar, later identified as the younger brother of the late Gulshan Kumar of T-Series fame. Krishan Kumar's number was taken under technical surveillance after due authorization. Little did the police officer know that his routine move to take the Delhi number, and six other local numbers constantly in touch with it under surveillance, was going to shake up a game once patronized by gentlemen and synonymous with all that is upright and fair. I am, of course, referring to the game of cricket played across twenty-two yards.

The inspector, no keen follower of the game, was bewildered to hear chatter on cricket while listening to telephonic conversations under his lawful surveillance. He heard the name of Hansie Cronje, perhaps for the first time, who was meeting one Sanjeev Chawla in the lobby of a New Delhi hotel and planning to make his South African team underperform at Chawla's behest. One thing led to another and the lid on a large-scale betting and fixing scandal was blown, involving none less than the South African captain himself. All hell let loose as news of the scandal broke. The Crime Branch registered a case on 23 March 2000 and arrested Krishan Kumar, Sunil Dara aka Bittu and Rajesh Kalra—all associates of Sanjeev Chawla who had fled to London. Another accused, Manmohan Khattar, absconded likewise.

Public and media reactions ranged from shock, utter disbelief to revulsion. Strong denials followed from Hansie Cronje with the South African cricket board and Hansie's teammates rallying behind him. Incurable critics and detractors of the Delhi Police continued to be sceptical of the exposé despite the transcripts of Hansie's telephonic intercepts being made public.

At 3 a.m. on 11 April, eighteen days after the Crime Branch had registered the case against Hansie Cronje and others, Ali Bacher, the South African cricket board's managing director, was jolted out of sleep by a young man who had been unable to catch a wink of sleep in days, perhaps weeks. It was the voice of a man who had waged a fierce and lonely battle with himself, before deciding to surrender to his own conscience—a man who would turn the cricketing world topsy-turvy with an intrepid confession that was, at the time, like a verbal bolt of lightning from the blue. Hansie Cronje did not mince words and it did not take long for Ali Bacher to realize their enormous import. All sleep deserted Bacher as the South African captain told him that 'he had been dishonest' in his activities on the last tour of India and confessed to having received huge sums of money from 'undesirable people'. Hansie's coming clean not only shut the mouths of the Doubting Thomases in India, but also left the cricketing world benumbed. Many a lover of cricket swore not to watch and follow the game ever again. When role models and symbols of utmost rectitude and probity like Hansie Cronje came crashing down, avid followers of the game felt utterly betrayed, disillusioned and dejected. One such person, among the millions, was me.

I was then posted in the CBI as joint director (Economic Offences Wing 2 and 3). As an officer on deputation from the Delhi Police, I felt proud of the achievement of my parent organization and, particularly, of Inspector Ishwar Singh, who, as a young sub-inspector, had served with me from 1989 to 1992, during my tenure as the DCP, South district of Delhi.

The public uproar following the exposé was deafening. Rumours had already been rife for some time of the involvement Indian cricketers' in betting and fixing, and their less-than-chaste nexus with shady characters who hung around in dressing rooms and players' boxes. Demands for a CBI inquiry rang in the air. Some years ago, Manoj Prabhakar, a former member of the Indian team, had gone to the extent of giving an interview in the 11 June 1997 edition of *Outlook* magazine, alleging involvement of senior players in betting and fixing. The interview had attracted wide media and public attention, leading to the Board of Control for Cricket in India (BCCI) ordering an inquiry on 20 June 1997 by Justice (Retired) Y.V. Chandrachud, the former Chief Justice of India. However, the inquiry committee had given a clean chit to everyone connected with cricket and had summarily dismissed the allegations. The only person faulted was Manoj Prabakar. The one-man committee had observed, rather interestingly: 'It will be a sad day if the common men and women on whose support the game has occupied its pride of place believe that bookies, not the chosen eleven, play the game.'

Despite Justice Chandrachud absolving everyone of any wrongdoing, doubts lingered in the minds of Indian cricket lovers and observers of the game. Now that the South African captain had been caught on tape fixing deals with bookies, and a criminal case had been registered, the public demand for a CBI inquiry into the ills plaguing Indian cricket gathered momentum all over again.

The matter reached the Parliament and the Government of India decided to order the CBI to go into the entire gamut of malpractices existing in Indian cricket. On 2 May 2000, the CBI commenced its inquiry. The team heading the inquiry was Joint Director Ravi Sawani, an IPS officer, a year junior to me in service. The cricketing world waited with bated breath on what the CBI would expose, and the CBI waited for a breakthrough.

Within a few weeks of the CBI undertaking the inquiry, an old and trusted informant from my Delhi Police days sought time and met me in my office on 26 June. He told me that the man the CBI might be looking for in connection with the match-fixing inquiry, namely M.K. Gupta, wanted to meet me. Ignorant of Gupta, I asked the informant, 'Gupta who?' He was surprised I was unaware of M.K. Gupta—the *baap* (father) of all bookies and fixers of cricket. Even further intrigued, I asked the informant, 'Why would he want to meet me?' 'Sir, you are the only person in the CBI whom he has heard of,' he replied. I further queried, 'How and when did he hear of me?' He said, 'Sir, he has approached me because I know you.' I asked, 'Does he wish to surrender to the CBI?' He answered, 'Sir, he would first like to meet you first and then decide.'

I asked him to wait in my office until I got clearance from my bosses. Now, the CBI is the sort of organization where the unwritten code of conduct is rather stiff. Meeting a shady person like M.K. Gupta, allegedly a bookie and a fixer, without taking superiors into confidence, was not kosher. So I called on my immediate superior—Special Director P.C. Sharma—and shared the details of my meeting with the informant. On hearing of the informant's offer, he was quite excited about the prospects it held for the match-fixing inquiry at hand. He immediately took me to Director R.K. Raghavan and shared the information with him. I got the go-ahead without any hitch as, prima facie, the input augured well for the onerous task of solving the cricket match-fixing riddle the organization had been assigned.

The informant called up a number and then turned to me. He said, 'Sir, MK is waiting for you in Room 650 of Hotel Oberoi. You can meet him right now.' It took me only ten minutes to reach the Oberoi as the CBI headquarters and the hotel are closely located. When I rang the bell of the hotel suite, a fairly tall and wheatish-complexioned, ordinarily dressed man greeted me respectfully. He introduced himself as M.K. Gupta. There were two other men in the living room of the suite, who too were introduced to me and we all sat down on the sofa. Soon, two other men emerged from the adjoining bedroom. For a moment I thought it was some kind of a trap I had unwittingly walked into. Even though I trust my instincts in most situations, I began to think that on this occasion I had pushed the envelope a bit more than necessary. Why on earth had I not called the man to the lobby first? Why had I chosen to come all by myself? As these thoughts hung over me like a dark cloud that obstinately refuses to let any ray of light in, I felt more than a wee bit uncertain and uncomfortable. But then my thoughts took me to the informant, who I knew was too trustworthy to betray me. The two men, whose sudden emergence on the scene had alarmed me, greeted me respectfully and sat down, putting me at ease.

MK offered me tea but I declined. Without prevaricating, he came straight to the point.

'*Sir, main surrender karna chahta hoon. Saare fasaad ki jad main hoon.* (Sir, I wish to surrender. I am at the root of all trouble.)' He was referring to the match-fixing controversy.

Though unaware of how he was connected, I pretended I knew the entire background. I asked him, '*Aap kehna kya chahte hain?* (What are you driving at?)'

Without beating about the bush, he began to narrate the story of his life. He was a clerk in a bank and was given to betting small amounts on cricket. He gathered as much knowledge as he could about the game and began placing intelligent bets which won him more money than other bettors. Through a customer in his bank, he was introduced to one Anand Saxena, a big-time punter in cricket and other sports. Gradually, in Saxena's company, MK's turnover in betting increased manifold, as did his profits. He decided to quit his secure but 'boring' bank job and become a full-time bookie in partnership with Anand Saxena.

Once in 1988, while watching a club-level cricket match in Delhi, MK saw a young cricketer make a century with a flourish and was deeply impressed with his talent. MK met the budding talent after the game and gave him 2000 rupees as a token of his appreciation. He also shared his contact number with the cricketer, asking him to get in touch whenever he needed any help, financial or otherwise. Little did the fledgling cricketer realize that he had unwittingly bitten the bait thrown at him by someone determined to become the pioneer in fixing cricket matches worldwide.

MK candidly admitted to me that he had made an investment in a young talent, almost certain that the club-level cricketer would make it big. It was then that MK would reap the benefits of his investment.

The Delhi cricketer kept in touch with him and a relationship developed between the two, where MK was the benefactor and the player the beneficiary. Sure enough, he was picked for India's tour of New Zealand in 1990. Another player from Delhi in the Indian team, waiting to be trapped by MK, was a promising all-rounder, on whom the shrewd MK had set his hawk-eyed sights.

During the New Zealand tour, the young Delhi cricketer 'groomed' by MK provided critical inputs over the phone to the bookmaker about pitches, weather conditions, composition of teams, chances of India winning or losing, etc. MK used such inputs to his advantage and made big money, both in betting and taking bets from other punters.

The Indian cricket team returned home from New Zealand in March 1990, having lost the three Test series 0–1. Later, the same year, India was to tour England but the Delhi player was dropped. On MK's request, he introduced him to his close friend, the Delhi all-rounder. MK paid 40,000 rupees to his second catch as an advance for providing services similar to what the earlier one had provided from New Zealand. In addition, MK promised to buy him a Maruti Gypsy on return, if the all-rounder gave him (MK) useful inside information. Manoj Prabhakar did more than was expected of him. Besides providing inputs about pitch, weather, etc., he underperformed in one of the Test matches which ended in a draw. India lost the three Test series 0–1.

True to his word, MK bought the cricketer a wide-wheeled Maruti Gypsy on his return from England. The all-rounder then introduced MK to several international- and national-level players. The list, which is long, included the most venerated names from across the entire spectrum of the cricketing world. (It is pointless for me to repeat who did what or didn't for MK, in return for considerations, small or big, cash or kind; the details were sordid, to say the least.) In the interim, MK fell out with the all-rounder over money. MK suspected he had begun to 'work' for other bookies as well. MK again turned to his first collaborator, his long-term 'investment', who introduced MK to the Indian captain, and the rest is history. The fact that different courts of law in India have exonerated the Indian skipper and the others on 'technical' grounds must be mentioned to set the record straight. However, their careers as cricketers representing their country were over, their new roles as commentators or even MPs notwithstanding.

What shocked me further was MK's revelation about umpires, physios, sports journalists and groundsmen, who, according to him, could all be compromised for a price. He gave specific examples of how he had done it on different occasions. I realized MK was a prized catch and a gold mine of information on the underbelly of the game of cricket. My organization, the CBI, would be only too happy to tap into MK, the fountainhead of all ills that plagued the 'gentlemen's game'.

MK had his conditions, though. He should not be subjected to the rough-and-ready treatment, normally associated with the police in India, by the officers handling him. I assured him that what he had heard did not apply to the CBI.

As the conversation between MK and me progressed, I gradually realized that the other men present in the suite were all big-time bookies owing allegiance to MK. They treated MK with due deference. Their names elude my failing memory, except for one called Vinod Chembur. He was, and perhaps still is, a big-time bookie from the Chembur area of Mumbai. There was another one from Indore, one from Jaipur, and so on. Presumably, they were all there to lend moral support to their big boss as he had decided to come clean before a CBI officer.

I returned to the CBI headquarters later in the afternoon and reported the details of my meeting with MK to my superiors. Needless to say, they were elated. The riddle the organization had been struggling to solve seemed relatively simple now. I was asked to take over the inquiry, but I politely declined. I told them I was already snowed under work and would be happy to hand over MK to my colleague supervising the inquiry. To tell the readers the truth, whenever a case or inquiry is transferred to another team from one already dealing with it, it always results in bad blood. During my career, I have been confronted with similar situations several times when I was asked to take over cases being investigated by other officers as my team, by chance, had made a breakthrough in those cases. But I have scrupulously avoided creating any ill-feeling or malice by usurping cases or credit which, in the normal course, were not mine.

The following day, Ravi Sawani, the joint director heading the cricket match-fixing inquiry by the CBI, accompanied me to Hotel Oberoi at a pre-scheduled time. I introduced Ravi to MK with his avalanche of information and left. In the weeks to follow Ravi Sawani's team made headlines day after day. Media frenzy overtook the cricketing world as those named by MK, big or small, were called one by one to the CBI headquarters on Lodhi Road for questioning. All through the day, hordes of TV cameras and reporters lined up outside the entrance to the headquarters. Anyone called for questioning had to wade through the media glare, much like movie celebrities walking the red carpet at Cannes.

As is common knowledge, based on the CBI's findings, several Indian cricketers were banned for life and several others for varying periods of time. The CBI inquiry gathered and processed enormous data based on oral, technical and documentary evidence. Its report dated October 2000 makes fascinating reading. But the fact remains that it revolves mainly around what MK disclosed.

Sometime during the inquiry, about whose proceedings I learnt every day from the media, I came to know that two big names of Indian cricket were likely to be summoned to the CBI headquarters. Obviously, when they came, they would perforce have to walk the 'ramp'. I, at a deeply personal level, felt anguished at the prospect of such a thing happening. For the first and only time that I spoke to my dear colleague Ravi Sawani during the course of the inquiry, I said, 'Yaar, if you call and parade these two players before the media, what would be left of this game? For millions of kids and cricket fans, the ultimate idols of the game would be reduced to dust. You may be calling them as witnesses, but the world would take it that they are involved. Can't you speak to them in the privacy of the premises of their choosing?' It is to Ravi's credit that he didn't call the big two to his office. They were indeed spoken to but away from the media gaze. I will forever remain indebted to Ravi for concurring with me and respecting my feelings.

~

But tracing MK was not going to be my only brush with the ills of cricket. Not many know that the first formal case ever registered in connection with match-fixing in cricket was in England in October 1999 by the New Scotland Yard. The case of the Delhi Crime Branch against South African cricketers was registered much later, in March 2000. Allegations in the London case, curiously, again pertained to an Indian who was a resident of Delhi. It was alleged in the Scotland Yard case that he had attempted to compromise Bob Willis, an English fast bowler, and Stephen Fleming, the New Zealand captain. He planned to predetermine the outcome of the third Test between England and New Zealand played at Old Trafford, Manchester, between 5 and 9 August 1999. A noted film distributor from Mumbai and a British newsagent of Indian origin were allegedly the Delhi resident's comrades-in-arms.

David Jones was then a senior detective at the New Scotland Yard, whom I had met in London in 1994, when I visited the Yard to seek assistance in the extradition of Iqbal Mohammad Memon aka Iqbal Mirchi, wanted in several drug and mafia killings of Mumbai. Ever since, David and I have been friends, helping each other in official work, both formally and informally (see 'Atithi Devo Bhawa' for one such case). Dave, as I call him, telephoned me in late April 2000 to say that two detectives from the New Scotland Yard would call on me to seek help in an important matter. As always, I assured Dave I would do my best to help them.

After a couple of days, two detectives of the Yard, namely Bruce Hornbury (since deceased) and Martin Hawkins, were in my office to seek help in pursuing local inquiries on the Delhi resident. I extended whatever help the team needed and was possible at my end. They returned a happy lot. This, more or less, coincided with the commencement of the cricket match-fixing inquiry by the CBI. Later, I was informed that the Scotland Yard's inquiry did not lead to prosecution of the suspects, and all three are a free lot today. Reportedly, the Delhi resident is a movie actor, director and producer now.

~

Thirteen years rolled by and April 2013 came. Much like Sub-Inspector Ishwar Singh's serendipitous listening into the telephonic chatter of Hansie Cronje, the late Inspector Badrish Dutt of the Delhi Police Special Cell, while monitoring phones connected with terrorists and underworld elements, heard conversations between individuals who sounded like cricket bookies, attempting to contact cricketers playing the Indian Premier League (IPL), season six. The inspector informed his superiors, including me, immediately. I was then the commissioner of police, Delhi. The progress of the operation was monitored closely as it held promise. One lead in the monitoring of phones led to another and three cricketers and numerous bookies were now on our radar.

The interceptions revealed a wide network of bookies and fixers taking orders from none other than Dawood Ibrahim himself, through an intricate web of intermediaries. Three cricketers playing for Rajasthan Royals seemed compromised, ready to do the bidding of fixers. For money, they were prepared to underperform after giving specific signals from the playing arena to their respective 'handlers' present in the stands.

We waited for them to translate their respective promises into visible action. On 5 May 2013, before a match between Rajasthan Royals (RR) and Pune Warriors commenced at Sawai Mansingh Stadium, Jaipur, at 8 p.m., a player from RR was in conversation with a former cricketer, which was intercepted at 5.54 p.m. The RR player was asked to give away fourteen runs in the second over of his spell after giving a signal. The player said he would pull his tucked-in T-shirt out of his trousers and do as he was told.

In the pursuance of this plan, the player did squander away fourteen runs but forgot to give the predetermined signal. The fixers Chandresh Patel aka Jupiter was furious as his syndicate failed to make the windfall gains it had hoped for. Even though the RR player was not caught on camera doing the bidding of the fixers, we had adequate evidence otherwise—technical, material, documentary and verbal to book him after the completion of our investigation.

The next cricketer to commit hara-kiri was a player who had played for India and was now in RR as their strike bowler, and also the enfant terrible of Indian cricket, known for his antics on and off the cricket ground. He was fixed by another syndicate, again working under the overall command and control of the D-Company, to give away fourteen or more runs in an over. The match in which this player was to perform his 'feat' was scheduled to be played on 9 May 20013 between Rajasthan Royals and Kings XI Punjab at Mohali. This player was approached and compromised by the same former IPL cricketer who had 'fixed' the earlier Royal.

As planned, before his second over, the young cricketer took out his hand towel and tucked it in the front of his slacks. His warm-up was longer than usual, as mutually agreed upon between him and the bookies, following which he did his best to throw away fourteen runs, but the batters could milk him only for thirteen. The bookies, however, were satisfied with his 'sincere' effort to do their bidding. We had intercepted the audio conversation of the deal and videotaped its execution during the course of the match.

Aware of another such 'deal' to be closed on 15 May 2013 between yet another RR player and spot-fixers, we lay in wait till the rookie cricketer made his false move. Meanwhile, the Delhi Police in general and I, in particular, had come under strong attacks by the media and civil society owing to the rape of a minor girl by her neighbour in east Delhi. Coming within four months of the ghastly Nirbhaya incident of 16 December 2012, my detractors—including some I had hunted down in the CBI for economic offences—the media and self-styled social activists had been on an overdrive targeting me. My officers in the Special Cell suggested we go public with our unearthing of the spot-fixing racket without waiting for the third RR player to be netted. We already had information on two cricketers and a wide network of bookies and fixers with their mafia connections under our belt. Waiting for six more days was ridden with risk, as any leak from any quarter could mess up the entire operation. A premature media disclosure of our operation owing to such a leak, my officers feared, would considerably neutralize its news value. However, if we went public ourselves, the tide of adverse media attention against the Delhi Police and its beleaguered commissioner, might turn in our favour. I disagreed with them, rejected their 'considerate' suggestion and decided that we must wait.

I had experienced and endured similar assaults of adverse media and public opinion following sensational killings, terror attacks and serial murders on many an occasion during the thirty-seven years of my police career. Public and media opinions are as fickle as the English weather. As soon as the murder is solved or the serial killer arrested, everything changes dramatically and sunshine returns in all its glory. In my mind, there was only one path we could tread—complete the investigation, net our last quarry and endure the disparagement in the interim. Moreover, the raging anti-police storm was largely motivated, without any rational basis, and I knew it would pass.

Tragically, on 11 May, we lost Inspector Badrish Dutt, our main investigator of the case. He was killed in a grisly incident in Gurgaon, found dead with bullet wounds, alongside his paramour Geeta Sharma, a self-styled private detective. In all probability, one had shot the other and then shot oneself. It was a huge setback for the investigating team, but we put the loss of a good officer behind us and soldiered on.

On 15 May, we watched the live coverage of the contest between Rajasthan Royals and Mumbai Indians with bated breath. Our police teams lay in wait to move in, both in Mumbai and Delhi. True to his word, the third RR player gave away fourteen runs, as he had promised to the fixers in lieu of Rs 60 lakh. A go-ahead was given by us and, just as the match ended, a crackdown by our teams followed. In a swift operation, the Delhi Police Special Cell boys arrested fourteen persons, including bookies, financers and the three fixed cricketers during nightlong raids on 15–16 May. Several computers, mobile phones, TV sets, handwritten diaries and incriminating papers were recovered during the raids. The lid on the first case of spot-fixing in Twenty20 cricket had been blown.

On the afternoon of 16 May, we triumphantly addressed a press conference informing the world about our momentous operation. The disclosures, quite expectedly, rocked the world of sports and once again numbed millions of cricket-crazy Indian fans. The Indian media got enough fodder to chew on for a fortnight. Our campaign to apprehend and book the last culprit involved in the racket carried on, taking the number to thirty-six.

For us in the Delhi Police, the tide had turned in our favour, from relentless hostility of the media and adverse public opinion to benign positivity. It was both amazing and amusing to see the turnaround in the fourth estate. The very same celebrity anchors, senior correspondents and resident editors, who had been baying for my blood till the other day, seeking my sack or resignation, were now pursuing me for one-on-one interviews. The same purveyors of relentless criticism and cynicism were now effusive in their praise. How the wheel of fortune had turned!

During the media frenzy, to my horror, I heard from a reporter that the Hansie Cronje case registered in March 2000 had never been charge-sheeted. Incredulous, I asked my officers in the Crime Branch to check if the news were true. After a bit of inquiry, they confirmed that the information was indeed correct. I decided to ensure that the case reaches the court within the couple of months remaining of my service. Thanks to the efforts of senior officers of the Crime Branch, we succeeded in filing the charge sheet in the case in the last week of July. Five of the six accused in the case (the late Hansie Cronje was the sixth), including Sanjeev Chawla, a London-based restaurateur; Krishan Kumar; Sunil Dara aka Bittu, a Delhi-based punter-cum-bookie; Rajesh Kalra and Manmohan Khattar (still absconding), both local businessmen of Delhi; were charge-sheeted and await trial.

On 30 July 2013, a day before I hung up my boots, happily the first charge sheet in the spot-fixing case also reached the court. I retired a content man the following day, having completed what I had planned to do.

On 5 August, I left for London to visit my daughter who had been blessed with a baby girl two weeks earlier. During the three weeks of my much-needed sojourn, I went to meet a friend at Luton, a large town in Bedfordshire, fifty kilometres north of London. In the evening, my friend took me to the Indians Cricket Club in Luton Town for a drink. As I settled cozily in a sofa, sipping my single malt, I heard an announcement requesting me to come to a small stage set up in one corner of the club hall. The secretary of the club made a brief speech welcoming me and made a mention of the police investigations into the malpractices in cricket I had been associated with, mainly the IPL-6 spot-fixing case. He then went on to invite the president of the club to present me with a handsome glass trophy with the inscription: 'Thank you for making the cricket world a better arena to play in'. The gesture was overwhelming, especially because, in sharp contrast, no such recognition had come my way back home. It had not occurred to any of the cricket bodies of my own country, or the various Delhi clubs of which I am a member, to come forward and recognize the good work done by the Delhi Police under my charge. Perhaps, contrary to the old Christian saying 'Praise loudly and curse softly', we Indians believe in doing just the opposite. Nonetheless, the little glass trophy sits pretty on my writing desk, bringing a cheer to me constantly.

Willy-nilly, but happily so, destiny brought me to be part of four major inquiries/investigations into the malpractices in cricket. I was exposed to the rot that has set in a game played once by lords and royals on sunny afternoons in white flannels in the bucolic greens of England. It was common for a batsman to 'walk' even if declared not out, if he knew he had nicked the ball and had been caught behind. If given out when he was not, the batsman would still walk. Such was the spirit in which the 'gentleman's game' was played that any human act considered unfair was embodied in the phrase 'that's not cricket'. As the game became popular in faraway lands, particularly in Britain's erstwhile colonies, as it brought in big money by way of endorsements and sponsorships with the advent of television and shorter versions of the game, as value systems in general among human beings deteriorated, the virus of betting on the outcome of a cricket match crept in. Crooked and 'enterprising' minds, such as the protagonist of this story, brought in the idea of 'fixing' of players and others associated with the game. The arrival of cell telephony made it that much easier for bookies and fixers to operate.

While most connected with cricket fight relentlessly to retain its pristine glory and integrity, a few rotten eggs have muddied the waters and given the game a bad name, so much so that if someone today were to say 'that's not cricket', referring to something unfair or unjust, you and I might laugh at the folly!

Acknowledgements

To write a book has always been a dream. However, self-doubt and the sense of unhurriedness kept me from making any such attempt. Until one day, destiny brought me face-to-face with S. Hussain Zaidi—the celebrated chronicler of the Mumbai underworld—at a book launch in Delhi. For some unknown reason, after an hour-long conversation, he thought I had stories to tell and that I could write. He shared his thoughts with Chiki Sarkar of Penguin Random House who straightaway sent me a contract to write a book with a demanding deadline. Neither of them had read a line written by me. I can never thank them enough for the blind faith they reposed in me. That I have not let them down is my fervent hope.

My daughters Arunima and Ankita, and my sons-in-law Manav and Kushagra had similar faith in my untested writing skills. They have been after my life to write a book, knowing not whether it would find any takers. Although I don't need to thank them, I must admit that it is their love and support that has kept me going. They were my first sounding boards, always giving useful feedback and suggestions, which kept me on course. May God bless them!

A special word of thanks to my nephew Akarsh Sahay for preparing the site diagrams of three chapters after visiting the spots and walking long distances to get his bearings right.

My dear friend Sayantan Chakravarty of *India Empire*, and one of India's finest investigative journalists of yesteryear, was a fierce critic till, one day, I asked him politely to go easy on me. After all, I am not a consummate and professional writer as he is. He was gentler thereafter but kept giving me a reader's perspective. His contribution in making this book materialize is immense. Thank you, Sayantan. I owe you a lunch.

Since most of what I have recounted was based on memory, I needed hard facts to beef up the stories. While researching, I had to reconnect with police officers at all levels in Mumbai, Kolkata, Delhi, Gujarat and the CBI. Their response and support were always spontaneous and refreshing. Part of the joy in putting together this book was speaking with them and feeling the abiding bonds of police fraternity and its e*spirit de corps* that surmount time, age and retirement. I owe a debt of gratitude to my batchmate D. Sivanandhan, Rakesh Maria, K.M.M. Prasanna and Senior Inspector Sandbhor of the Mumbai Police; Kuldip Sharma and Sudhir Sinha of Gujarat Police; Rajeev Kumar of Kolkata Police; ACP (Retired) Prithvi Singh and Inspector Ishwar Singh of Delhi Police; Virendra Singh (formerly a close colleague in the CBI and now in the Income Tax Department); Satish Jha and O.P. Chhatwal (my SPs then),

Raman Tyagi, Ajay Bassi, M.C. Sahni, V.S. Shukla and D.S. Shukla of the CBI; and countless others who helped me in my research for the book. If I have missed out someone, I beg their pardon.

A big thank you to Haripad N. Ravi Kumar, my personal assistant from my CBI days, and to Inspector Khurshid Ali, member of my personal staff in Delhi Police, for rendering me the secretarial help I desperately needed.

I wish to thank the CBI of the years of my tenure, my bosses and, most of all, the members of my team who worked alongside me during the operations on which these stories are based. I owe the success of these missions equally to my superiors and subordinates in the CBI.

I can never thank Raja Vijay Karan enough for writing the foreword to the book at such short notice. I had the proud privilege of working under him when he served the Delhi Police as its commissioner in the late 1980s. He gave me the break to head a district as a young DCP. His abiding love and affection for me are evident in the kind words in the foreword.

Equally, for their encouraging endorsements, my heartfelt thanks to Aroon Purie, Suhel Seth and Ravi Shastri. Each one of them is a busy person and for them to spare time, read the first proofs and send their comments so promptly shows how blessed I am by their friendship.

To Milee Ashwarya and Penguin Random House, who ventured to publish the book, and to Gurveen Chadha, my young editor, who worked tirelessly to bring the manuscript to its present shape, I owe a big debt of gratitude. I also thank Richa Burman for doing a scrupulous and thorough job of line-editing; and Shatarupa Ghoshal and Shanuj V.C. for their close reading of the text.

Last but not least, a big hug to my dear wife, Mala, who sacrificed several hours of our being together to let me write and made do with watching the channel Zindagi. She, as always, remained my sheet anchor as I struggled with the book, often giving me critical advice and the encouragement I needed at crucial junctures.